John Capgrave

The Life of Saint Katherine

Middle English Texts

General Editor

Russell A. Peck
University of Rochester

Associate Editor

Alan Lupack
University of Rochester

Advisory Board

Rita Copeland
University of Minnesota

Thomas G. Hahn
University of Rochester

Lisa Kiser
Ohio State University

Thomas Seiler
Western Michigan University

R. A. Shoaf
University of Florida

Bonnie Wheeler
Southern Methodist University

The Middle English Texts Series is designed for classroom use. Its goal is to make available to teachers and students texts which occupy an important place in the literary and cultural canon but which have not been readily available in student editions. The series does not include those authors such as Chaucer, Langland, or Malory, whose English works are normally in print in good student editions. The focus is, instead, upon Middle English literature adjacent to those authors that teachers need in compiling the syllabuses they wish to teach. The editions maintain the linguistic integrity of the original work but within the parameters of modern reading conventions. The texts are printed in the modern alphabet and follow the practices of modern capitalization and punctuation. Manuscript abbreviations are expanded, and *u/v* and *j/i* spellings are regularized according to modern orthography. Hard words, difficult phrases, and unusual idioms are glossed on the page, either in the right margin or at the foot of the page. Textual and explanatory notes appear at the end of the text. The editions include short introductions on the history of the work, its merits and points of topical interest, and also include briefly annotated bibliographies.

John Capgrave

The Life of Saint Katherine

Edited by
Karen A. Winstead

Published for TEAMS
(The Consortium for the Teaching of the Middle Ages)
in Association with the University of Rochester

by

Medieval Institute Publications

WESTERN MICHIGAN UNIVERSITY

Kalamazoo, Michigan – 1999

Library of Congress Cataloging-in-Publication Data

Capgrave, John, 1393-1464.
  [Life of St. Katharine of Alexandria]
  The life of Saint Katherine / John Capgrave ; edited by Karen A. Winstead.
    p. cm. -- (Middle English texts)
  Includes bibliographical references.
  ISBN 1-58044-053-3 (alk. paper)
   1. Catherine, of Alexandria, Saint--Legends--Poetry. 2. Christian women
saints--Egypt--Alexandria--Legends--Poetry. 3. Christian poetry, English (Middle) I.
Winstead, Karen A. (Karen Anne), 1960- II. Title. III. Middle English texts (Kalamazoo,
Mich.)

PR1846.C3 L53 1999
821'.2--dc21
                                      99-045139

ISBN 1-58044-053-3

Printed in the United States of America

Cover design by Linda K. Judy

For

Phil Neal, Karl Matthias, and Beth Gasho

Ohio State University 1998

Contents

Acknowledgments

First let me acknowledge two extraordinary debts. My graduate research assistant, Maureen Novak, worked on this project from its inception in 1994 until she left Columbus for Yale Law School in 1998. Besides helping me prepare glosses and check my transcription against the original manuscript, she was a wonderful consultant on a whole host of editorial matters. When funds were unavailable, she contributed her time. My husband, Carl Winstead, used his computer expertise to generate a word list that greatly enhanced my understanding of the language of Rawlinson poet. 118. He helped me think through many a textual conundrum and read this manuscript at several different stages, as always, going far beyond what one could ask of even the most generous friend and spouse.

This edition benefited enormously from the comments of numerous colleagues and students at The Ohio State University, particularly Nick Howe, Lisa Kiser, Ethan Knapp, Terry Odlin, Dan Reff, Chris Zacher, Melanie Chapin, Frank Darwiche, Bryan Davis, Karen Dollinger, Joe Grossi, David Kinkade, Stacy Klein, Wendy Matlock, Jesse Montaño, Robin Norris, and Vicki Schwab. Pamela Sheingorn generously participated in a workshop on the Introduction and Book 2 during a visit to Columbus. Peter Lucas kindly supplied me with offprints of his work and with advice about editing. Chris Manion, my editorial assistant during the final months of the project, tracked down some especially arcane allusions. I am grateful to Russell Peck for his support of this project, to Mara Amster for her scrupulous work on my transcription, and to Alan Lupack and Eve Salisbury for their reading of the edition in its final stages. Finally, at Medieval Institute Publications in Kalamazoo, Michigan, Thomas Seiler and Juleen Eichinger have given the manuscript one last reading, for which I am grateful.

A Seed Grant from The Ohio State University provided for a research quarter, a graduate research assistant, and the purchase of microfilms of all four Katherine manuscripts. A Grant-in-Aid from the College of Humanities and Office for Research enabled me to travel to the British and Bodleian libraries to work with the manuscripts themselves. The Department of English funded research assistants for the summer of 1994 and the summer and autumn of 1997. I am grateful to The Bodleian Library, University of Oxford, for permission to publish this edition of MS Rawlinson poet. 118.

Phil Neal, my undergraduate research assistant for 1997, reviewed the manuscript carefully and gave me invaluable advice on tailoring the text and apparatus to undergraduates. I dedicate this edition to him and to two other friends and former students, Karl Matthias and Beth Gasho, who challenged me to think about teaching and its relation to research in new ways.

The National Endowment for the Humanities has provided generous support to the Middle English Text Series.

The Life of Saint Katherine

Introduction

John Capgrave's life of Saint Katherine of Alexandria belongs to the most popular genre of medieval narrative: hagiography, or writings about the saints.[1] From the earliest centuries of Christianity, accounts of the lives, deaths, and miracles of exceptionally holy men and women proliferated. These stories, which were written in Greek, Latin, and all the medieval vernaculars, were extraordinarily varied. Some sketched the saint's life in just a few sentences, while others expended thousands of lines of verse or prose on their subject. Some were full of meditations, prayers, and moral and theological exposition, while others were fast-paced and funny, sometimes racy. Hagiography could serve many different purposes, from affirming Christian dogma to promoting political and social agendas. Though most saints' lives were written by the clergy, they were directed to men and women from all walks of life and, indeed, were constantly being reshaped to fit the needs and values of new audiences.

Though saints' lives claim to be "true," they defy the modern reader's sense of historical accuracy.[2] To begin with, the earliest biographies of so many saints, including Katherine of Alexandria, were produced centuries after their protagonists were supposed to have lived. Moreover, there is a certain sameness about the genre, which signals the legends' fictiveness. The lives of countless saints draw on a few standard plots, stock characters, and conventional incidents. Miraculous escapes, violent and sexually charged conflicts, and ingenious methods of inflicting death figure prominently. Medieval readers of saints' lives — much like contemporary fans of James Bond movies, slasher flicks, bodice-busters, or whodunits — relished the repetition of familiar plots and motifs. Yet such repetition also conveyed a religious "truth," namely, that all saints *are* the same, in that all live a common life of holiness

---

[1] For an excellent general introduction to the genre, see Thomas Head, "Hagiography," in *Medieval France: An Encyclopedia*, ed. William Kibler and Grover Zinn (New York: Garland Pub., 1995), pp. 433–37.

[2] On medieval views of truth and historicity, see Ruth Morse, *Truth and Convention in the Middle Ages: Rhetoric, Representation, and Reality* (Cambridge: Cambridge University Press, 1991), and Gabrielle M. Spiegel, *Romancing the Past: The Rise of Vernacular Prose Historiography in Thirteenth-Century France* (Berkeley: University of California Press, 1993).

(*vita sanctorum*) modeled on the life of Christ.[3] As long as the contours of that universal, spiritual life were sharply drawn, the hagiographer could use his (or, less often, her) imagination to fill in the details, or could borrow those details from previous legends.

The Katherine of Alexandria legend exemplifies one of the most popular hagiographical formulas, the virgin martyr legend, an account of the trial and execution of a beautiful Christian who defies all authority to uphold her faith. Like most virgin martyrs, Katherine probably never existed: although her martyrdom is set in the early fourth century, the earliest mention of her dates from the ninth century, and a full account of her passion was not composed until the eleventh century. According to that account, known as the Vulgate version, Katherine was a learned young queen of Alexandria who confronted Emperor Maxentius as he presided over pagan ceremonies in her capital. Consternated by her learned denunciation of paganism, Maxentius summoned fifty philosophers to trounce her in a public debate, but Katherine instead converted them all to Christianity. Outraged, Maxentius resorted to violence, only to be thwarted at every turn by heavenly intervention. When he starved Katherine, angels fed her; when he scourged her, they healed her; when he built a machine with which to mangle her, they shattered it, showering the pagan spectators with the lethal fragments. To make matters worse, Katherine converted the emperor's wife and his best friend. Unable to sway his prisoner through torture, intimidation, reason, or flattery, Maxentius had her beheaded. As proof of her purity, milk gushed from her severed neck, and angels transported her body to Mount Sinai, where her relics continued to perform miracles.[4]

Though saints' legends tended to be highly formulaic, each saint was distinguished by some attribute or incident, often one that inspired the adoption of that saint either as a personal patron or as the patron of a certain cause or vocation. For example, scholars adopted St. Nicholas because he resurrected three students who had been robbed, killed, diced, and pickled by an innkeeper.[5] Because the virgin martyr Apollonia was tortured by having her teeth yanked out, she became the patron saint of toothache sufferers and was portrayed gripping a tooth with pincers.[6]

---

[3] I am using the term coined by the sixth-century author and theorist of hagiography Gregory of Tours. See his *Life of the Fathers*, trans. Edward James (Liverpool: Liverpool University Press, 1985), p. 2.

[4] A version that circulated in England of this standard *vita* has been edited by S. R. T. O. d'Ardenne and E. J. Dobson in *Seinte Katerine*, EETS s.s. 7 (Oxford: Oxford University Press, 1981), pp. 132–203. Nancy Wilson Van Baak has translated a somewhat different version of this *vita* in *La festa et storia di Sancta Caterina: A Medieval Italian Religious Drama*, ed. and trans. Anne Wilson Tordi (New York: Peter Lang, 1997), pp. 249–91.

[5] Charles W. Jones, *Saint Nicholas of Myra, Bari, and Manhattan: Biography of a Legend* (Chicago: University of Chicago Press, 1978).

[6] See Leslie Abend Callahan, "The Torture of Saint Apollonia: Deconstructing Fouquet's Martyrdom Stage," *Studies in Iconography* 16 (1994), 119–38.

Likewise, Katherine is shown with a wheel, recalling the torture on a machine of spiked wheels that Maxentius planned for her. Katherine's learning and sovereignty established her by the end of the Middle Ages as one of Europe's most popular saints. The clergy, who were largely responsible for producing and disseminating saints' legends, identified with her as a fellow scholar; as Capgrave puts it, "Because thou were so lerned and swech a clerk, / Clerkes must love thee — resoun forsoth it is" (*Katherine*, 3.38–39). Laypeople, who were becoming increasingly important as readers and patrons of saints' lives, could appreciate the public Katherine, a lady of affairs with property to manage and worldly obligations to discharge. The drama of a queen besting an emperor obviously appealed to medieval artists, since they frequently depicted Katherine in full regalia trampling the prostrate Maxentius, her sword piercing his neck or gouging out an eye.

A striking indicator of the interest Katherine aroused was the metamorphosis of her legend during the thirteenth century, when hagiographers began prefacing the traditional account of her confrontation with Maxentius and martyrdom (the "passion") with elaborate descriptions of earlier events. These expanded narratives often recount the deeds of Katherine's forbears and tell of her birth, family life, education, and eventual ascension to the throne. Moreover, they all contain some version of the saint's conversion and her transportation to heaven, where she marries Jesus in a mystical wedding ceremony that literalized the ancient *sponsa Christi* motif.[7] This episode of Katherine's legend may have captured the imagination of Margery Kempe and other late medieval holy women, for many of them reported mystical marriages of their own. The earliest extant English legend to cover Katherine's life before her martyrdom was written in the Anglo-Norman dialect of French near the middle of the fourteenth century.[8] This was followed, c. 1420, by a Middle English life in prose, later incorporated into a popular collection of saints' lives, the 1438 *Golden Legend*.[9] Some twenty-five years later, John Capgrave produced the legend presented in this edition, which is, to my knowledge, the longest and most intricate Katherine legend written during the Middle Ages, either in Latin or in any vernacular.

---

[7] Virgin martyrs had for centuries been referred to as Christ's spiritual brides. For a discussion of Katherine's literal representation as Christ's bride, see Millard Meiss, *Painting in Florence and Siena after the Black Death: The Arts, Religion, and Society in the Mid-Fourteenth Century* (Princeton: Princeton University Press, 1951), pp. 107–13.

[8] London, British Library, MS Addit. 40143.

[9] *The Life and Martyrdom of St. Katherine of Alexandria*, ed. Henry Hucks Gibbs (London: Nichols, 1884). A shorter and later version of this prose life has been edited by Saara Nevanlinna and Irma Taavitsainen, *St. Katherine of Alexandria: The Late Middle English Prose Legend in Southwell Minster MS 7* (Cambridge: D. S. Brewer, 1993). The introduction by Nevanlinna and Taavitsainen provides a valuable survey of this popular Katherine legend.

Capgrave and his Milieu

Capgrave spent much of his seventy-one years in the thriving port of Lynn on the estuary of the Ouse River in northwestern Norfolk.[10] At his birth in 1393, Lynn was the ninth largest city in England, with a population of around 5000, and boasted some seventy-five craft guilds and a merchant class that thrived upon the trade in wool, cloth, grain, and wine. At the center of town stood a prestigious convent belonging to the Augustinians, an order of friars committed to preaching and service in urban areas.[11] Perhaps emulating an earlier John Capgrave, who may have been his uncle, Capgrave joined the order in his mid-teens and was ordained c. 1416. He pursued a standard course of studies, mastering the basics of grammar, logic, and philosophy at local Augustinian institutions before tackling theology at their London convent. He concluded his training at Cambridge University by attaining (in record time, at the age of thirty-four) the highest and most prestigious teaching degree available, that of *magisterium*, or doctor of divinity.[12] In the process, he mastered debating skills that surely contributed to the unusual length and intricacy of the disputes in his Katherine legend, first between Katherine and her barons and later between her and the fifty philosophers.

That Capgrave belonged to a religious order by no means implies that he was an otherworldly recluse. Though we can only speculate about his student days, one set of rules for Augustinians studying in London anticipates plenty of mischief among the aspiring theologians: laughing and whistling in church, shouting and banging dishes at meals, sneaking food or unauthorized visitors into the rooms or selling their furniture for spare cash, patronizing taverns, and staying out all night.[13] In Lynn, Capgrave would have been in the thick of affairs, for the Augustinians were frequently called upon to mediate conflicts between civic factions such as the merchants and the craft guilds. He would also have met the major political figures who lodged with the Augustinians while visiting Lynn; indeed, in 1446 Capgrave, as prior, was responsible for entertaining King Henry VI. His experience of the world was further broadened by travel. He visited Rome in 1449 on Augustinian business and did enough sightseeing to write a guide to that city, *The Solace of Pilgrimes*. Capgrave grew prominent within his order. He was prior of the Lynn friary, the largest Augustinian house in England, from c. 1441 to 1453, and was subsequently elected Prior Provincial of England by

---

[10] For more on Capgrave's life and milieu, see the studies by De Meijer, Fredeman, Gibson, Lucas, and Seymour. For a study of Lynn itself, see Vanessa Parker, *The Making of King's Lynn: Secular Buildings from the 11th to the 17th Century* (London: Phillimore, 1971).

[11] For a detailed study of the Augustinian order in England, see Roth; and Aubrey Gwynn, *The English Austin Friars in the Time of Wyclif* (London: Oxford University Press, 1940).

[12] Roth, 1.174.

[13] Fredeman, "Life," p. 214.

unanimous vote. From 1453 to 1457, he oversaw thirty-four houses with more than 500 friars and served as liaison with the Prior General in Rome.

Despite his administrative obligations, Capgrave was a prolific author. His oeuvre includes the lives of Saints Katherine, Norbert, Augustine, and Gilbert; a chronicle of England; a collection of historical biographies about people named Henry; a guide to Rome; several theological treatises; and numerous commentaries on the Bible. He may, indeed, have viewed his writing as an extension of his responsibilities first as head of the Lynn friary and then as head of all English Augustinians, for he dedicated his works to patrons who could aid his house and his order: Kings Henry VI and Edward IV, bishops and heads of religious houses, Duke Humphrey of Gloucester, and the Norfolk magnate and bully Sir Thomas Tuddenham.[14] Generating goodwill among such magnates was especially vital as political chaos mounted, breaking out in open civil war in 1455 (the Wars of the Roses). All of Capgrave's works except his *Katherine* survive in manuscripts — including lavish presentation copies — that he himself produced or supervised the production of, perhaps at a scriptorium within the Lynn convent.[15]

Political unrest did not thwart the development of a rich culture in southeastern England. Capgrave's East Anglia abounded with authors whose endeavors were encouraged by local bibliophiles and patrons of the arts.[16] In the decades following Chaucer's death in 1400, John Lydgate, John Metham, and Osbern Bokenham were, through tributes to their predecessor and adaptations of his work, shaping a "Chaucer Tradition" in England.[17] Religious drama flourished, and during the 1430s, Margery Kempe, also of Lynn, a businesswoman, traveler, and mother of fourteen, completed her extraordinary *Book*, an amalgam of autobiography, hagiography, mysticism, and social criticism. That a laywoman could produce such a work at a time when the Church in England, fearing the spread of heresy, was overtly hostile toward amateur theologizing, attests to a certain tolerance in East Anglia, a survival of the openness to spiritual creativity that had enabled the anchoress Julian of Norwich to record her unusual visions a generation earlier.[18] Capgrave's *The Life of St. Katherine* was very much a product

---

[14] H. S. Bennett discusses Tuddenham's doings in *The Pastons and Their England* (New York: Cambridge University Press, 1922).

[15] Lucas, "Scribe and Publisher."

[16] See especially Gibson and Moore.

[17] For discussions of the roles of Lydgate and Bokenham in the formation of a Chaucer tradition, see, respectively, Seth Lerer, *Chaucer and His Readers: Imagining the Author in Late-Medieval England* (Princeton: Princeton University Press, 1993) and Delany.

[18] For discussions of the religious climate in late-fourteenth- and fifteenth-century East Anglia, see Gibson; Staley; and David Aers and Lynn Staley, *The Powers of the Holy: Religion, Politics, and Gender in Late Medieval English Culture* (University Park: Pennsylvania State University Press, 1996).

of East Anglian culture. Though Capgrave acknowledges only one English source for his narrative (a possibly fictional legend relayed by a London priest), his *The Life of St. Katherine* reads as if it were written by someone who had read Chaucer, was conversant with the works of Lydgate and Bokenham and with biblical drama, and knew of Margery Kempe's *Book*.[19]

Capgrave's *The Life of St. Katherine*

In his prologue, Capgrave tells us that his *The Life of St. Katherine* derives from a long-lost biography composed by Katherine's disciple Athanasius, which was translated from Greek into Latin by a fifth-century scholar named Arrek and from Latin into English nearly a millennium later by a parson of St. Pancras in London. Unfortunately, Capgrave explains, the anonymous priest died before he could complete his project; moreover, his dialect was so obscure that his translation was known to only a handful of scholars — and even they could not understand it. Having come upon the incomplete manuscript, Capgrave undertakes to translate his predecessor's "derk langage" into proper English and to supply the missing account of Katherine's martyrdom from an authoritative Latin source. Yet if Capgrave was, as he avers, faithfully translating preexisting sources, those sources have not survived.[20] Certainly Capgrave did not originate the events that he narrates; all are found in earlier Katherine legends. However, medieval authors were not loath to invent authorities (Lollius in Chaucer's *Troilus and Criseyde* is a famous example), and we should not accept Capgrave's assertions without question.

Capgrave's *The Life of St. Katherine* stands apart both from other known narrations of Katherine's life and from English hagiography generally. To begin with, at five books totaling about 8,000 lines of rhyme-royal verse, his legend is rather long for a saint's life. Its length is not unprecedented; during the 1430s, Lydgate had written "epic" lives of Saints Edmund and Alban, along with *The Life of Our Lady*, all of which comprise several thousand rhyme-royal lines and are divided into multiple books.[21] Lydgate may have been emulating Chaucer's *Troilus and Criseyde*, which was widely admired by fifteenth-century readers. Although Capgrave borrows literary devices favored by Chaucer and Lydgate, he makes no pretensions to high art. His stanzas jingle with the fillers, tags, and formulas that abound in popular

---

[19] On Capgrave's familiarity with Chaucer, see Pearsall, Stouck, and Winstead ("Chaucer Tradition").

[20] See Kurvinen's discussion and partial transcription of the Latin *vita* that most closely resembles Capgrave's.

[21] Karen A. Winstead, "Lydgate's Lives of Saints Edmund and Alban: Martyrdom and *Prudent Pollicie*," *Mediaevalia* 17 (1994), 361–76.

romances.[22] These features, along with broad humor, colloquialism, and irregular meter, distinguish Capgrave's *Katherine* from his only other verse narrative, the far more decorous *The Life of St. Norbert*, composed c. 1420 and dedicated to John Wygenhale, abbot of the Premonstratensian priory of nearby West Dereham.

Capgrave's casual style does accord with his stated goal of making Katherine's long-lost *vita* known "more openly . . . / . . . of woman and of man" (Prol., lines 45–46). Yet he does not tell a simple story, as so many popular writers did; rather, he transforms Katherine's life into an encyclopedic narrative holding something for everybody: for the antiquarian, digressions on Greek and Roman history, with the occasional reference to "Brytayn, the londe in whech we dwelle" (4.111); for the political theorist, divagations into theories of just and unjust rule and justifiable versus unjustifiable rebellion; for the entrepreneur, numerous references to money, merchandise, and commerce; for the doting parent, descriptions of King Costus and Queen Meliades coddling the baby Katherine and of attendants bustling about her nursery; for the aspiring *gentil*, accounts of pageants, jousts, and feasts.

Attuned to the interests of women, who were avid readers and patrons in 1440s East Anglia, Capgrave develops those aspects of the virgin martyr's relationship with her heavenly spouse that provincial wives could understand: her longing for her absent husband, for example, and her anxiety over the safety of her household and property during dangerous times.[23] Through his portrayal of other women — the Virgin Mary, Maxentius' wife, and Katherine's mother — he further engages a female audience. Widows who had themselves struggled to secure their children's inheritance could appreciate the maneuvers of Meliades. Shortly after her husband's funeral, she summons a parliament in Alexandria, the ancient seat of kings, without telling anyone why (1.512–18); then, having propitiated the magnates of her husband's realm with lavish entertainments, she has Katherine crowned, effecting her daughter's prompt and smooth succession at a time when many people were grumbling at the prospect of being governed by a girl.

For Capgrave, addressing a broad audience does not mean avoiding complex social and philosophical issues but rather engaging ordinary readers in those issues. The long debate in

---

[22] See Pearsall.

[23] For discussions of East Anglian women as patrons and readers, see Delany; Gibson; and Ralph Hanna III, "Some Norfolk Women and Their Books, ca. 1390–1440," in *The Cultural Patronage of Medieval Women*, ed. June Hall McCash (Athens: University of Georgia Press, 1996), pp. 288–305. For more on the responsibilities of provincial wives, see Coss; Ann S. Haskell, "The Paston Women on Marriage in Fifteenth-Century England," *Viator* 4 (1973), 459–71; and Sarah McNamer, "Female Authors, Provincial Setting: The Re-Versing of Courtly Love in the Findern Manuscript," *Viator* 22 (1991), 279–310. See also *Wife and Widow in Medieval England*, ed. Sue Sheridan Walker (Ann Arbor: University of Michigan Press, 1993).

Book 2 over a woman's fitness to rule sets forth contradictory yet equally compelling arguments about government, tradition, and gender, and it concludes with no clear-cut winner. Books 3 through 5 treat weighty doctrinal matters at length, despite the Church's opposition to theologizing in English.[24] Indeed, Capgrave does not shrink from adumbrating parallels between Maxentius' persecution of Christians and the Church's persecution of the Lollards (followers of John Wyclif who advocated, among other things, that ordinary people should read and discuss the Bible in their own language).[25] For example, Christians are denounced by "[a] byschop . . . with mytere and with crose" (4.309) and persecuted for engaging in unlicensed preaching (4.1431–35), while Capgrave puts into the mouth of an idolatrous pagan the very arguments by which the Church defended the veneration of devotional images (4.1499–1512). With equal temerity, Capgrave implicitly criticizes the current English monarch, Henry VI.[26] Like Katherine, Henry was widely accused of being overly pious, inattentive to matters of state, and insufficiently manly. If these traits led a great saint's kingdom to ruin, where were they likely to lead Henry's? As a shield for these dangerously topical allusions, Capgrave adopts a quintessentially Chaucerian device: he interposes between himself and the text an intrusive narrator whose digressions, contradictions, and bizarre interpretations can only frustrate the reader looking for simple truths.

The Text

Capgrave's *Katherine* survives in four fifteenth-century manuscripts. I have based this edition on Bodleian Library MS Rawlinson poet. 118, which, scholars have long agreed, best preserves Capgrave's language and orthography. Indeed, F. J. Furnivall's foreword to the Early English Text Society's 1893 edition of the legend castigated its editor, Carl Horstmann, for editing the wrong manuscript, British Library MS Arundel 396, and apologized to the Society's members for the resulting "waste of some of their money."[27] We can be so certain about Capgrave's language because all his writings except *Katherine* survive in autograph or

---

[24] Nicholas Watson, "Censorship and Cultural Change in Late-Medieval England: Vernacular Theology, the Oxford Translation Debate, and Arundel's Constitutions of 1409," *Speculum* 70 (1995), 822–64.

[25] For classic studies of the Lollards, see Anne Hudson, *The Premature Reformation: Wycliffite Texts and Lollard History* (Oxford: Clarendon Press, 1988) and Margaret Aston, *Lollards and Reformers: Images and Literacy in Late Medieval Religion* (London: Hambledon Press, 1984). On the parallels Capgrave establishes, see Winstead, *Virgin Martyrs*, pp. 175–77.

[26] Winstead, *Virgin Martyrs*, pp. 168–74, and "Gynecocracy," pp. 367–71.

[27] *The Life of St. Katharine of Alexandria*, p. xxiv.

holograph manuscripts. The orthography of these manuscripts is remarkably consistent.[28] For example, Capgrave almost never uses the guttural "ght," preferring instead "th" — thus, "rith" rather than "right," and "lith" rather than "light." Although the language of the Rawlinson manuscript is closest to Capgrave's, its orthography — though clearly based on Capgrave's — is extravagantly variegated, reflecting the idiosyncrasies of at least three different scribes.[29]

Since students might find the varied spellings of the same pronouns especially confusing (Middle English "hir," "her," and "here" are at various times used to designate modern English "her," for example), I have normalized the pronouns in accordance with Capgrave's own practices. Hence, in this edition, Modern English "her" is consistently written "hir," Modern English "their" is written "her," and Modern English "them" is written "hem." The scribe of Rawlinson poet. 118 frequently writes "who" for Modern English "how." Though Capgrave himself preferred "who," I have for clarity transcribed "who" as "how" on the grounds that the "who" spelling does not represent a pronunciation different from the "how" spelling. To further facilitate comprehension, the second person pronoun, which is generally spelled "the" in Rawlinson poet. 118, is consistently spelled "thee" in this edition. Final "e" that is long and given full syllabic value is written "é."

The Rawlinson manuscript is sloppily written but well preserved. However, it is missing several leaves (3.188–263, 4.1888–1963). I have supplied the missing text from Arundel 396. Following the policy of the Middle English Texts Series, I have spelled out all numerals; expanded all abbreviations; replaced thorn with *th* and yogh with *g*, *y*, or *gh*; and used the modern equivalent for *i/j* and *u/v*. I have emended what seem to be obvious errors in the manuscripts, documenting substantive alterations in the notes.

Punctuation and capitalization follow modern conventions. According to the policy of the Middle English Text Series, all pronouns and certain nouns (God, Lord, Son, Ghost, and a few others) referring to the Christian deity are capitalized; when designating Christ's mother, "lady" is also capitalized.

---

[28] See Lucas, "Toward a Standard Written English" and "Consistency and Correctness" (both reprinted in *From Author to Audience*).

[29] For a study of this manuscript and its scribes, see Lucas, "William Gybbe" (reprinted in *From Author to Audience*).

The Life of Saint Katherine

Select Bibliography

Manuscripts

Oxford, Bodleian Library MS Rawlinson poet. 118.

London, British Library MS Arundel 396.

London, British Library MS Arundel 168.

London, British Library MS Arundel 20.

Edition

The Life of St. Katharine of Alexandria. Ed. Carl Horstmann. EETS o.s. 100. 1893; rpt. Millwood, N.Y.: Kraus Reprint, 1987. [Edition of MS Arundel 396, with MS Rawlinson poet. 118 edited on facing pages for Books 1–3.]

Studies

Beadle, Richard. "Prolegomena to a Literary Geography of Later Medieval Norfolk." In *Regionalism in Late Medieval Manuscripts and Texts: Essays Celebrating the Publication of "A Linguistic Atlas of Late Mediaeval English."* Ed. Felicity Riddy. Cambridge: D. S. Brewer, 1991. Pp. 89–108.

Colledge, Edmund. "John Capgrave's Literary Vocation." *Analecta Augustiniana* 40 (1977), 187–95.

Coss, Peter. *The Lady in Medieval England, 1000–1500.* Mechanicsburg, Penn.: Stackpole Books, 1998. [A beautifully illustrated study, recommended for readers wishing to understand Capgrave's treatment of Katherine in light of what is known about the lived experience of gentlewomen in late medieval England.]

Delany, Sheila. *Impolitic Bodies: Poetry, Saints, and Society in Fifteenth-Century England: The Work of Osbern Bokenham.* Oxford: Oxford University Press, 1998. [A study of the writings and milieu of Capgrave's fellow East Anglian poet, Osbern Bokenham. Especially relevant is the discussion of Bokenham's Katherine legend, with passing reference to Capgrave, in ch. 7.]

De Meijer, Alberic. "John Capgrave, O.E.S.A." *Augustiniana* 5 (1955), 400–40 and 7 (1957), 118–48, 531–75.

Doyle, A. I. "Publication by Members of the Religious Orders." In *Book Production and Publishing in Britain, 1375–1475*. Ed. Jeremy Griffiths and Derek Pearsall. Cambridge: Cambridge University Press, 1989. Pp. 109–23.

Fredeman, Jane. "The Life of John Capgrave, O.E.S.A. (1393–1464)." *Augustiniana* 29 (1979), 197–237.

———. "Style and Characterization in John Capgrave's *Life of St. Katherine*." *Bulletin of the John Rylands Library* 62 (1979–80), 346–87.

Gibson, Gail McMurray. *The Theater of Devotion: East Anglian Drama and Society in the Late Middle Ages*. Chicago: University of Chicago Press, 1989. [This rich study of fifteenth-century East Anglia does not discuss Capgrave but provides essential information about his milieu.]

Goodman, Anthony. "The Piety of John Brunham's Daughter, of Lynn." In *Medieval Women*. Ed. Derek Baker. Oxford: Basil Blackwell, 1978. Pp. 347–58. [To my knowledge, this essay contains the first comparison of Capgrave's Katherine to Margery Kempe (p. 354, n. 35).]

Heffernan, Thomas J. *Sacred Biography: Saints and Their Biographers in the Middle Ages*. New York: Oxford University Press, 1988. Pp. 167–84.

Horrox, Rosemary, ed. *Fifteenth-Century Attitudes: Perceptions of Society in Late Medieval England*. Cambridge: Cambridge University Press, 1994. [Includes overviews of such subjects as education, government, religion, urban society, and women.]

Johnson, Ian. "*Auctricitas*? Holy Women and their Middle English Texts." In *Prophets Abroad: The Reception of Continental Holy Women in Late-Medieval England*. Ed. Rosalynn Voaden. Cambridge: D. S. Brewer, 1996. Pp. 177–97. [Includes a discussion of Capgrave's prologue to *Katherine*.]

Kurvinen, Auvo. "The Source of Capgrave's *Life of St. Katharine of Alexandria*." *Neuphilologische Mitteilungen* 61 (1960), 268–324. [Provides a partial transcription and translation of the Latin life of Katherine that most closely resembles Capgrave's legend.]

Lewis, Katherine J. *The Cult of St. Katherine of Alexandria in Late Medieval England*. Woodbridge: Boydell and Brewer, 1999. [This study focuses on the popular prose life of Katherine.]

———. "Model Girls? Virgin-Martyrs and the Training of Young Women in Late Medieval England." In *Young Medieval Women*. Ed. Katherine J. Lewis, Noël James Menuge, and Kim M. Phillips. New York: St. Martin's Press, 1999. Pp. 25–46. [Lewis draws most of her examples from Middle English lives of St. Katherine.]

Lucas, Peter J. "John Capgrave, O.S.A. (1393–1464), Scribe and 'Publisher.'" *Transactions of the Cambridge Bibliographical Society* 5 (1969), 1–35.

———. "Consistency and Correctness in the Orthographic Usage of John Capgrave's *Chronicle*." *Studia Neophilologica* 45 (1973), 323–55.

———, ed. *John Capgrave's Abbreuiacion of Cronicles*. EETS o.s. 285. Oxford: Oxford University Press, 1983. [Provides an invaluable introduction to Capgrave's entire *oeuvre*. Extensive bibliography covers all of Capgrave's writings, Latin and English, as well as his life, language, and scriptorium.]

———. "William Gybbe of Wisbech: A Fifteenth-Century English Scribe." *Codices manuscripti* 11 (1985), 41–64. [A study of the Rawlinson poet. 118 MS (containing the version of Capgrave's *Katherine* edited here) and its principal scribe.]

———. "John Capgrave, Friar of Lynn." *The Historian* 44 (1994), 23–24. [Condensed version of a lecture given in 1993 to celebrate the 600th anniversary of Capgrave's birth.]

———. *From Author to Audience: John Capgrave and Medieval Publication*. Dublin: University College Dublin Press, 1997. [A collection of previously published essays on Capgrave.]

Moore, Samuel. "Patrons of Letters in Norfolk and Suffolk, c. 1450." *PMLA* 27 (1912), 188–207 and *PMLA* 28 (1913), 79–105.

Introduction

Murphy, James J. *Rhetoric in the Middle Ages: A History of Rhetorical Theory from Saint Augustine to the Renaissance*. Berkeley: University of California Press, 1974. [Enormously helpful for understanding the rhetorical underpinnings of Katherine's two debates.]

Pearsall, Derek. "John Capgrave's *Life of St. Katharine* and Popular Romance Style." *Medievalia et Humanistica* n.s. 6 (1975), 121–37.

Reed, Thomas L., Jr. *Middle English Debate Poetry and the Aesthetics of Irresolution*. Columbia: University of Missouri Press, 1990. [Useful for understanding the intellectual and generic contexts of the two debates in *Katherine*.]

Roth, Francis. *The English Austin Friars, 1249–1538*. 2 vols. New York: Augustinian Historical Institute, 1966, 1961. [Vol. 1: *History*; Vol. 2: *Sources*.]

Seymour, M. C. "The Manuscripts of John Capgrave's English Works." *Scriptorium* 40 (1986), 248–55.

———. *John Capgrave*. Authors of the Middle Ages 11. Brookfield, Vt.: Variorum, 1996.

Staley, Lynn. *Margery Kempe's Dissenting Fictions*. University Park: Pennsylvania State University Press, 1994. [Valuable study of fifteenth-century intellectual, social, and spiritual issues.]

Stouck, Mary-Ann. "Chaucer and Capgrave's *Life of St. Katharine*." *American Benedictine Review* 33 (1982), 276–91. [Discusses structural correspondences between *Katherine* and *Troilus*.]

Winstead, Karen A. "Piety, Politics, and Social Commitment in Capgrave's *Life of St. Katharine*." *Medievalia et Humanistica*, n. s. 17 (1990), 59–80.

———. "Capgrave's Saint Katherine and the Perils of Gynecocracy." *Viator* 25 (1994), 361–76.

———. "John Capgrave and the Chaucer Tradition." *Chaucer Review* 30 (1996), 389–400.

———. *Virgin Martyrs: Legends of Sainthood in Late Medieval England*. Ithaca: Cornell University Press, 1997. [Ch. 4 treats Capgrave's *Katherine* together with the prose life composed c. 1420.]

Winstead, Karen A., trans. *Chaste Passions: Medieval English Virgin Martyr Legends*. Ithaca: Cornell University Press, 2000. [Includes a translation and transcription of the prose life of St. Katherine.]

Wogan-Browne, Jocelyn, Nicholas Watson, Andrew Taylor, and Ruth Evans, eds. *The Idea of the Vernacular: An Anthology of Middle English Literary Theory, 1280–1520*. University Park: Pennsylvania State University Press, 1999. [The excerpts and essays included in this volume provide an invaluable resource for understanding the vexed issue of the vernacular in Capgrave's day.]

Wolpers, Theodor. *Die englische Heiligenlegende des Mittelalters*. Tübingen: M. Niemeyer, 1964. Pp. 330–42.

The Life of Saint Katherine

Prologue

[The History of This Legend]

	Jesu Cryst, crowne of maydenes alle,	
	A mayde bare Thee, a mayde gave Thee soke;	*bore; suckled you*
	Amongis the lilies that may not fade ne falle	*i.e., the saints*
	Thou ledyst these folk, ryth so seyth oure boke.	*lead; exactly; book*
5	With all her hert evyr on Thee thei loke;	
	Her love, her plesauns, so sore is on Thee sette	
	To sewe Thee, Lord, and folow thei can nott lette.[1]	
	Ryth thus be ordyr we wene Thou ledyst the daunce;	*Exactly; by; know; dance*
	Thi modir folowyth Thee next, as reson is,	
10	And aftir othir, thei goo rith as her chaunce	*their share*
	Is schap to hem of joye that may not mys.	*given; them; fail*
	But next that Lady above alle othir in blys	*i.e., the Virgin Mary*
	Folowyth this mayde weche we clepe Kateryne.	*call*
	Thus wene we, Lord, because that Thou and Thyne	*suppose*
15	Have gove to hir of grace so grete plenté	*given; her*
	That alle the privileges weche be in othir found	
	Ar sett in hir as in sovereyne hye degré,	*her*
	For in alle these rychely doth she habound.	*abound*
	Loke alle these seyntis that on this world so round	*Consider; saints*
20	Levyd here sumtyme, and in sum spyce or kynde,	*Lived; formerly; manner*
	Her vertues shal we in this same mayde fynde:	*Their*

---

[1] Lines 5–8: *They look to you with all their heart; / Their love, their joy, is so earnestly fixed on you, / Lord, that they cannot stop pursuing and following you*

Thou gave to Jon, Lord, the grete evangelyst,
Thin owne presens whan he hens shuld wende;   *presence; go*
That same presens, rithe evene as Thou lyste,   *just; wished*
25   Thou gave this mayde at hir lyvys ende.   *her*
A welle of oyle eke Thou wold hir sende   *oil also*
Out of hir grave, as had Seynt Nycholas;
And for hir clennesse Thou graunted hir that gras   *purity; grace*

Weche Seynt Poule had — mylke ryth at his throte
30   Ran out with bloode, men sey, in tokenyngis
That martyrdam and maydenhod ryth in o cote   *identical (in one person)*
Were medelede togydyr. Thou, doutir onto the kyngis,   *mixed; daughter*
So had thou fully as these holy thingis.
To araye thi grave His aungellys eke Godd sent,   *also*
35   Ryth as He dyd sumtyme for Seynt Clement.

And as Seynt Margarete had hir petycyoun
At hir last ende graunted of Godd allmyth —   *almighty*
What maner man or woman that with devocyoun
Askyth a bone of hir, he hath it ryth   *favor; truly*
40   As he wyl have, if he ask but ryth,   *correctly*
For ellis fayleth he, it is not to his behove[1] —
The same grace hast thow of Godd, thi love,

Purchasyd, lady, onto thi loveris alle.   *Obtained*
Therfor wyl I thee serve so as I can
45   And make thi lyffe, that more openly it schalle
Be know abowte of woman and of man.
Ther was a preste, of flesch he was ful wan,   *very pale*
For grete labour he had in his lyve
To seke thi liffe yerys thyrtene and fyve.[2]

50   Yet at the last he found it, to his gret joye,
Fer up in Grece i-beryed in the grownde.   *Far*
Was nevyr no knyth in Rome ne eke in Troye   *knight; nor also*

---

[1] *For if he fails [to receive his request], it (what he asked for) is not for his profit*

[2] *To seek your life (biography) for eighteen years*

16

Mor glad of swerde or basnett bryght and rownde — *helmet bright*
Than was this preeste whan he had it fownde:
55 He blyssed thee ofte, and seyd all his laboure — *you often*
Was turned to solace, to joye and socowr. — *relief*

He mad thi lyff in Englysch tunge ful well, — *very well*
But yet he deyed or he had fully doo. — *died before; finished*
Thy passyon, lady, and all that scharp whele
60 He left behynd—it is yet for to doo;
And that he mad it is ful hard ther-too, — *what he wrote is very hard to read*
Ryth for straungenesse of his derk langage. — *obscure language*
He is now ded, thu hast gove him his wage. — *given; reward*

Now wyl I, lady, more openly make thi lyffe — *more clearly write*
65 Oute of his werk, if thu wylt help ther-too;
It schall be know of man, mayde, and of wyffe,
What thu hast suffrede and eke what thu hast doo. — *done*
Pray Godd, oure Lorde, He wyll the dore on-doo, — *undo the door*
Enspire oure wyttys with His pryvy grace — *Inspire; special*
70 To preyse Him and thee that we may have space. — *praise; capacity*

Thys preeste of whom I spake not longe ere
In his prologe telleth all his desyre,
How that he travayled many a londe to lere — *traveled [through]; learn*
The byrth, the cuntré, the langage, of this martyre, — *country; martyr*
75 Who was hir modyr and eke who was hir syre; — *father*
Aboute this mater he laboured yerys eytene — *eighteen years*
With prayere, fastyng, cold and mekyll tene. — *great hardship*

So at the last had he a revelacyoun
All mysty and derk, hyd all undyr clowde.
80 He thowte he sey thoo in his avysyoun — *thought; saw; then; vision*
A persone honest, clothed in precyous schrowde, — *respectable; fine vestments*
Whech evyr cryed upon the preest ful lowde: — *loudly*
"Beholde," he seyth, "thu man, what that I am,
What thyng I schew, and eke why I cam." — *reveal*

85 For in his hand he held a boke ful elde, — *old*
With bredys rotyn, levys dusty and rent; — *covers; pages; torn*

17

And evyr he cryed upon the preest, "Behelde!
Here is thi labour, here is all thin entente.
I wote ful welle what thu hast sowte and ment;　　*know; sought and intended*
90　Ope thi mouth, this book muste thu ete;　　*Open*
But if thu doo, thi wyll schall thu not gete."　　*unless*

"A, mercy, lorde!" seyd this preeste to him.
"Spare me now!　Who schulde I this book ete?　　*How*
The roten bredys, these levys derk and dyme,　　*covers; pages*
95　I may in noo wyse into my mouth hem gete:　　*way; them*
My mouth is small and eke thei be so grete,
Thei wyll brek my chaules and my throte —　　*jaws*
This mete to me is lykly to do noo note."　　*food; good*

"Yys," seyd he, "thu mote nede ete this book —　　*must*
100　Thu schalt ellys repente. Ope thi mowth wyde,　　*otherwise*
Receyve it boldly — it hath no clospe ne hook.
Let it goo down and in thi wombe it hyde;
It schal not greve thee neyther in bak ne syde;　　*harm; back*
In thi mowth bytter, in thi wombe it wyll be swete,
105　So was it sumetyme to Ezechyell the prophete."　　*As; formerly*

The preeste tho toke it into his mowth anon;　　*then; at once*
It semed swete, ryth as it hony were.　　*as if it were honey*
The other man is passed and i-gon;
The preest is stoyned as thow he turned were.　　*astonished; though; demented*
110　New joye, new thowte, had he than there.　　*ideas*
He awoke and was ful glad and blythe;
Of this dreme he blyssyd God ofte sythe.　　*often since (many times)*

Aftyr this not long, depe in a felde,
I-clad wyth flowres and herbys grete and smale,　　*plants*
115　He dalf and fond this boke whych he behelde　　*dug*
Before in slepe, ryght as I told my tale.
There had he salve to all his byttyr bale.　　*suffering*
It was leyd there be a knyte that men calle　　*laid; knight*
Amylion fytz Amarak, of Cristen knytes alle　　*son of*

120	Most devoute as onto this mayde.
	He fond it among old tresoure in Cipire-londe.
	In Kyng Petris tyme, as the cronycle sayde,
	Of that same Cipre where he this boke fond
	And in Pope Urban tyme, as I undyrstond,
125	The fyfte of Rome, fell all this matere
	Wheche ye have herd and yet ye schall more clere.

Cyprus (121)
Cyprus (123)
i.e., Urban V; happened (125)

There was a clerk with this same Kateryne
Whos name wc clepe in Latyne Athanas; *call; Athanasius*
He tawte hir the reules, as he cowde dyvyne, *as he could understand them*
130 Of God of hevyn, of joye, and of grace,
And sche him also, for be hir he was *by her*
I-turnyd onto Crist and to oure feythe;
He was hir leder, as the story seythe.

He wrote the lyfe eke of this same mayde;
135 He was with hir at hir last ende,
He say hir martyryd, as himselve sayde. *saw*
He mote nede have hir lyfe in mynde — *must certainly*
He was a servaunt onto hir ryth kynde. *true nature*
What schuld I lenger in his preysyng tary? *spend more time praising him*
140 He was hir chauncelere and hir secretary.

He gate hir maisterys thorowowte the partes *got; teachers*
Of all grete Grece, hir fadyres empyre,
To lerne hir be rowe all the sevene artes; *teach her in order*
This same man payd hem all her hire, *them; their salaries*
145 He was as in that courte fully lord and syre.
He knew hir kynne and hir counsell also, *family; advisers*
Hir fadyr, hir modyr, and all the line therto;

Hir holy life he knew, hir conversacioun, *habits*
All hir holy customys wyll sche levyd here. *while*
150 He stode be hir in hir grete passioun. *by*
He say the aungelis, how thei hir body bere *saw; how*
Fer up into Synay and leyde it down there; *Far; Mount Sinai*
He saw the venjauns, eke, how it was take *vengeance, also*
On many a thousand eke for hir deth sake;

19

155	He sey eke Maxense, how he was slayn,	*saw*
	Dropped from a bregge down in a revere,	*bridge; river*
	Deyd so ful sodeynly in ful byttyr payne,	
	Forthe was he draw into hell-feere —	*fire*
	Aungellys bare hir, the develys bare hys beere.	*bore; bier*
160	Behold the sundry reward of vertu and of syne:	*different*
	On is in hevene, the other is hell withinne.	*One*

	Long aftyr the deth of this Maxencyus,	
	Byschop in Alysaunder, Katerynes cité,	*Alexandria; city*
	Was this sam man, this Athanasius,	
165	In whech he suffred ful mech adversyté.	*much*
	I wot not veryly yef it were he	*know; if*
	That made the psalme whech we clepe the crede,	*call*
	Whech we at pryme oft-tyme syng and rede.	*read*

	He deyd evyn there an holy confessoure,	*right there*
170	And aftyr his deth myth unneth be knowe	*might hardly*
	The lyvyng, the lernyng, of this swete flowre	
	And martyr Kateryne, of hy ne of lowe	*i.e., of any class*
	Tyl on Arrek dyd it new i-sowe,	*Until a certain man Arrek sowed it anew*
	For owt of Grew he hath it fyrst runge,	*Greek; i.e., translated*
175	This holy lyff, into Latyne tunge.	

	This clerk herd speke oft-tyme of this mayde,	*i.e., the priest*
	Bothe of hir lyffe and also of hir heende,	*end (death)*
	How sche for lofe hir lyffe hath thus layde	
	Of oure Lorde Cryste, oure gostly spouse kende.	*our dear heavenly spouse*
180	This made him sekere into that londe to wende,	*determined; travel*
	To know of this bothe the spryng and the welle,	
	If any man coude it any pleynere telle.	

	Twelve yere in that londe he dwelt and more,	
	To know her langage, what it myght mene,	
185	Tyl he of her usages had fully the lore	*fully understood*
	With ful mech stody, tary, and tene.	*much; time; hardship*
	Ful longe it was or he myght it sene,	*before; might see*
	The lyff that Athanas made of this mayde;	*Athanasius*
	But at the last he cam, as it is sayde,	

190	Ther as he fonde it from mynde all i-ded,	*i.e., out of circulation*
	For heretykys that were thoo in that londe	*heretics; then*
	Had brent the bokys, bothe the leffe and the brede,	*burned; pages and covers*
	As many as thei soute and that tyme fonde;	*sought*
	But, blyssyd be Godd of His hye sonde,	*through His high decree*
195	This boke founde thei not in no manere wyse —	*way*
	Godd wolde not that the nobyll servyse	

Of His owne mayde schulde be thus forgete.
A hundred yere aftyr it was and more
That this Arrek this new werk had gete

200	Fro the tyme of Athanas, for so mech before	*Athanasius; so long ago*
	Was he hens pased, i-ded and forlore	*dead and forgotten*
	As from every tunge, bothe his boke and he,	
	Of every man and woman in that cuntré.	*country*

And be this preste was it onto Englischmen

205	I-soute and founde and broute unto londe,	
	Hyd in all counseyll among nyne or ten.	*Known only by nine or ten people*
	It cam but seldom onto any mannes honde;	
	Eke whan it cam it was noght undyrstonde	
	Because, as I seyd, ryght for the derk langage.	*obscure*
210	Thus was thi lyffe, lady, kept all in cage.[1]	

	Nevyrthelasse he dyd mych thyng ther-too,	*accomplished much*
	This noble preste, this very good man:	
	He hath led us the wey and the doore on-doo,	
	That mech the bettyr we may and we can	
215	Folow his steppes. For thow he sore rane	*though he ran hard*
	We may him ovyrtake, with help and with grace	
	Whech that this lady schall us purchass.	

	He is now ded, this goodeman, this preste;	
	He deyd at Lynne many yere agoo;	
220	He is ny from mynde with more and with leeste;	*nearly forgotten by everyone*
	Yet in his deying and in his grett woo	*as he was dying*

---

[1] *Thus the [story of] your life was kept locked up (little known)*

21

This lady, as thei sey, appered him unto: *i.e., Katherine*
Sche bad him be gladde in most goodely wyse;   *manner*
Sche wolde reward him, sche sayd, his servyse.

225   Of the west cuntré it semeth that he was
        Be his maner spech and be his style;   *manner of speech*
        He was sumtyme parsone of Sent Pancras   *formerly*
        In the cité of London a full grete whyle.
        He is now above us ful many a myle;
230   He be a mene to Kateryne for us,   *intermediary*
        And sche for us alle onto oure Lorde Jhesus.

        Aftyr him nexte I take upon me
        To translate this story and set it more pleyne,   *write it more clearly*
        Trostyng on other men that her charyté
235   Schall help me in this caas to wryght and to seyne.
        Godd send me part of that hevynly reyne
        That Apollo bare abowte, and eke Sent Poule;   *Apollo bore*
        It maketh vertu to growe in mannes soule.

        If ye wyll wete what that I am,   *wish to know who*
240   My cuntré is Northfolke, of the town of Lynne;
        Owt of the world to my profyte I cam
        Onto the brotherhode whech I am inne.
        Godd geve me grace nevyr for to blynne   *cease*
        To folow the steppes of my faderes before,
245   Whech to the rewle of Austen were swore.   *Augustinian Rule*

        Thus endyth the prologe of this holy mayde.
        Ye that rede it pray for hem alle   *read*
        That to this werk eythere travayled or payde,   *either worked on or paid for*
        That from her synnes with grace thei may falle
250   To be redy to Godd whan He wyll calle
        With Him in hevyn to drynke and to dyne,
        Thorow the prayere of this mayde Kateryne.

Book 1

[Katherine's birth, education, ancestry, and coronation]

Chapter 1

	Sumetyme there was a grete kyng in Grees,	
	Of Surré and Cypre bothe lord and syre,	*Syria; Cyprus*
	As clerkes tel us in elde storyes.	
	All thyng was rewlyd at his desyre,	
5	He governed full sadly that ilk empire:	*soberly; same*
	Costus men called this kyng thoo be name.	
	A losyd lorde was he and of ful grete fame,	*respected*
	A lombe to the meke, a leoun to the prowde,	*lamb; meek; lion*
	Thus was he noted, if ye lyst to lere.	*desire to learn [about him]*
10	He was so wel i-know bothe styll and lowde,	
	All dede him homage bothe fer and nere:	*far*
	Kyng, duke, erle, baron, and bachilere,	
	For her behove to his presens soute	*profit; presence; sought*
	And to his help eke whan hem nedyd oute.	*anything*
15	Many yldes longed thoo onto his grete lande	*islands belonged*
	And alle were thei buxum at his request.	*they all obeyed his commands*
	The grete see holy had he in his hande	*sea entirely under his control*
	And all the havenes both est and west —	*harbors*
	He welded hem alle ryth as him lest.	*ruled them all just as he pleased*
20	Were thei marchauntis, were thei marineris,	*sailors*
	Alle were thei than to him as omageris.	*subjects*
	This kyng in pees regned many yeres,	*peace*
	And because he was fayre and strong of bones	
	He was wele beloved of all his omageres;	*subjects*
25	A noble man, thei sayde, he was for the nones,	*for the occasion*

Gracious in feld, peisible in wones,[1]
Fre of his speche, large of his expens,   *Well-spoken; generous*
Ful gladly with peynes wold he dispens.   *dispense with punishments*

Was no lorde besyde that him wold do wrake   *harm*
30 For what man that dede he shuld it sone wayle   *soon regret*
Whan that he gan venjaunce to take —   *began vengeance*
Preyer as than wold not avayle.
To many a kyngdom made he asayle   *attacked*
And many a castell beet he ryth down
35 Whan thei to his lawes wold not be bown.   *bound*

A goode man was he, this is the grounde: *reason*
Meke as a mayde, manful at nede,   *Meek*
Stable and stedfast evyrmore i-founde;
Strong man of hand, douty man of dede,   *valiant*
40 Helper of hem that to him hade nede;   *needed him*
Wrong thinges tho wroute he nevere,   *did*
Petous of spiryt and mercyful was he evere.   *Compassionate*

Pees wold he put debate evyr above;   *Peace*
That vertu cleymyd he only to himselve.   *claimed*
45 Alle his noble werkys onto pees and love   *peace*
Were mad as mete as ex onto helve. *suited to each other as an axe to its handle*
Among all the lordes that men dyd thoo delve   *study*
He was most worthy and eke most wys.
Synne hated he hertly, harlatrye and vyis.   *Sin; heartily, harlotry and vice*

50 Ful grete pyté onto oure thowt it is   *we think it is*
That swech a trew man schuld hethen be,   *such*
But rith thus wrote thei that were ful wys:
Oute of the harde thorn brymbyl-tree
Growyth the fresch rose, as men may see;
55 So sprong oure Lady oute of the Jewys   *i.e., the Virgin Mary*
And Kateryne of hethen, this tale ful trew is.

---

[1] *Honorable on the battlefield, a peacemaker at home*

Chapter 2

	Too cytes had this kyng among all othere	*cities*
	Largest and grettest above hem alle:	
	The on cost of gold ful many a fothere	*one; a great amount*
60	Or he had made it with toure and with walle;	*Before*
	The other was made, as bokes sey alle,	
	A full longe tyme er he was bore,	*before*
	In whech all kynges thoo crowned wore.	*were*

The fyrst hyth Amaleck; in Cypre it stant.   *is called*
65   The other hyth Alysaunder; in Egypt it is.   *Alexandria*
The same lond of Cypre nothyng doth want,   *lack*
But is ful of plenté and full of blys,
Of gold, sylvyr, frute, and men, iwys;   *indeed*
A grete lond, closyd with the see abowte,   *surrounded by the sea*
70   On the northwest syde of Surré, it is no doute.   *Syria*

Therfore this kyng, ryght as for a keye   (*see note*)
Of all his kyngdame, set his town there;
Who come to Surré mote come that weye.   *must*
There may no shypp this cours forbere,   *avoid this route*
75   Were it in pees or ellis in were.   *Either in peace or in war*
It had a havene ful huge and ful grete,   *harbor*
And castelle strong with turrettis feete,   *pretty*

Open onto marchauntis, to alle that wille come.
Because hir fredomys were large and fayre,   (*see note*)
80   Both oute of hethnes and of Cristyndome,
It was a place of ful grete repayre.   *a popular destination*
Undir him there the kyng made a mayere   *mayor*
To kepe his lawes; thei shuld not fayle
Too stuf it with men and eke with vytayle.   *provision it; also; victuals*

85   Thus myght this lord from Alisaunder ryde   *Alexandria*
(In schyppes I mene) to this grete cité,
And evyr on his owe lordchippe abyde;   *without leaving his own realm*
For on alle cuntres principale lorde was he,
Were it of felde, of town, or of see,

90   Whech stode betwyx the grete cytes too.

            All was it do there as he bad it doo.   *Everything was done as he commanded*

            The other cyté, Alysaundre be name,

            On the bordyre of Egypt it stant ful fayre;

            A gret place, a large, and of hye fame.   *lofty*

95   Thei of Egypt mote nedys repayre   *must necessarily go*

            Onto this cyté, thorow wey and thorow wayre,   *by road and by river*

            If thei to Affryk or to Cartage goo;

            And thei of Affryk the same mote alsoo,

            If thei in Egypte wyll bye or selle.

100   Thedyr was Seynt Mark the evangelyste   *There*

            Sent be Seynt Petyr there for to dwelle,

            To preche hem the gospell of oure lord Cryste.

            He prechyd so there that hem alle twyst   *turned*

            Fro all her maumentrye and fals beleve;   *heathen practices*

105   He mad hem in Cryst for to beleve.

            He that wyll know this more plat and pleyn,   *clearly*

            Rede Philo, in his book whech he dyd calle   *Read*

            De vita theorica. There schall he seyn   *see*

            That thorowoute the cyté, in towre and in walle,

110   It was thoo fulfyllyd with hermytes alle,

            Monkys and prestys and swech holy men,   *Monks; other such*

            Here thirty, here twenty, here nyne, here ten.

            The cuntré all abowte was full of these men,

            And ful of martires, ful of confessoures,

115   Of maydenes, wydowys, and chast women:

            Who coude noumbyr all the fayre floures

            That growe in the mede aftyr swete schowres,   *meadow; showers*

            Than myght he noumbyr hem, I trow not he may. *might; them; believe*

            There were thei putte in ful scharp asay,   *tested sorely*

120   These vessells of gold, martires I mene,

            With fyre and with yryn i-slayn and i-brent,   *iron slain and burned*

            In furnes of sorowe were thei mad clene;   *furnace*

            Was non that scaped but or that he went   *escaped unless before*

	He schuld be dede or turn his entent.	*i.e., renounce his faith*
125	There was the fyrst exercyse of dyvyn scole,	
	Whech is a scyens that longith to noo fole,	*discipline; is mastered by; fool*
	For on Pathenus, as seyth oure book,	*a certain Pantaenus*
	Full many a yere red there with besy entent,	
	And aftyr him Clement the scole up toke;	
130	Orygene was the thirde aftyr that Clement	
	(Not Clement of Rome but another that us lent	
	Many a good coment and many a holy exhortacioun,	
	Most specyali in that book whech is called *Stromatum).*	
	Thys same Alysaundre whech I spak of now	
135	Was large, ryche, ful of puple eke,	*people*
	For that fame every man thedyr drow.	*drew every man there*
	Every knyght and marchaunt gune it than seke;	*did; seek*
	Thei thowt it was enow, whan thei schuld speke,	*enough*
	A kyng to be lorde ovyr thys alone,	
140	Thow he had not ellys longyng to his trone.	*no other lands in his realm*
	Eke for the grete welth that was in that wonis,	*property*
	Thei called her kyng none other name:	*their*
	"Kyng of Alysaundyr," thei seyd, "alone he is.	
	He is a lord; he is worthy swech fame.	*of such*
145	Mote every tunge be doum and every kné lame	*May; dumb*
	That oure noble lord neyther love ne drede;	
	And thei that do it, well mote thei spede."	*i.e., honor him; prosper*
	Too hundred and fourty yere aftyr Crystys byrth	
	Was even and no more to these kynges dayes.	*equal*
150	He levyth thus in joye and in mekyll myrth,	*lived; great happiness*
	And honoured swech goddes as longed to his layes.	*belonged to his faith*
	Or he wan his land he had scharp asayes,	*won; vigorous attacks*
	But to othir thing we wyl go now pleyn	*directly*
	To telle forth oure tale as the cronycles seyn.	*say*

Chapter 3

155 Almyty God that althing makyth growe
  Doth many more merveyles than we can cast,   *imagine*
  For whosoevyr men heryn or ellis sowe,   *however; heed; follow*
  It is sumtyme fyrst we wene shuld be last.   *suppose*
  Oure witte onto His witte is but a gnast;   *compared to; spark*
160 It mote nede be thus whan He wil have it so —   *must necessarily*
  All His wyll only mote nede be do.

  Whan thyng is ferthest from oure opynyon,
  Than werkyth He His wondres ryth at his wyll.
  Beholde now the spede and the savacyon   *prosperity; salvation*
165 Of the chyldryn of Israel; God wold hem not spylle   *them; abandon*
  But to kepe hem in daunger and miserye stille,
  In whech thei were falle only for synne.   *sin*
  He halpe hem owte whan that thei cowde blynne; *might have perished*

  If He had sonere holp hem, thei myth a went   *have supposed*
170 It had not be Goddes myght but her owne dede.
  Therfor chaunged He all her entent: *minds*
  He wold not help hem tyl that thei had nede.
  Whan thei were in dyspeyre and myght noght spede, *despair; prosper*
  Than sent He His help and His socoure.   *relief*
175 Thus doth oure Lord; thus doth oure Savyoure.

  Ryght in this wyse wrowt oure Lorde here: *did*
  He wold send a chyld ful onlych to other   *unlike any other*
  To these elde folk whech lyved all in dwere   *doubt*
  To hafe any chyld, most specyaly the modyr.
180 The kyng had levere than of gold a fothyr   *rather; large amount*
  He myght be sekyr of wych a new chaunce.   *certain*
  Zacharye and Elysabethe stode in this traunce.   *predicament*

  So dede Abraham with Sarra, his wyff;
  Sche conceyvyd not tyll sche was in age.   *elderly*
185 Joachym and Anne had the same lyff —
  Maryes forth-bryngers — and the same wage.   *reward*
  God can ful well make of swech a rage   *torrent*

A ful fayre floode; blessed mote He be.   *river; must*
So Kateryne is not alone in this degré,

190 For God to Himselfe this mayden had i-chose
     As for His owyn spouse and for His wyffe dere.
     Of swech speke all Crysten, as I suppose,
     "God send us part of hir good prayere!
     Of all save on sche is Him most nere;   *i.e., the Virgin Mary*
195 Sche may, and sche can, and sche wyll alsoo
     Pray to oure Lord that we may cume Him too."

Chapter 4

     Whan Godd, oure Lord, wold the seson schuld be
     That this fayre lady to lyth schuld be born,   *light*
     He ordeynd and sett it in swech a degré   *arranged*
200 That of too folkes whech lustes had lorne   *had lost their passion*
     Schuld this mayde spryng, as rose oute of thorne.
     This world wondred that this thing myght be soo,
     How so elde a lady with chyld schuld now goo.

     Many a man and woman at this thyng low.   *laughed*
205 Summe of hem sayd, "It is but a lye.
     The kyng is ful febyll, the qween ful eld now.
     Schal sche now grone? Schal sche now crye?
     Schal sche in this age in chyldebede lye?
     This thyng is not lykly!" Thus seyd thei alle,
210 Ladyes in the chaumbyr and lordys in the halle.

     But the tyme is come: Sche begynnyth to grone,
     Cryeth, and wayleth, as do alle women,
     For of that penaunce was Mary alone
     Excused, and no moo, thus oure bokes ken,   *no others; make known*
215 Whech that were writyn of ful holy men.
     Kateryne thei named that fayre mayd yinge.   *young*
     Hir fader men called Costus the kyng.

     Hir moder, thei seyd, sche hyght Meliades;   *was called*
     The kynges dowter sche was of Ermenye.   *daughter; Armenia*

220	Of bewté sche had prys in every prees	*beauty; stood out in every crowd*
	Thorowowte the londe of alle Sarcynrye.	*Saracens*
	Me lyst not in hir preysyng lengere to tarye:	*wish; longer in her praise to tarry*
	Sche was full fayre and full goode eke;	
	It is schewyd in hir dowter, that men now seke	*daughter; seek*

225	To be her help in myschefe and in nede.	*their; trouble*
	But whan thre dayes were pased and i-gon,	
	This chyld for to hylle, to lulle, and to lede	*clothe; rock; supervise*
	Too worthy ladyes were ordeynd anon.	*Two; appointed at once*
	And not only thei to travayle there alone,	
230	But of other women a ful grete rowte,	*staff (company)*
	Ryght for this cause: to bere it abowte,	

	To kepe it, to wasche it, and for to clothe;	*it (the child)*
	To lyft it, to lull it, and to fede it eke;	
	To bathe it, to wyp it, and to rokke it bothe.	
235	Thei had her labour newly be the weke;	*They had their new duties every week*
	Thus is it kept, it schuld not be seke.	*sick*
	The kyng had of it a comfort ful hye;	*took great joy*
	The qwen coude not ther-fro kepe now her hye.	*take her eyes off [the child]*

	Thus was it norched, this nobyl goodly chylde,	*nurtured*
240	This gracious lady, tyll sche cowde goo.	*walk*
	Sche was fro hir byrth bothe meke and mylde.	*meek*
	Mercy fro the tetys grew with hir alsoo	*teats*
	And lested with hir all hir lyffe ther-too.	*lasted all her life*
	Sche was ful sone plesyd whan sche made mone;	*quickly gratified; cried*
245	No wondyr it is: thei hafe but hir alone.	

Chapter 5

	Thus provyd this princesse evyre more and more.	*matured*
	Sche was set to book and began to lere	*learn*
	All the letteres that were leyd hir before,	
	For of all the scoleris that are now or were	
250	Sche is hem above; for neyther love ne feere	
	Mad hir to stynt whan sche began to ken	*stop; learn*
	The lettyres and the wordys that sche spelled then.	

Sche had maystyres fro ferre that were full wyse   *from far away*
To teche hir of rethoryk and gramere the scole;   *knowledge*
255   The cases, the noumbres, and swych manere gyse;   *information*
The modes, the verbes, wech long to no fole.   *which can be mastered by no fool*
Sche lerned hem swetly, withowte any dole,   *grief*
Bothe the fygures and the consequence,   *forms; logic*
The declynacyons, the persones, the modes, the tens.   *declensions; moods; tenses*

260   Among all othir, a wyse man there was
And ful sad therto; he was hir chauncelere.   *serious at that; chancellor*
Men called him be name Mayster Athanas.
He was survyoure to all that there were,   *supervisor*
And, as I seyd ere, he payed her hyere.   *salaries*
265   He was an hye clerk and a sovereyne.   *high and distinguished scholar*
All the seven artes coude he ful pleyne,   *knew; clearly*

And ovyre this lady was his most cure   *concern*
That sche schuld be occupyed all the long day
In doctrine and stodye, save in mesure: *but in moderation*
270   Sumtyme among had sche hir play;
Sumtyme to hir mayster wold sche sey nay —
Whan he bad hir play, sche wold sit stylle.
To stody and goodenes inclined was hir wylle.

Sche lerned the Greke, sche lernyd the Latyn tunge.
275   Sche lerned of nature the pryvy weys alle   *all the secrets*
That ony philosophyre be his doctrine had runge.   *wrung [from nature]*
Sche knew the effectis as thei schuld falle
Of all the bodyes whech we the planetes calle.
This was thorow besynes of Athanas the clerk,   *through the efforts*
280   Whech tended onto hir and set hir thus on werk.   *supervised her studies*

God of His grace, as seyth the story,
Agens alle heretykys that reygned thoo there   *Against; at the time*
Wold all His conquest and His victory
Schuld be arered only be hir.   *accomplished*
285   Therfor lern sore, thou yong Goddys scolere: *earnestly; scholar of God*
Thu schall ovyrcome heresye and blaspheme
Thorowowte all Grek, thorowowte all thi reme.   *Greece; realm*

	Ryght as be twelve ydyotes, seynt Austyn seith	*illiterate men*
	(He meneth the Aposteles, for thei not lerned were),	
290	Thorowowte the word was sowyn oure feyth	*world*
	That every man may know and every man lere,	
	Godd wold not wynn us with wysdam ne fere	*fear*
	But with holy boystysnesse, if I schuld sey soo.	*simplicity (humility)*
	Ryght thus, as me thinkyth, in this caas hath He doo,	
295	For whan that His chyrch was at gret neede	
	He ordeynd this lady for to geve batayle	*do battle*
	Ageyn all the word; thei schall hir not ovyre lede,	*Against; world; overcome*
	Ne alle her argumentis schal not avayle.	*their*
	Sche schal so be lerned that all her asayle	*attacks*
300	Schall fayl and falle bothe cunnyng and bost.	*boast*
	Sche schall be myty with strength of Goost.	*mighty; Holy Spirit*

Chapter 6

	Hir fader, that sche schuld lern these artes alle,	*so that*
	This nobyll lady, his owyn douter dere,	
	Ded mak a paleyse large and ryalle	*royal*
305	In whech he wold that sche schuld lere.	*desired*
	Bothe knytes and clerkes, all dwelt thei there	
	Whech were ordeynd to hir owyn servyse.	
	Now to make hir rest, now for to make hir ryse,	
	And eke new norture to tell hir and to teche,	*lessons*
310	Many maysteres therfore thethyr were fett.	*fetched*
	As fer as her cunnyng myght strech and reche,	
	Thei lerned this lady withowte any lett.	*taught; impediment*
	Alle her wyttys were only on hir sett.	*their*
	Ye may well suppose in youre owne dome,	*judgment*
315	Evyr as sche grew, the grettere mayster come.	
	Her stodyes there full craftily were i-pyght	*furnished*
	With deskys and chayeres and mech othir gere,	*chairs; gear*
	Arayed on the best wyse, and glased full bryght.	*well-lighted*
	Every faculté be himselve, for thei of gramere were	*discipline by itself*
320	Sett on the west syde, and eke thei that lere	*study*

Astronomye on the est, ryght for thei schuld loke   *look*
Sumtyme on the hevyn, sumtyme on her boke.   *book*

All the other artes betwyx hem stode arowe,   *in their place*
Ryght aftyr her age and aftyr her dygnyté.   *according to*
325   Every man that cam there myght well i-knowe
Whech was worthyere and hyer of degré.
Hir fadyr the kyng seldom wold hir se:
Onto these clerkes he hath hir thus take   *teachers; he turned her over*
As thow he had hir only now newly forsake;

330   For lettyng of hir lernyng dyd he than soo.   *To avoid hindering*
Sche wex fast in body and lerned eke sore.   *grew; fervently*
Whan o mayster was goo, anothir cam hir too.   *one scholar went*
Thus chaungyng of maystirys and eke of lore   *learning*
Had this noble mayde. Sche lerned mych the more.
335   Ye may wete nature lovyth variaunce: *know*
Sumtyme men stody; sumtyme thei daunce.   *dance*

The kyng dyd make there for hir alone
A paleyse wallyd ryght on the sowth syde,
Open to the sune there was hir trone —   *throne*
340   There is no swych now in this worde wyde.   *nothing like it; world*
It was made for Kateryne there to abyde
Whan sche wold stody be hirselve sole.   *alone*
In the grete garden was most hir scole.

It was fer awey fro every manere wyght.   *person*
345   It was made and ordeynd at hir owyn devyse.   *design*
There wold sche ly sumtyme, stody and wryght.   *write*
It was sett full of trees, and that in straunge wyse.   *uncommon*
There wold sche sytte, and there wold sche rise;
There was hir walkyng and all hir dysporte.   *leisure*
350   Solitary lyf to stodyers is comfort.   *"studiers"*

Sche bare the key of this gardeyn — there had it no moo.   *no one else had it*
Whan sche went in, sche schett it full fast.   *shut it securely*
It was speryd ful treuly went sche to or froo,   *fastened securely*
For of many thynges was sche sore agast   *dismayed*

355   But most of inquietude. Stody may not last
      With werdly besynesse, ne with his cure: *worldly occupation; its care*
      The olde wyse sey thus, I yow ensure.   *wise ones*

      The walles and the toures were made nye so hye,   *nearly*
      Ful covertly with arches and sotelly i-cast;   *artfully; cleverly engineered*
360   There myght not cume in but foule that doth flye.   *birds*
      The gatis, as I seyd, were schett full fast
      And evyr more hirselve wold be the last.
      The key eke sche bare, for sche wolde soo.
      Thus lyved this lady in hir stody thoo.   *then*

Chapter 7

365   Sche lerned than the liberall artes seven.
      Gramere is the fyrst and the most lyth;   *enjoyable*
      He tellyth the weye full fayre and full even,   *exactly*
      How men schall speke, and how thei schall wryte.
      Retoryk, the secunde, is sett in this plyte: *can be described thus*
370   He doth ny the same, save that he arayeth   *nearly*
      His maters with colourys and with termes dysplayeth.

      The thyrde sciens calle thei dialetyk: *discipline; dialectic*
      He lerneth men within a lythyll throwe;   *while*
      If he be stodied there is non to him lyke
375   The trewth fro the falshed that techeth for to know.[1]
      Aftyr him than folowyth ryght be rowe   *in order*
      Arsmetryk, in whech the cunnyng so stant   *Arithmetic; is such that*
      Nowmbres schall thu know, thu schall not want.   *lack*

      Thei tawt hir also the scyens of musyk;   *taught; discipline*
380   Ful wel grownded was sche in this melodye.
      Sche had a maystir — there was none him lyke —
      He departyd this scyens in thre, withouten lye: *divided*
      Into metyr, to ryme, and to armonye   *harmony*

---

[1] Lines 374–75: *If it be studied, there is nothing like / Dialectic for teaching one the difference between right and wrong*

	(Armonye is in voyse, in smytyng or wynde;	*striking [of musical instruments]*
385	Symphonye and euphonye arn of his kynde).	*are*

In geometrye was this lady lernyd also,
In Euclidis bokys with his portraturys.   *figures*
That is a sciens mech stody longeth ther-too,   *it requires much study*
For to know the letterys and the figures.
390   If I speke therof I schal make forfetures   *errors*
Ageyn this sciens — I can not of that arte   *know*
But swech as he can that makyth a carte!¹

In astronomye this lady eke so hye steye   *i.e., is so learned*
Sche know the strenght and the stondyng stylle   *position*
395   Of alle the planetis that regnen upon hey,   *reign on high*
Whech are of goode wyll and whech are of ille,
Whech wyll help a mater and whech will it spille,   *ruin*
And these she lernyd both more and lesse.
Sche mowled not, I trow, in no ydylnes.²

400   Thus for hir lernyng had sche swech fame
That hir fader dede gader thorowoute the land
All the grete clerkys that were of any name   *reputation*
Ryth to this entent, as I undirstande:
To wete yf his doutir dare take it unhand   *know; in hand*
405   To be apposyd of so many wyse men.   *challenged by*
Thei were gadred in that place thre hundred and ten:

Eche of hem schall now do all his myght
To schew his cunnyng; if any straunge thyng   *uncommon*
Hath he lernyd his lyve, he wyll now ful ryght
410   Uttyr hit, for his name therby schall spryng.   *reputation; grow*
But there was ryght nowt but Kateryn the yyng   *no one; young*
Undyrstod all thyng and answerd ther-too;
Her problemes all sche hath sone ondoo.   *soon solved*

---

¹ Lines 391–92: *I know no more [geometry] than a cart-maker*

² *No moss grew on her, I believe, on account of idleness*

"O good Godd," seyd these clerkes thane,
415 "This mayd hath lerned more thyng in hir lyve
Than we supposyd, for more than we sche can.   *she knows more than we do*
We wondyr how sche may oure argumentis dryve
For hir conclusyoun now; in yerys fyve
Cune we not lerne that sche doth in one."
420 Thus seyd these wysmen be row everychon.   *each one in turn*

Thei tok than her leve at the kyng alle;   *took leave of*
Home to her cuntré, certeyn, will thei goo.
"This mayd, youre doghtyr, lord," thei seyd, " sche schall
Be a wondyr woman, and sche may leve ther-too.   *if she lives*
425 Of us nedyth sche noght; we hafe not here to doo.   *nothing to do here*
Sche can that we can, and therto mech more."   *knows what we know*
Thus seyd thei, certeyn, the wyse that there wore.   *wise men; were*

Thys noble kyng hath reward hem full weele,
Gove hem grete gyftys and grete liberté —
430 Lordes dede so thanne; clerkes had every deel,   *bit*
All that thei spent, of the liberalyté
And of the bountyfnesse of swech lordes fre.   *generosity; liberal*
Thus are thei rewardyd and home everychoone,   *everyone goes home*
And Kateryne in stody is left thus alone.

Chapter 8

435 Whan all was welle and sekyr, as sche wende,   *secure; thought*
Than cam deth to hows and dyd his duté.   *home; duty*
Of all hir joye he made sone an ende,
For he hath take awey hir owyn fadyr fre   *noble*
And owte of this world hath ledd him, where he
440 Is in swech place as longyth onto him.   *is appropriate to*
He is logged there with lordys of his kyne   *lodged; family*

Whech deyd withouten feyth, withowt Crystendome;
Kateryne is swech on, yet sche schall not be long.   *such a one*
Owte of all Grece the grete lordes come:
445 But thei had do soo, thei had do grete wrong.   *Unless*
All her grete worchep oonly dyd honge   *honor; depend*

36

Upon the noble kyng; he lyght there now ded. *lies*
Thei closyd him in clothe and aftyrward in lede. *enclosed; lead*

Thei led him to the temple with solemnité
450 (If wepyng and waylyng schuld be called soo).
There was noon othir noyse than in that cité
But "Welaway! Alas, what schul we doo?
Oure lord is now gone — we gete him no moo.
Who schall bere the crown now he is deed?
455 He left us non eyre for to be oure heed *heir; head (i.e., ruler)*

"But a yong mayde. What schal sche doo?
Sche is but a woman! Yet had sche weddyd be
Or tyme that hir fadyr went thus us froo *Before*
It had be more sekyrnesse and more felicyté. *certainty*
460 There is no more to sey, but sekyrly we
Are likely to be subject onto othir londys.
We bounde sumtyme; now mote we suffyr bondys."[1]

The noble qween eke, what sorow that sche made
It is pyté to here, to telle, and to rede.
465 There cowde no solace hir hert that tyme glade; *gladden*
The teeres fell down evyr as sche yede. *went*
The yung lady Kateryne hath chaunged hir wede, *dress*
And hir coloure eke is now full pale.
What schuld I of her sorow make lengere tale?

470 The kyng was leyd in a toumbe made of golde and stones
Ful ryaly, ye may wete, for he was her kyng, *royally; know; their*
Anoynted eke with baume, that neythir flesch ne bones *balm*
Schuld rote ne stynke — swech was the beryyng *the practice of burying*
In that tyme to lordes — and mych other thyng
475 Was seyd and do, whech nedyth not to rehers, *need not be rehearsed*
For happyly summe folk myght than be the wers *perhaps; be the worse*

---

[1] *Once we bound [others]; now we must suffer bonds*

	To here swech maumentrye and swych maner rytes.	*learn of; idolatry; rites*
	The lordes abode there styll in that same place,	
	Both dukys and erlys, bischoppys and knytes,	
480	Thyrty dayes evyn, for so usage was.	*custom*
	The dayes rone fast and begune to pace.	*pass*
	The lordes that there were, thei seyd that her kyng	
	Mote hafe a memoryall for any maner thyng,	*Must certainly have*

And that of swech lestyng whech schuld not fayle. *permanence*
485 Thus seyd thei all ryght with oon entent. *all in agreement*
Peyntyng and wrytyng and graving in entayle, *ornamental engraving*
It wyll wanyse and wast, roten and be brent. *vanish; waste; burned*
Therfore to this ende are thei all consent:
The grete cyté whech her lord dyd make *their*
490 Schall chaunge now his name for her lordes sake. *its name; their*

It schall no lengere hyght thus, the gret Amaleck. *be called*
His name wyll thei turn thorowoute all the cost. *change; coast*
Whosoevyr thedyr come, with cart or with sek, *there; sack*
Thei mote called it now the citee Famagost. *must; Famagusta*
495 Thus mad thei crye than thorowoute al the hoost *assembly*
That all men of Grece mote have it in mowth, *speak of it*
Dwelle he est or west, dwelle he north or sowthe.

And this is her cause: "For that cyté he made. *reason*
In the same dwelt he most," thus seyd thei alle,
500 "In this cyté mych myrth and mych joye he had;
In this cyté to deth eke he down dede falle.
For these same causes his name bere it schalle.
Evyr whyll it on grounde stant, it schall nevyr be lost, *stands; i.e., forgotten*
But evyr be in knowlech the cyté of Famagost." *Famagusta*

505 Thus it is called now and evermore schall be,
With a G sett there the C schuld stande:
The grete noble Famagost that stant on the see. *Famagusta; sea*
Thus it is named thorowout every lande,
There walkyth many a foote, and werkyth many hande.
510 Thus schal the name of wordy men sprede, *worthy*
And schrewes shul sterve nameles, swech is her mede. *wretches; die; reward*

Book 1

Chapter 9

	The qween sett a parlement at hir owe coste	*expense*
	Att Alisaundre the Grete, to whech sche wolde	*desired*
	Every lorde that held of hir husbonde Coste	*was bound to*
515	To this parlement nedis goo or ryde shold;	
	But he come wylfully, he may be ful bold,	*Unless; rest assured*
	He schal be compelled. Sche sent ferre and nye	
	For alle the lordis, and no man wyst why.	*knew*

	But why that sche sette the parlement in that place	
520	O cause there was, for in that same cité	*One reason*
	Alle kynges of that lond, as usage was,	*custom*
	Hadd receyved the crowne wyth solemnyté.	
	And for a costom long hold may nott brokyn be	*because*
	But yf it turbel meny men, therfore she held it there.	*disturb*
525	Many lord and lady att that parlement were.	

	Anothir cause there was: for the kynrode of hir	*reason; her kin*
	Had founded this cité and refounded eke,	
	Be whom and be whos dayes ye shal sone here	*About them and their times*
	If ye wyl be stylle and no man now speke	
530	But I myselve. Ye schal not nede to seke	*seek*
	Mo cronycles or storyes; ye schal lere of me	*More*
	Alle the lyne and the lordes aftyr her degré.	*according to*

	Ther was a lord sumtyme that the soudon was	*sultan*
	Of Surré and of Egipt: Babel was his name.	*Syria*
535	He beldyd Alysaundre in that same place:	*built Alexandria*
	He called it Babilon, in haunsyng of his fame,	*to enhance*
	That it schuld not falle ne nevyr be lame.	
	This was his wyll; and aftyr many a day	
	It was called Babilon, sothly for to say,	*truly*

540	Not Babilon alone, but Babilon the lasse,	*the lesser*
	For differens of the other that stant in the est.	*To distinguish it from*
	Who wyll owte Egypt into Affryk passe,	*Africa*
	Goo or ryde wheydir he wyll, this wey is the best:	*where*
	This was anothyr cause why this gret fest	

545   Was hold in that place, for hir ryall kyn   *royal*
    Oute of this Babell cam, bothe the more and the myn;   *the greater and the lesser*

    The third cause was this, as seyth Athanas —
    Grettest of hem alle, as semyth onto me —
    This same cyté in the londe of Egipt was,
550   In whech there reygned another kyng than he,
    So was he called than for diversyté   *to distinguish between them*
    Kyng of Alysaundyr alone, ryght for differens   *to distinguish himself*
    Of the kyng of Egypt, this is the sentens.   *reason*

    Thys wote I well of Athanases resoun
555   Whech that he makyth of the fundacyoun[1]
    Of this same Alysaundyr, whech oft with tresoun
    Was nye disceyvyd of many straunge nacyoun.   *nearly*
    But now wyll we leve all that declaracyoun   *leave*
    And tell forthe of Babel and of othir men
560   Whech long to the kynrod, mo than nyne or ten.[2]

Chapter 10

    Thys same Babell had a sone aftyr him;
    Madagdalus he hyght. He was lord alsoo   *was called*
    Of this Babilon many yere. And forth the same kyn
    Reygned in that same place mo than on or too,   *more*
565   For his son hyght Antiochus, the story seyth soo
    (Not Antiochus the grete, of whech spekyth Machabe,
    But another before, as ye schall sone se).

    Thys Antiochus had a son men cleped Gorgalus.   *called*
    A worthi man he was, of Surré lord and syre.
570   He begate a sone men clepyd Antiochus,
    And aftyr Antiochus, reygned in that empyre
    His sone Seleucus. He sett ryght in a mire   *swamp*

---

[1] Lines 554–55: *I know this well from Athanasius' account of the foundation*

[2] *Which belong to that family, more than nine or ten*

The cyté men clepe Seleuce for his owyn fame,
And Antyoche he beldyd in his faderes name.   *built*

575 This is the fyrst lyne of this ych Gorgalus,   *same*
For we mote turn ageyn, if we truly telle.
This same Gorgale yongere son hyght Mardemius;
A manly man he was and of hert felle.   *fierce*
Gret Alysaundyr sprong of him as strem owt of welle,   *Alexander (the Great)*
580 For unto this Mardemy wedded was this fayre
Meliore, the noble mayde of Macedonye the ayre,   *heir*

And of this Mardemye and Meliore the mayde
Cam Kyng Phylyppe, fadyr to Alysaunder the Grete.   *Alexander*
Thus went the secund lyne, as oure auctour sayde.
585 Oute of Gorgales yong son the fyrst have we lete   *abandoned*
But for a lytyll whyle, for we wyll now trete
Of the woundres that this Alysaundyr sowte in his lyffe — *Alexander sought*
All his labure yet in every mouth is ryffe.   *rife*

He conquered the kyng of Pers whych Dary hyght;   *Persia; Darius*
590 He toke Arabe and Fenice, and eke his owyn cosyne, *Arabia; Phoenicia*
Antiochus Gorgalys sone, he ovyrcame be myght.
He wan this Babylon from him with gune and engyne;   *cannon and catapult*
There cessed the name of Babylon and forevyr gan lyne, *ceased; went to rest*
For he chaungyd it to his, and thus he called it than
595 Alysaundyr aftyr him because he it wanne.   *conquered*

Ten cytes mad this lord even oute of the grounde.   *founded*
All ten thei hafe his name, Alysaundyr thei hyght.   *Alexandria*
Too cytes he chaunged and kept hem hole and sounde: *Two; renamed*
Alysaundyr he wolde thei schulde hyght be ryght.
600 In twelve yere he wan this worlde with ful grete myght.
Whan he schuld dey, he partyd his londe on twelve   *divided*
Whech he had governed alone sumtyme himself.

To his lordes gave he his londes for to holde.
Surry and Alysaundyr, Fenice and Palestyne,   *Phoenicia*
605 That gafe he to Seleucus, myghty man and bolde.   *mighty*
He was to this Alisaundyr of kyn ryght cosyne

41

Of Gorgalus bloode, as I seyde, of the fyrst lyne
At whech I than left and now begynne ageyne.
Alle thing may not be seyd at ones, as clerkis seyne.

Chapter 11

610	Too and thirty yere reigned Seleucus there.	
	He had an eyre aftyr him, kyng of that place,	*heir*
	A noble man thei called Antiochus Sothere.	
	Twenty wyntyr evene among hem he was,	*i.e., years*
	And aftyr had the crown, the sceptyr, and the mace	*staff*
615	His son, whech thei calle Antiochus Theos.	
	He reygned fiftene yere and aftyr him than roos	*rose*

A man thei call be name Seleucus Galericus.
There reygned he twenty wynter, and than Selecus Garanne
Thre yere bare the crown, and efte Antiochus
620 Whech is called the Grete. He reygned thanne
Sex and thirty wynter. Jewes yet him banne   *still curse him*
For the sorow that he dede onto her lond and hem
Whan he robbed the temple at Jherusalem.

	The noble book of Machabe wryghtyth his dedys,	
625	His cruelnesse, his ire, and his treson, eke	*also*
	His feyned repentauns. Therfore his mede is	*reward*
	Sorow for synne, for whan he was seke	*sin; sick*
	He askyd mercy but not worth a leke.	*leek (i.e., worthlessly)*
	He left a sone nye of that same plyte;	*nearly of the same condition*
630	Seleucus Philophator men seyn that he hyght.	*was named*

	He synnyd be his doghtyr ful onkyndely,	*against nature (i.e., incestuously)*
	Therfore was he brent with the bryght levene.	*bright lightning*
	In *Appollony of Tyre* ye may rede the storye,	
	How many lordes were dede be sex and be sevyn	*i.e., by the dozen*
635	For thei coude not gesse his problemes evyn.	*solve his riddles*
	He reygned there eleven yere, withowten any lees.	*i.e., to tell the truth*
	His son aftyr him hyght Antiochus Epiphanes.	

His yeres were eleven and his son hyght thus,
Antiochus Eupatere. He leved yeres too,
640   And aftyr him sekyrly reygned Demetrius.
Thre yere he bare the crown, the story seyth soo.
Antiochus Sedites kyng was there thoo
Nyne yere evyn, and aftyr him reygned there
Anothir kyng thei calle Demetrius Sothere.

Chapter 12

645   In his tyme the Romaynes whon fro him
Mech of his londe and eke that gret cyté
Whech that he helde, and so had all his kyn,
I mene Alysaundyr. Thei set there her see —   *capital*
The Romaynes dyd so. For he was fayn to flee   *Although he wanted to*
650   Forth into Egypt, he held him ryght there.
Thus led he his lyffe in sorow and in feere;   *fear*

He lost all the londes whych his faderes wonne.
Foure-skore yere even reygned the Romaynes there
And in this servage newly thus begunne   *new state of servitude*
655   Reygned the same kyng the tyme of twelve yere.
Alysaundyr, his son, than dede the crown bere
Nyne yere evyn, and than Demetrye, his brother.
He reygned foure yere and aftyr him anothir,

Men calle him in bokes Antiochus Griphus.
660   He governed twelve yere all this forseyd londe.
In these foure kyngis tyme, myne auctour seyth thus,
All this ilke cuntré to the Romaynes was bonde   *same*
Tyll that Fortune turned so hir honde
Whan Helyus Adrianus emperour was of Rome,
665   Whych weddyd his doghtyr to on thei call Phalone.

This Phalon was sone onto the seyd Demetrius.   *son*
Be him cam Surry to ryght hold ageyn,   *its rightful governors*
And all her subjeccyoun to Rome cessed thus.
Solaber was the name of the mayd thei seyn;
670   Ryght soo hyght sche. Thei that hir there seyn   *saw*

Seyn nevyr swych anothir; thus seyd thei alle.   *Saw*
This same Phalon — summe men so him calle —

Had a ful fayre sone be this same Solabere.
Zozimus he hyght, kyng aftyr his fadyr he was,
675   And Archenon and Archibelon reygned also there,
Than aftyr Antigonus, and than cam Claudace —
Sune aftyr fadyr, all reygned in that place —
Than aftyr Borus, ryght thus haf I founde,
And thanne ageyn Claudace called the secunde.

680   This same Claudace Costus fadyr was,   *was Costus' father*
And this same Costus fadyr to Kateryne.
Here may ye se of what men and of what place
Cam this woman, this lady, this virgyne;
Here is it schewyd hooly all the lyne.   *Her entire line is shown here*
685   Thus I behyte you that I schuld doo.   *promised*
In this reknyng myne auctour and I are too,   *account; are in disagreement*

For he acordeth not wyth cronicles that ben olde   *agrees; are*
But diversyth from hem, and that in many thyngis.   *departs*
There he acordyth, there I him hold,[1]
690   And where he diversyth in ordre of these kyngis
I leve him, and to othir mennys rekenyngis   *other men's accounts*
I geve more credens, whech before him and me
Sette alle these men in ordre and degré.

Butte men wyll sey now and happely replye,   *perhaps*
695   "What menyth this lyne and this rehersayle,
To rekene so many men and to multiplye
Noumbres and yerys whech may not avayle?   *are of no use*
And eke, us thynkyth, it doth sumwhat fayle,   *is rather pointless*
For thow thei were men of grete lordschype,   *though*
700   The kynrod of schrewys to God is no worchepe."[2]

---

[1] *Where he agrees [with the old chronicles], I follow him*

[2] *The lineage of heathens does God no honor*

I answere hereto as do Seynt Jerome:
"Crist cam of schrewys," he seyth, "for this skylle   *heathens; reason*
The principall cause why to this world He come
To corect synneris; that was His wylle."
705   For many men that synfull were and ille   *evil*
Are in His genelogie, ye may hem there fynde,
My lady Kateryne stante in this same kynde.   *situation*

Chapter 13

Now to telle forth even as I fyrst sayde:
The lordys are come whech clepyd were.   *summoned*
710   Agens the parlement the cité is arayd   *arrayed for the parliament*
With plenté of vitayle and all odyr gere.   *food; other gear*
Men lakked ryth nowt that were logged there;   *Lodgers lacked nothing*
Gret chepe had thei, all maner vitayle;   *abundance*
It is stuffyd so be resoun it may not fayle.   *stocked*

715   The reall lordys wyth baroun and bacheler   *royal; knight*
Are com now thedyr to do her servyse.   *their*
Byschopis and clerkys togedyr in fere —   *in company*
Thei wyll now schew her wyttys wyse;
Thei schall have nede or that thei ryse.   *before they go*
720   Summe lordys are come eke homage to make,
And ladys many ryth for the qwenys sake.

This mayde is crownyd with all the observawns   *rituals*
Whech servyd that tyme in stede of the Masse.   *were practiced; Mass*
Thei prayd to Jupiter he schuld hir avauns   *bless*
725   And to all the goddys, both more an lasse,
There was no god whech thei lete thoo passe.   *overlooked*
The lordys swore all how that thei schuld
Her servyse evyr sewe and her sutes holde.   *follow; claims*

Thanne begunne the festes, I trow gret inow,   *believe great enough*
730   As in that cuntré custome was thane.
To lord and to lady, and to povert low,   *the lowly poor*
Full foyson was there; to every man   *plenty*
Many mo deyntys than I rehers can.   *delicacies*

Every man had plenté in hale and in halle; *tents and in halls*
735 Thoo men that servyd it nedyd not hem to calle, *did not need to be called*

Swech rewle and ordinauns was there i-had.
There was no gate warnyd to no maner wyte, *closed to anyone*
But that every man schuld be ryth glad *so that*
Thei were kept opyn both day and nyth. *night*
740 The bordes evyr cured and the mete dyth, *tables; tended; food prepared*
Whan on had his mele in cam anodyr.
Of sylvyr vessell there was many a fothir. *vessels; a large amount*

No place was voyd, neydyr parloure nor chaumbyr, *empty; neither*
But all were thei full of women or of men.
745 The grete paleys that stante at Alisaundyr,
It was full of puple, no man seyd "go hen" *people; "go away"*
Save reverens was had; lordes — here nyne, here ten — *respect*
Thus kept her astate. The cité eke all abowte
Was full of gentylys withinne and withowte. *gentlepeople*

750 Lordes and ladyes that were there of hir kynne
Onto that feste come, both on and odyr, *i.e., one and all*
And all were thei loggyd in full riall ine. *lodged; royal dwelling*
Summe were of hir fadyrs syde, summe were of hir modyr.
Of curtesye and gentylnesse, game and non othyr, *pleasure*
755 Was than her carpyng. Save summe spoke of love, *conversation; Except*
Every man spak of thing whech was to his behove. *benefit*

Justys were there, and thoo with the best; *Jousts; those*
Summe had the bettyr and summe had the werre. *worse [luck]*
The grete theatyr there had ful lytyll rest: *theater*
760 Evyr was there fytyng, but there was no werre. *war*
Many noble men whech were come fro ferre *afar*
In that same place were asayd ychoon, *tested each one*
As well in wrestyllyng as puttyng at the ston. *wrestling*

And aftyr all this is endyd and eke i-don,
765 Justis, revellis, and festes gune to slake. *began to wind down*
Thei toke her leve, homward for to goon,
But yet or thei fully had her leve i-take *before; taken their leave*

46

	Ech lord whech had there any lady and make	*mate*
	Was gove two courseres (of whech the on	*given; horses*
770	Was blak as cole, the other wythe as bon)	*black as coal; white as bone*
	With sadyll and brydyll of gold and of sylke.	
	Many moo rewardes eke than I can now seye:	
	Summe were gove mantellis wyght as the mylk	*cloaks white*
	On whech were many a broche and many a beye.	*ornament*
775	Thus ryd thei homwarde foreth in her wey.	
	There is noght ellys now but farwell and goo,	*nothing else*
	"I pray God be with yow." Thus is the parlement doo.	*finished*

Chapter 14

	Thys lady, as the story even forth telleth,	
	Kepyth hir chambyr and holdyth hir thus inne.	*Stays in; keeps to herself*
780	With hir modyr the qween as yet sche dwellyth.	
	Hir bokes for to loke on can sche noght blyne;	*cease*
	Whosoevyr lett hir, he dothe full gret synne.	*prevents*
	To offende his lady, what wene ye it is?	
	There was no man that tyme that durst do thys.	*dared*
785	It was oonly hir joye, all hir entent,	*i.e., study*
	For hir hert that tyme was set to nowt elles.	*nothing*
	Ful hye honour therby aftyrward sche hente.	*gained*
	Bothe wit and wysdome owte of hir hert welles	*surges*
	Evyn as the streme rennyth fro the welles;	
790	Swych fayre frute in stodye dyd sche fynde	
	With besy conceytes whech sche had of kynde.	*a sharp mind; by nature*
	There was no wyght that in hir presence	*person*
	Durst onys touch of ony ille dede;	*ever allude to*
	And if he dyd, he had hir offens.	*he offended her*
795	Forevyr more he coude not aftyr spede	*prosper*
	As for to be hir servaunde, that is no drede.	
	Sche hated not the persone, but only the synne.	
	Of vertuous spech coude sche not blynne.	*cease*

There was nevyr wrong founde in that may.   *maiden*

800 The cors of hir governauns was evyr so clene,   *pure*

Bothe pryvy and aperte; at every asay,   *private and public; trial*

Stedfast and stable was evyr this qwene.

Sche was a very seynt, truly as I wene,   *believe*

Thow sche were not baptized. So was Cornelius: *Cornelius was too*

805 His prayere was herde — scripture seyth thus —

Of oure Lorde Godd or he baptized were,   *By*

And therfore was Petyr sent unto him,

The articles of the feyth him for to lere.   *teach*

He had feyth befor, but it was dyme.   *faint*

810 He was made to Cryst a ful ryght lyme.   *limb*

His feyth was not cause of his good werkes,

But his werkes causyd feyth, thus seye these clerkys.

Thys same lady eke, thow sche not baptized were,

Sche hauntyd holy werkys be steryng of the spryght   *practiced; stirring; spirit*

815 Whech made hir of synne for to hafe fere   *fear*

And to love vertu bothe day and nyght.

The soule nedyth vertu as mech as yye lyght;   *eyes need light*

This wote thei well that feel experyens.   *who have learned by experience*

This was the cause that hir noble presens

820 Was noryschere of vertu and qwenchere of vyce,   *nourisher*

For whan sche coud aspye any mysdrawte   *perceive; misconduct*

Of man or of woman, that thei were nyce,   *foolish*

For fere or for lofe wold sche leve nawte,   *not hold back for fear or love*

But soone schuld thei full wysyly be tawte.   *taught*

825 "It may not be thus," sche sayd, "it is not honeste.

A man, but he be reulyd, he is but a beste.

"What wene ye now whan ye trespace?   *What are you thinking of*

Thow I not aspye yow, I sey yow trulye.   *see; tell*

There is oon above that loketh on oure face

830 And on all the membrys of oure bodye;

If he ony fowle dede may in us aspye,

He deynyth oure servyse. This is my preve.   *disdains; contention*

Sey clerkys what thei wyll, thus I beleve,

"For wele I wote, above Jupiter and alle
835   Is a maystir-rewler, and eterne He is;
Upon this world whatsoevyr schall befalle,
Falle whan it schall, He is evyr in blysse,
And thei that love vertu schall not want, iwysse,   *lack, indeed*
Nevyr His gode lordschop. He may, as it is skylle,   *proper*
840   Make goddes of men whan that evyr He wylle."

Thus wold sche sey, that noble lady dere   *dear*
Onto hir servauntes and hem all exhorte.
Sche was homly as thow sche were her fere.   *unpretentious; their equal*
The dredfull and sekely wold sche comfort.   *frightened and sickly [people]*
845   Mery and glad was sche at every disport,   *amusement*
Sad eke ther-to whan sche schuld sad be,   *Serious*
Godely of hir spech, of hir expens fre.   *generous*

Chapter 15

What is a lond whan it hath non hed?
The lawes are not kept, the lond desolate,
850   The hertes hangyng and hevy as lede,   *lead*
The comonys grucchyng and evyr at the bate.   *people complaining; quarreling*
There is kept non rewle, kept non astate.
Thus seyde the puple of Surry alle aboute: *people*
"Oure kyng is now ded; oure lyth is nye owte.   *light; nearly*

855   "Othir londys spoyle us, and that withoute mercy.   *ravage*
We mote nede suffyr — we may non odyr doo.   *must; nothing else*
Thow we speke and calle and for help cry,
There is no man gladly wyll cum us to.
We have alleway thouth that it schuld be so.   *always thought*
860   Wythowte a kyng, how schuld a cuntré stand?
We have lost forevyr oure name and oure land.

"We have a qween: sche comyth among no men;   *i.e., keeps to herself*
Sche loveth not ellys but bokys and scole.
Late all oure enmyes in lond ryde or ren,   *run*
865   Sche is evyr in stody and evermore sole.   *alone*
This wille turne us all to wrake and to dole!   *bring us; harm; sorrow*

But had sche a lord, yet all myth be wele.   *might*
O thu blynd Fortune, how turnyst thou thi wheel

"Now hye, now lowe; now he that was above
870   Lyght low benethe in care and myschef eke,
And he that supposyd to conqwer now his love,   *expected*
He schall noght haf hir of all this next weke!
Sumtyme be we heyle; sumetyme be we seke.   *healthy; sick*
O very onsikyrnesse! O chaungand and variable,   *uncertainty; changing*
875   Thu wordly lyffe, for evyr art thou unstable.   *worldly*

"How schall this londe withoute kyng now stande?
It was nevyr seyn yet that the Sarsynrye   *Saracen lands*
Was left alone unto a womannes hande.
Sche must be weddyd, this mayd — and that in hye —   *in a hurry*
880   Onto summe kyng. Oure lond may thus not lye.
Fy upon rychesse, but if thei worchep doo
To man that weldyth hem, for thei are mad ther-too.   *controls*

"We schall fare ellys as thise negardes doo: *otherwise; misers*
Ley up her gold and evyr wyll thei spare;
885   In all her lyffe thei may not tend ther-too
To hafe any myrthe or ony welfare.   *derive any pleasure or benefit from it*
Ryght evyn thus now are we lyke to fare:
We schul haf rychesse and it schal do noo goode.
Godd forbede eke that this ryall blode

890   "Of oure noble kyng schuld cesse thus in this mayde.
We wyll require hir on all manere wyse
For to be wedded." Thus the puple sayd:
"There is noo reule in lorde ne in justyse:
Thei sett the schyere, the cessyons, and the cyse
895   Ryght as hem lyst. Will for reson goth now.[1]
This governauns is nothyng unto oure prow!   *profit*

---

[1] Lines 893–95: *[Without a king] there is no regulation of lords nor of justices: / They arrange the shires, sessions, and the assizes (courts) / Just as it pleases them. Self-interest is disguised as reason*

"And if we to batayle schuld us enbrace,	*if we go to war*
Who schuld lede us? Who schall be oure gyde?	*guide*
A woman kende nevyr yet able was	*known*
900 To reule a puple that is so grete and wyde,	
To sette the standard the wengys on the syde.	*(see note)*
And if we chese to capteyn any other lorde	*as captain*
Envye and rancure wyll cause sone dyscorde."	*rancor*

Thys was her lay thorowowte all the londe:	*opinion*
905 "Why is oure qween thus long withowte a kynge?"	
Bothe hye and lowe, all had this on honde.	
"Why is sche unweddyd, this yung, this fayre thynge?	
Sche is full wyse, sche is full lykyng,	*pleasing*
Sche is ful able a husbond for to have:	
910 Sche mote so nedys yf sche wylle us save!"	*by necessity must do so*

Upon this matere evene wyth a comon asent,	
Thei made a gaderyng wythoute auctorité.	*assembly*
For serteyn lordes ryth sone have thei sent,	
That thei shal come the common profyth to se.	*attend to*
915 Among hem alle this was than her decré:	
Upon this matere a lettir wylle thei wryte.	
In most goodly wyse, thei wyll that lettir endyte	*compose*

In whech thei shal onto her lady the qwen	
And to hir modir, whech is her lady eke,	*their*
920 Wryte and pray that thei wyl to hem seen,	*take care of them*
As thei be ladies both mercyful and meke,	
Thei suffyr no more the lordes thus of Greke	*Greece*
Ovyrryde hem so — it was not the old gyse.	*Oppress; old way*
The lettir, certeyn, was wrytyn in this wyse.	*indeed*

Chapter 16

925 "Onto oure ladyes, the elder and the yonge,	
Be it now knowe that thorow all Surry-lond	
It is seyd and spoke ny of every tunge	*almost*
That thei were nevyr so lykly to be bonde	
To othir londes whech have the hyer hond	*upper hand*

51

930 As thei are now. Wherfore togyder thei crye
Onto yow, ladyes, that ye wyll have mercye

"Upon youre men, upon youre lordes eke.
Thei may not lyve but thei defended be.   *unless they be defended*
Youre hertys be so petouse and so meke,   *compassionate*
935 Ye wyl not lete this matere slyde, pardé!   *by God*
What is a lord but yf he have mené?   *subjects*
What is a puple but yf thei have a lord?
Loke every kyngdam thorowout all this world:

"But yf thei have a man that dare wele fyth,   *Unless; fight*
940 Thei are put undir. It was not sene or now
That Surré and Cipre and that ylde that hite   *island; was called*
Candé the rych, whech hath a see ful rowe,   *Candia; rough sea*
Shuld be thus kyngles. To God we make a vowe:
We may not lyve thus long in rest and pes;   *peace*
945 Of clamoure and cry wyll we nevyr i-ses   *cease*

"But evyr beseke you, as oure ladyes dere,   *beseech*
Ye wyl be governyd and werk be counsayle.   *act according to counsel*
Thynk ye be to us both leef and dere,   *beloved*
And think oure servyse may yet sumwhat avayle.   *be helpful*
950 Lete sum peté owt of youre hertys hayle!   *pity flow from your hearts*
Suffyr youre puple have sum of her desyre.
This was the losse certeyn of men of Tyre:

"Thei had no kyng, therfore thei had no grace.
Whan Appolony was ded, fro hem passed and goo,
955 Every man as there his owe maystir was.
God forbede forevyr that it were so
In Surré-lond, for than were it undo.   *then it would be ruined*
It was nevyr sene, forsoth, ne nevyr schall be,   *truly*
And if it were, farewele than felicité!   *then*

960 "This we desyre now, schortly for to telle,
And thus desyrith all the lond bedene;   *together*
This is conclusioun of all oure gret counselle:
That oure yong lady mote nede weddyd bene.

	Late hir have choys; sche is wyse, we wene.	*Let; choice*
965	Chois hath sche, for many on wold hir have.	*many a one*
	Deliver this matere, so God youre soulys save.	*Act upon*

"This thing is all that we wylle sey as now.
We aske a answere, and that in hasty wyse.
We pray to God, to whom we alle mote bowe,
970 He sette yow soo and lede in swech a gyse   *such a way*
That ryth tomorow or ye owt of bed ryse
And er ye come owte into the halle,
That ye dysyre as we desyre now alle."

Chapter 17

The qwene answeryd and wrot rith thus ageyn.   *i.e., Meliades*
975 Sche seyd, "This thyng allgatys moste be do.   *surely*
To lyve alone in stody, it was nevyr seyn
That ony lady ony tyme dyd so."
Therfor hir wylle is fully sette ther-to
That hir dowtir, qwene of that empyre,
980 Schall be weddyd hastyly to sum syre.

And upon this hir lettir hath she sent   *thereupon*
Ryth in this forme and in this maner stylle:
"The Qween of Surry, of Cypre that was brent,
Of Candy eke lady and of many a myle,   *Candia*
985 Wyffe onto Costus, whech but a lytyle whyle
Is passyd and ded, onto her puple sche seyth,
She aloweth ful wele her manhode and her feyth;   *acknowledges; their valor*

"Sche wyl as thei wyll, and hath do many a day,
That hir doutir onto sum kyng shuld be
990 Maryed or wedded. She seyd yet nevyr nay
But evyr hir wylle hath be into this degré,
Loke where ye wyll and whanne, for so wyl sche.
Sche wold ful fayn that this thing were i-doo;   *wishes very much; done*
It had be fynyschyd ful long tyme agoo   *It would have been*

995 "Yf it had ley in hir or in hir wylle.   *very reasonable*
       Sche thynkyth, certeyn, reson that thei say   *very proper*
       To have a kyng it is ful goode skylle
       Because a woman neithir can ne may
       Do liche a man ne sey, it is no nay.   *Do or speak as a man; no doubt*
1000 Go loke youreselve, for ye be wyse men alle.
       My doutir, I trowe, onto youre wyll schal falle;

       "She was nevyr yete asayed in no degré   *questioned at all*
       Of you, ne me, ne of no maner with.   *By you; no other person*
       As in this matere sche seyd nevyr nay ne yee.
1005 We may not blame hir in no maner plyth: *any way*
       She doth to us as yet nothyng but ryght,
       Ne non she cast, truly, as I suppose.   *she intends none*
       We wyll ful sone hir of this thing appose.   *examine*

       "Yf she consent, than have we al i-doo.
1010 But this same thing, certeyn, touchith us alle:
       It longyth nowth only to on or too,   *not*
       But all oure reme herto must we calle,   *realm*
       For grete perell ellys therof myth falle.   *peril; might arise*
       Yt longyth to the ferthest as wele as to hem   *pertains*
1015 That dwelle here ny. Ye wote ful wele, hir em   *uncle*

       "The Duke of Tyre mote nede know this thing,
       The Duke of Antioche eke, hir owne cosyn.
       If we shul have a lord or ellys a kyng,
       Thei mote consent, thei mote make the fyn.   *conclude the matter*
1020 Lete this matere no lenger slepe ne lyne: *rest*
       We wyll send oute now in all hastly wyse
       That every man shal com in his best gyse   *array*

       "Onto this Alisaundre, there we dwelle as now.   *where*
       Thei shal sey and here alle that evyr thei wylle.   *hear*
1025 There shall no man, to God I make a vowe,
       Be lettyd for us, speke he loude or stylle."   *hindered by us; softly*
       This was the sentense of the qwenes bille.   *content; letter*
       The puple red it and was ful wele apayde.   *satisfied*
       "God save oure lady!" wyth o voys thus thei seyde.   *one*

54

1030   Thus endeth this boke of this clene virgine
        In whech hir byrth, hir kynrod, and hir countré
        Is declared, so as she wold enclyne   *be inclined*
        Hir gracious help to send onto me.
        Now ferthermore a newe boke begynne wyl we
1035   In whech we schall onto hir worchep wryte,   *honor*
        So as we can in oure langage endyte,   *compose*

        The grete conflicte betwyx the lordes and hir,
        Ryth in the parlement whech was ful realy hold   *royally*
        At grete Alysaundre. Many a ful stout syre
1040   Onto that cité at that tyme cam ful bold.
        It wyl be long or that this tale be told;   *is finished*
        Therfore I counsell that we make here a pause   *take a break*
        And eke a rest ryth evene at this clause.

Book 2

[The Marriage Parliament]

Prologue

Loke, whanne ye see the sparkes fayre and bryth
Spryng fro the fyre and upward fast to goo,
Ye may suppose be reson and be ryth
Summe fyre is nye; experiens telleth you soo. *near*
5   There go no sparkes, neithir to ne fro,
But there as fyre is; this se we ryth at eye. *we see this with our eyes*
In this same maner of this same lady I sey:

These holy wordes, these holy dedes eke,
Whech sche spake and used here lyvand, *did while she lived*
10   Alle thoo were tokenys that hir hert gan seke *those; tokens; did*
Hir gostly spouse; sche lefte not tyll sche found *spiritual; stopped*
That blyssyd Lord. Sche knowyth not yet His hand
As sche schall aftyr, but sche have tokenys gode, *and yet; tokens*
And all of God. Sche knowyth not yet the rode, *way*

15   Sche knowyth not Crist, sche hath not herd His lore, *teachings*
But yet the fyre of charité and of love
Brennyth in hir so that evyr more and more *Burns*
Hir hert is sette on oon that sytte above. *i.e., Christ*
I trowe that dowe the whech upon Crist dide hove *dove; hover*
20   Whanne He was baptized had mad in hir His nest.
This wote I wele: sche cannot now have rest, *know*

But all hir spech is now to comend
The grete vertu whech we virginité
Amongys us name. Who coude thanne a wende *have thought*
25   That on this vertu so dewly thynk wold sche, *duly, i.e., conscientiously*
For swech exaumples want in that cuntré. *are lacking*

Ther is no man desyryth sche be a mayde —
"Sche mote be weddyd nedys," thus thei sayde.

And as we see, the more is leyde to brenne,   *burn*
30   The gretter fyre there is, it is no dowte,
For drawe awey the schydys fro it then,   *shides, i.e., firewood*
Sone wyll the fyre be qwenchyd and be owte.
The more this lady vertues is aboute,
The more thei grow; thei have a full gode grownde.
35   Her cours, thei sey, as sercle it is rownd,   *circle*

For every vertu folowyth ryth aftyr othyr:
Whanne on is come he callyth ine his felaw;
Thei love togydir as systir or as the brother,
Ech of hem all his besynesse doth to draw
40   Tyll all be come; ryth swech, lo, is her law.   *their nature*
Begynne ageyn whan thu hast used the last;
Her serculed cours ryth thus lo have thei cast.   *circular*

Thys made hir hate these fleschly lustys alle,
For in this sercle sche is so farre i-paste   *she has so greatly excelled*
45   That from that whele sche cast hir not to falle.   *resolves*
Hir hert and thei be teyd so wondyr fast,   *i.e., virtues; tied*
Of hem it hath take so swetly the tast,   *taste*
Thei are mette and mates now and evyr more,
Thei are now bownd togedyr wondyr sore.   *securely*

50   It acordeth full weel, me thynk, to hir name   *is appropriate*
That vicyous lyfe in hir schuld have no place;
These Latyn bokys, I suppose, sey this same.
Hir name, thei seyn, it is so full of grace
That synfull lyfe it can distroy and race,   *raze*
55   For thus it menyth, certeyn, it is no nay:
"Cata" in Grew in Englysch is thus to say,   *Greek*

"Ovyr all" or "all"; and "ryne" in oure langage
Sownd "fallyng," as who schuld sey, in hir
Of synne and schame all the sory rage

60 Destroyd was; it neyhyd hir not nere.[1]
   These holy vertues were to hir so dere,
   Thei putte awey of synne all the flok;
   Thei are schyt owt and sche speryd the lok.   *shut out; closed the lock*

   O noble lady that art now us above,
65 Suffyr oure tungys, thow thei unworthy be,
   To telle thi lyfe, thi langoure, and thi love,   *distress*
   That thu had here in thi devoute secré,   *i.e., inner-most heart*
   To telle the sorowe eke and that adversité
   Whech with thi Lordys thu suffyrd as a clerk.   *scholar*
70 We wyll now streyte dresse us to that werk.   *immediately apply ourselves*

Chapter 1

   Now is not ellys but ryde, go, and ren: *ride, go, and run*
   Messagerys are oute on hasty wyse   *in a hurry*
   To calle to parlement alle maner menne,   *all kinds of men*
   That thei come alle now in her best gyse.   *attire*
75 Clerkis must come, for thei be so wyse,
   And lordes, eke, becawse thei be strong.
   This gaderyng hardely was not taryd long,   *delayed*

   For, as I rede, withinne wekys thre
   Thei be come thydir, and that with gret pryde: *splendor*
80 The Prince of Capadoce wyth a gret mené;   *Cappadocia; company*
   The Erl of Joppen cam ryth be his syde —   *Jaffa*
   There myght men se who can best sytte and ryde.
   The Prince of Paphon is come thedyr allsoo;   *Paphos (in Cyprus)*
   The Duke of Damask, with many another moo.   *Damascus*

85 The Duke of Salence, the Duke of Garacen,   *Salins*
   Thei were there reall, and eke so was he,   *royally*
   The Erle of Lymason: ful many strong men   *Limousin*

---

[1] Lines 56–60: *The Greek word "Cata" means, in English, / "Over all" or "all"; "ryne," in our language, / Means "falling." Together (i.e., "Catherine") they connote that, within her, / All the turmoil of sin and shame / Was vanquished and never approached near her*

Had thei with hem, these reall lordes thre.
The Amerell of Alysaundyr, with solemnité   *Admiral*
90 He hath receyvyd hem; he was a full strong syre.
He is come also, the noble Duke of Tyre.

Last of all thedyr gan aproche
A worthy man, hir owyn ny cosyne,
Thei call him there the Duke of Antioche.
95 All this matere he schall now determyne,   *he will now settle the issue*
Thus wene thei alle, for oute of o lyne
Are thei come bothe; he may ryght nowt wante.   *cannot fail*
His wyll in hir hert ful sone schall he plante.

The day is come now whech assygned was.
100 The lordes are gadred togedyr all in fere.   *in company*
The lenghe of the halle fully too hundyrd pace
So was it, certen, in whech thei gadered were,
Syttyng in her cownsell. Thoo men that were there,
Thei mett it hemself, thei seyd it was soo —   *measured*
105 Swech howses in this world ar not many moo.

A grete lorde was chose there amongis hem alle
To tell her wylle; spekere thei sey he was —
I wot not veryly what that men him calle.
He went ful esyly forth a ful soft pas   *very quietly*
110 Tyll he was come ryght befor the face
Of this meke lady and than thus he seyd:
"Myn sovereyn lady, ye schull not be dysmayde.

"Ye schall forgeve — and that I pray yow here —
Thow I to yow sey treuth as I must nede.
115 I am a servaunt, for I hafe take wage and hyre   *wages and salary*
Of yow, my lady, and that in many stede.   *on many occasions*
I am chose eke the nedys for to bede   *to voice the needs*
Of all youre reume, of lordys and of othyr.   *realm*
I except ryght noon, for certenly youre modyr

120 "As in this case is ryght on of hem:
Sche wyll and thei, that ye, my lady dere —

59

So wyll my lord the Duke of Tyre, youre hem   *uncle*
(I sey not fals, for he is present here) . . . .
What schuld I lengere hyde now my matere:
125   Ye must now leve youre stody and youre bokys
And tak youre solace be feldys and be brokys.

"Thynk on youre kyn, thynk on youre hye lyne:
If ye lef thus the elde auncetrye   *live thus*
Schall fayle in yow. There is no dyvyne   *die out*
130   Ne phylysophre here wyll sey that I lye,
For I sey thus: onto oure goddys hardylye   *certainly*
It is not plesaunce that ye schuld thus doo;   *pleasure*
It pleseth hem bettyr and ye consent ther-too   *if*

"And eke youre puple that ye a husbond have,
135   A real lorde whech may us alle defende.
The goddys frenchep if ye wyll kepe and save,
Onto this purpose ye mote nede condescende —   *agree*
Youre puple gretly therby schuld ye mende.   *benefit*
Excuseth not that wyll noght be excusede;
140   There is swech choys, it may not be refusede.

"What lord is that if onys he myght yow see   *once*
But he wold have yow? Mech more, dare I sey,
If he knew youre cunnynge, as now do we,   *wisdom*
He wold desyre yow in all manere weye —   *in every way*
145   His crown, his kyngdam, wold he rathere leye   *lose*
Than he schuld want youre noble wyse presence.   *lack*
Who se yow onys desyryth not youre absence!   *Whoever lays eyes on you*

"Therfore, lady, youre servauntis are now here
Besekyng that ye wyll of youre grace   *Beseeching*
150   Ope youre eres and lyst to oure prayere.   *Open; listen*
For this cause only came we to this place
Ryght all in feere. Ye may us graunte solace
Or peyne and sorow, ryght as ye lyst to chese: *it pleases you*
Youre answere, lady, schall cause on of these."

Book 2

Chapter 2

155   Ful astoyned and all abasched sore *astonished; taken aback*
    Was this lady whan sche herd him than.
    "O noble Godd," thowt sche, "that I now wore *if only I were*
    No qwen ne lady, for I ne wote ne can *do not know how nor am able to*
    Voyde the sentens of this ilke wyse man. *Refute the wisdom; same*
160   My pryvy counsell, whech I hafe bore long, *private plan*
    Now must it owte, and that thynkyth me wrong, *be revealed*

    "For if I schewe that I so long hafe bore, *reveal; borne privately*
    The pryvyest poynt of my perfeccyoun, *most intimate*
    Me thynkyth swyrly than that I hafe lore *surely; will have lost*
165   The hye degré of my devocyoun.
    Whan veynglorye comth, vertu is than gon;
    Vertu serveth to plese Godd only
    And not the puple — ryght thus redd hafe I.

    "If I concelle my counsell, than schall I falle *conceal*
170   In indignacyon of all my puple here;
    If I denye her askyng in this halle
    And tell no cause, I put hem more in dwere: *doubt*
    Whech thing I do I fall evyr in dawngere. *Whatever I do*
    Yet wondyr I sore that my hert is sett *greatly*
175   On swech a poynte that I cannot lett, *abandon*

    "And yet it is ageyns myne owyn lawe,
    Whech I am swore to kepe and to defende.
    My mynd it faryth ryght as on the wawe *goes; waves*
    A grete schyppe doth, for whan he best wende *ship; thought*
180   To be escaped, than comth the wawys ende, *waves'*
    He fyllyth the schyppe and forth anon is goo. *at once*
    Onto this poynt I drede I am browte too. *brought*

    "I supposed ful welle to leve now at myn ese; *live as I please*
    Now must I leeve my stody and my desyre,
185   My modyr, my kyn, my puple, if I wyll plese.
    I mote leeve stody and wasch my boke in myre,
    Ryde owte on huntyng, use all new atyre. *fashionable dress*

Godd, Thu knowyst my pryvy confessyoun: *intimate thoughts*
I have made all anothyr professyoun.[1]

190   "If I myght kepe it, I schall yet, and I may   *if I may*
Contynue the same, to Godd I make a vowe.
Schuld I now chaunge my lyffe and myn aray
And trace the wodes abowte undyr the bow?   *ride through the woods; boughs*
I loved it nevyr; how schuld I love it now?"
195   Thus thowt this mayde be hirself alone,   *to herself*
And aftyr softly with syhynge gan sche grone.   *sighing; to groan*

Sche spak than lowde — thei myght here at onys: *hear*
"Gramercy, lordes," sche seyd, "of youre good wylle!   *Mercy*
Ye sey youre feldys and youre wonys   *fields; dwellings*
200   Are in poynt for me to scatyr and spylle[2]
But if I take a lorde now me untylle   *Unless*
Whech may put all this in governaunce;
Than schuld ye hafe bothe rest and abundaunce.

"I suppose weele that it schulde be soo.
205   Yet wyll ye graunte, pardé, of curtesye,   *by God!*
That syth this thing muste nedys goo ther-too   *since this must be done*
That I myselfe in whom all this doth lye
May hafe avysement. I am not schape to flye   *deliberation; about to*
Ne to fle neyther. Me thinkyth ye everychon   *every one of you*
210   Have ful gret hast and I haf ryght noon.   *haste*

"I am but yunge; I may full weel abyde:
Thus schuld ye sey to me if I had hast.   *haste*
Lete all this matere as for a whyle now slyde
Tyll mo yerys of myn age be past.
215   Therwhyles wyll I bothe lok and tast   *Meanwhile; try*
Where I wyll sett me and telle yow myn avyse.   *attach myself; plans*
I wold noght men seyd I were hasty or nyce,   *foolish*

---

[1] *I have professed a completely different lifestyle [than they wish for me]*

[2] *Are about to be dispersed and ruined because of me*

"For hasty schall I noght be in this matere.
I sewyre yow here I wyll no husbond take   *assure*
220   But if I telle my frendys whech be here,   *Without telling*
Lest that I renne in daunger and in wrake.   *come to harm*
What schuld I lengere to yow tale now make?
Tyme goth fast — it is full lyght of lope —   *it has a light step*
And in abydyng, men seyn, there lyghte hope.

225   "Thus schall we bothe with avysement werk.   *deliberation*
Best it is, me thinkyt, that we do soo.
Late the puple for a whyle jangyll and berk,   *complain*
Spek at her lust, so are thei won to doo.[1]
The choys is myne; I mote consent ther-too.   *must*
230   Tyme of avysement to have, I pray yow.   *deliberation*
Thys is all and sum that I wyll sey as now."

Chapter 3

Than ros a lord, a man of gret stature,
A rych man, eke, thei sey that he was.
His wordes were taut him with ful besy cure
235   Of a clerke there, the more and eke the lasse.[2]
His wytte was not sufficient as in this cas   *intelligence*
To speke in this matere, ryth thus he thouth.
"Myn owe lady," he seyde, "it is ful dere abowth,   *dearly paid for*

"The absens of youre fader now in this land.
240   I have lost myselve, and so have othir moo,
A thousand pownd that was thoo in my hand   *then*
Whan that he deyed and went us thus froo —
The same have othir men; I am sekyr it is soo.
We are come heder to here now youre entent   *here to hear*
245   In this matere, and ye haske avysement.   *ask for a waiting period*

---

[1] *Say what they want, as they are used to doing*

[2] Lines 234–35: *A clerk there had carefully taught him what to say, down to the least detail*

"Ye myth a be vysyd lady wele i-now
Long or this tyme if ye had lyste.[1]
In long abydyng is ful lytyl prowe.   *profit*
All that evyr I mene I wold that ye wyste:
250   It is more sykyr a bryd in youre fyste   *certain a bird in hand*
Than to have thre in the sky above
And more profitabyl to youre behove.   *success*

"'The gray hors whyl his gras growyth
May sterve for hunger,' thus seyth the proverbe.   *die*
255   Every wyse man as weele as I now knowyth
The sore may swelle long or the herbe   *before*
Is growe or rype — a grete clerke of Viterbe   *Viterbo, Italy*
Seyd so sumtyme and wroot it in his boke.
We have ful grete nede to spye and to loke   *inquire*

260   "That we now may have a kyng to rewle us and yow,
To governe the lawe that it schuld not erre,
To be to traytourys both cruel and row,   *rough*
To lede the lordys whan thei go to werre: *war*
Fro youre kend this governauns is full ferre!   *nature; far*
265   Youre blod is not so myty for to abyde   *mighty*
To se man be slayn be youre owyn syde,

"To se the boweles cut oute of his wombe
And brent befor him whyll he is on lyve,   *alive*
To se man served as thei serve a lombe,   *lamb*
270   Thorowoute his guttys bothe rende and ryve,   *tear and cut*
To se hem draw oute be foure and be fyve.
Youre pytous hert myght not se this chaunce,   *event*
For it wold mak yow to fall in a trauns.   *faint*

"Therfore it is best to yow, thus we think,
275   To take a lord that may suffyr all thys —   *endure*
Whech may se men flete and also se hem synk,   *float*
Suffyr hem to smert whan thei do amys,   *hurt; wrong*

---

[1] Lines 246–47: *Lady, you could have thought this over well enough / By now, if you had wanted to*

	Whan thei do weell, to hafe reward and blys.
	Ryght thus I mene, I mak no lengere tale:
280	But ye do thus, grettere growyth oure bale."

Unless; harm

Chapter 4

	Thys lady answerd onto this lord ageyn,
	"My faderes absence is more grevous to me
	Than to yow alle; this dare I savely seyn.
	And thow he levyd, he were no more, pardé,
285	But o man: withoute men what myght he[1]
	Doo or sey but as o man alone?
	What nedyth yow now for to make swech mone

safely
by God!

complaint

	"For losse of o man? Ye coude whyll he was here
	Defende youreself thow he with yow not yede.
290	Youre enemyes alle ye put in full grete dwere;
	Than were thei kept full low in full grete drede.
	My lord my fadyr whan dyd he you lede?
	Not many yerys befor that he went hens.
	As ye dyd than, dothe now in his absence.

went
doubt

295	"Ye chose a capteyn thoo, so may ye now,
	To whom obeyd as in that jornay
	Every lord, loked he nevyr so row —
	Thei durst not onys to him than sey nay!
	Goode serys all, of pacyens I yow pray,
300	Why may ye not do now as ye dyd thanne?
	What nedyth yow thus to gruch and to banne?

during that campaign
rough

complain and curse

	"Ye sey it is lost all that was sumetyme
	Wonne with swerde: I wote as weell as ye
	That many a theft and many a gret cryme
305	Was hyd fro him be craft and soteltè.
	And summe were punychyd — he wold it schuld so be —

i.e., King Costus; cunning

---

[1] Lines 284–85: *Even if he still lived, by God, he would be no more / Than one man: without others what could he*

And yet of this punchyng oft he knew ryght nowt.
May it not now in the same case be wrowte?   *be done in the same manner*

"I vouch save ye ryd and eke ye renne   *vouchsafe, i.e., permit; run*
310   To seke youre enmyes whech do yow this wrong,
Distroye her cuntré, her houses down ye brenne,   *burn*
The traytours eke be the nek ye hem hong.
What word seyd I evyr, eythere schort or long,
Schuld let your corage? I pray yow tell me now!   *hinder*
315   Be good to me ryght as I am to yow."

Chapter 5

Than ros a reall, a rych lord ther-with-alle;   *prince*
Thei called him Clarus, Prince of Capados.   *Cappadocia*
Upon his knees anoon he gan down falle.
"Madame," he seyd, "youre conseytes are full clos.   *thoughts; secret*
320   Youre name is spronge, your cunnyng and youre los,   *renowned; wisdom; fame*
All these are know; thei may not now be hyd.   *known*
And yet ye may neyther doo ne byd

"As may a man. Your fadyr — God hafe his sowle —
As seyd this lord is ded and go us froo.
325   Whatsoevyr men crye or elles gaule,   *yell*
We are full lykly to falle in care and woo.
Come now who schall, he is i-pased and goo,
And ye be left for to be oure qween.
It lykyght us weel that it schuld so been,   *pleases*

330   "But yet the chaunge is wondyrfull, me think: *incredible*
For a man a woman now we have —
And that a mayde. It may in no wey synk
In oure hertys that ye myght us save.
I schall sey treuthe, thow ye think I rave:
335   Ye wyll wepe and ye youre fyngyr kytte!   *if you; cut*
How schuld it than setyll in oure wytte   *could we be persuaded*

"Ye myght redresse all that was now spoke?
A kyng is ordeynd ryght to this entent:

66

To kepe his castelys that thei be not broke,
340   To kepe his puple that it be not schent.   *ruined*
Now is this werk all othyrwyse i-went:
To kepe all this a woman is not strong enow —   *enough*
We must enforce us therfore to kep yow.   *strengthen; protect*

"And thow ye be the fayrest that beryth lyffe   *is alive*
345   (For so wene I and so wene many moo)   *think*
It wyll become yow full welle to be a wyffe,
Myn owne lady, and ye wold enclyne ther-too   *if you would be so inclined*
To bryng forthe frute eythere on or too —
It schuld plese us thow that ye had twelve!
350   It schuld plese your modyr and eke youreselve.

"All youre rychesse, what schall it us avayle
Hyd in youre cophyr and kept now thus clos?   *coffer; guarded*
Ye may therwith make plate and mayle.   *armor*
I dare well sey the lond of Capadoos,
355   If ye had on whech myght bere up your loos,   *honor*
Wold pay a raunson with full good entent   *ransom; humor*
So that ye wold onto this thing consent.

"And thow ye be the wysest of this worlde,
Yet have ye not o thing that ye wante:
360   Therof youreself wyll bere me recorde.   *bear witness*
Nature can not — ne wyll not, pardé — plante
Myght and strength in women, for thei it want.
In stede of strength, of nature thei hafe beuté.
Thow ye be fayre and wyse, yet want ye   *Though*

365   "Bodyly strength wer-with ye schuld oppresse   *with which*
Thoo wykkyd dedys whech reygne now ful ryve.   *Those; rife*
With deth and vengeaunce schuld ye thoo so dresse,   *set right*
Were it in man, in mayden, or in wyffe.
I tell yow sekyr, this is a kyngys lyffe:
370   He may not hafe his worchepe all with ese;
Summe of his puple oft he must dysplese.

"Theyse thingis fall not, us thinkyth, to youre persone.[1]

Wherfore we wyll and ye consent ther-too   *if you*

Ordeyn a meen: ye schall not lyve alone —   *course of action*

375   Spouseles I mene — as ye yet evyr hafe doo.

This is oure erand; my tale is fully doo.

Sped this matere, hold us not long suspens,   *Expedite*

Than is it weele wared, bothe labour and oure expens."   *will rewarded*

Chapter 6

"Gramercy, syr," to him than seyd the qween,   *Mercy*

380   "Be the tendyrnesse that ye to me have,   *By*

Ye love me weell and that is now i-sene;

Ye love my worchep, my londys wold ye save.   *honor*

I thank you, syre, I sey not that ye rave,

But wysely spek all that ye have told.

385   And for this talkyng, I am to yow behold.   *beholden*

"But evyr me thynkyth whan I avyse me weell,   *consider well*

If it so streyt were as ye sey with yow —

Whech dyssese wold lek me nevyr a deell —   *would not please me at all*

For if it were thus as ye pretendyn now   *allege*

390   Ye schuld not hafe neyther feld ne plow

In no pes, if it were all as ye sey.

Therfore me thynkyth ye walk no trew wey.   *i.e., you mislead me*

"And as for conquest, seres, care ye ryght nowte.   *do not mind about that*

Youre lordchepys frely wune were to your handys

395   Or ye coude goo and or that ye were wrowte.[2]

Ye fawte nevyr yet for townes ne for no landys.   *fought*

Where ar your prisoneres whech ye led in bandys?

There was no werre syth that I was bore   *war since*

But on oure borderes, and ye care not therfore,   *about that*

---

[1] *We think these practices are not suitable to you*

[2] Lines 394–95: *Your lordships (i.e., the titles and properties) were nobly won / Before you could walk, even before you existed, and only later came into your hands*

400 "For we fynde the sowdyoures that be there. *provide for the soldiers*
Ye pay ryght not — ne nowte I coveyte ye doo. *nothing, nor do I desire you to*
Pluk up youre hertes and be nothing in fere! *fear*
Arme yow not but if we send yow too.
Ye dwelle in pees and so do many moo;
405 Pleyn yow nowte untyll ye fynd grevaunce. *Complain*
Ye sey also that I wold falle in trauns *stupor*

"If domys were kepte evene as thei schuld be *judgments were rendered*
And peynes gove to hem that schuld be ded. *punishments given; those who; executed*
I am a woman; therfore, it semyth not me *it is not fitting for me*
410 Ovyr swech bochery for to hold my hed — *Over such butchery to preside*
Myn hert wold drupe hevy as any led *sink*
For very pyté: thus ye gune replye
Ryght for ye wold I schuld be wedded in hye. *Because you wished; in haste*

"Her-to I answere as ye mote nede sey alle: *must all agree*
415 A kyng, ye wote weell, hath so gret powere
Ovyr his puple that whom he wyll he schall
To mak hem fre or make hem prysonere;
He may graunt lyffe to hem that be in dwere *dissension*
And ek in hope for to be hang and drawe. *expectation; drawn*
420 Thus may he doo; he is above the lawe.

"Than I myselve, rathere than I schuld swonne, *faint*
Myght graunt hem lyffe, thow thei not worthy were:
Thus dyd my fadyr full often in this towne —
Loke wel abowte for sume of hem be here
425 Whech were thus saved, I am nothing in dwere. *doubt*
I alowe youre motyves whan that thei be owte.[1]
I merveyle also that ye consydyr nowte

"That for because a kyngys gentyll hert
Hath swech fredam growyng ryght withinne, *generosity*
430 Whan he may not se men blede or smert,
Therfor his deputees, the more and ek the mynne, *lesser*

---

[1] *I accept your arguments, when they amount to anything*

69

Schuld punysch thoo schrewys that can not cese ne blynne   *wretches; desist*
Of her evyl dedys. Ilk day ye may this se —
It nedyth not herfore to legge auctorité.   *to cite authorities*

435   "Swech deputees, sere, hafe we many and fele   *sir; lots*
      That of swech materys nedys mote hem melle.   *must occupy themselves*
      What man that sle, fyght, robbe, or stele,   *kills, fights*
      Oure offyceres ful sikirly schul him qwelle —   *certainly; subdue*
      Nay not thei, but the lawe that is so felle,   *ruthless*
440   He sleth this meny; thei ar in this cas   *executes; group [of trespassers]*
      Servauntys to lawe, the more and eke the las.

      "All her powere, ye wote weell, of us thei have,   *they have from us*
      As thei had evyr in my fadyres lyffe.
      Let hem deme, lette hem spylle and save: *judge; execute and pardon*
445   This longyth to hem — I kepe not of this stryffe.   *is their duty; concern myself*
      Be it to man, be it to mayde or wyffe,
      That do amys, be hem thei dampned bene.   *wrong; condemned*
      I schall be to juges bothe kyng and qween."

Chapter 7

      The Erle of Jaff was called Syr Ananye.   *Jaffa*
450   He stode up than and to this lady sayde,
      Agens hir answere he gan ryght thus replye: *In response to*
      "It is full perlyous," he seyd, "to be a mayde
      And eke a qween. Ye may be full sone afrayde
      If any rysyng or ony scisme were sterde,   *schism; stirred up*
455   For of a kyng men wold be more ferde   *afraid*

      "Than thei of yow are, it is no dowte.
      The puple erryth: behold ye not how fele   *do wrong; how many*
      Thorowowte youre londe in every town abowte
      Renn as woodemen? Ye may it not consele: *Run; wildmen; conceal*
460   Thei fyght, thei flyght, thei robbe, and thei stele.   *fight; flee*
      All this aray me thynkyth ye sett at nowte;   *disturbance; treat as nothing*
      It faryth as ye of all this thing ne rowte!

       do not care about

"Ye sett more, be Godd that sytt above,   *You set more store*
Be on old boke and eke more deynté have   *pleasure*
465   Than be werre or justys, lust or elles love.
Men sey thei schall bryng yow to your grave.
What do your bokys? Pardé thei wyll not save
Neyther man ne best; thei dull a mannys mende,
Apeyre his body, his eyne thei make blynde.   *Impair; eyes*

470   "He that taute you fyrst this scole, I pray   *educated you*
He mote be hangyd — I trow he is worthy:
He hath yow browte and put in sweche aray   *habits*
That myrth and joye ye late hem slyde forby!   *let them pass you by*
Evyr at bokes ye sytte, knele, and lye.
475   Alas, madame, who lese ye youre tyme —   *lose*
I wepe so sore I may no lengere ryme!

"For Goddys lofe and for youre puples sake,
Chaunge now youre lyff and let your bok be stylle.
Loke no lengere upon thoo letteres blake,
480   For, be my trowth, stody schall yow spylle.   *truly*
Tend onto myrth; tak a lord you tylle: *unto you*
Than schal your body be full heyll and qwert,   *healthy; sound*
And mech more ese schull ye haf at hert."

Chapter 8

"Ye wold allgate that I schuld wedded be   *on all sides*
485   Ryght for this skylle: ye sey men drede me nowte;   *for this reason*
If any scysme were reysyd in this cuntré   *schism; raised*
It were not likly be me for to be browt
To ony good end — men sett at me ryth nowt.   *take no account of me*
Ye schuld drede more a man than ye do me.
490   And I sey thus: I knowe as wele as ye

"A man alone, be he nevyr so wyse
Ne eke so strong, he may no more, iwys,
But evyn as I may. His puple shal be nyse   *Indeed, he may do no more than I; foolish*
And eke evele tetched; the powere is not his   *ill-dispositioned*
495   To amend alone all that is amys:

His lordes must help to his governayle   *governance*
And elles his labour it wil lytyl avayle.

"Help ye on youre syde as I shal on myn!
Loke ye be trew onto my crowne and me,
500   Lete no treson in youre hertys lyn,   *lay*
Than schal this lond ful wele demened be.   *managed*
O noble God, who grete felicité   *what*
Shuld be with us if we were in this plyth;
We myth sey than oure levyng were ful ryght.   *living*

505   "Wyl ye now here how puple may make her kyng   *hear*
To erre sumtyme and sumtyme to do amys?
Ryth be ensaumple shal I prove this thing:
There was a kyng here besyde, iwys,   *indeed*
Fere in the est, that lyved in joy and blys   *Far*
510   In Babilony; evene Nabugodonoser he hyth.   *Nebuchadnezzar; was called*
His puple made him to do ageyn the ryth,   *do wrong*

"For he had with him in maner of a preest,
A ful goode man and of grete abstinense.
Ful pryvy thingis bare he in his breest;   *secret*
515   He coude telle all of derth and of pestilence.   *famine*
O thing there was in whech he dede offence:
He worchiped not swech goddes as we doo.   *the same*
Danyel he hyth. But among lyones too   *was called; two*

"Was he putt, ryth for the puple so wolde.   *because*
520   The kyng durst not wythstand hem in that cas;   *oppose them*
He must do soo, thow he wold or nolde.   *whether or not he wished to*
Ful sore repentaunt aftyrward he was,
For Danyell was saved ryth be Goddys grace.
(Whech God he servyd God, wold I myght Him know,
525   That noble Godd that made His myght so growe

"In swech lowe puple.) Here may ye see and ken   *know*
For puples crying a kyng may oftyn erre.   *Because of*
The woode opynyon of swech fonned men   *crazy; foolish*
Makyth a lord oft tyme to do the werre,   *worse*

72

530   To make him mevyd, to sett him oute of herre.   *incite him; off his hinge*
        Fy on her cry whan thei no reson hafe!
        Ye sey alsoo, for that ye wold me save,

        "I must leve book, I must leve stody eke.   *leave*
        My bokes, seres, Godd help, what greve thei yow?
535   This wordly governaunce were not worth a leke   *leek (i.e., worth nothing)*
        Ne were these bokes; thei are to mannes prow   *Were it not for; improvement*
        Full necessarye, for oure myndys are swech now
        It slydyth forby, all that evyr thei know,   *passes by forgotten*
        And be oure bokes ageyn full fast thei grow.

540   "How schuld we wete that the fyrst man of alle
        Had hyght Adam and eke his wyff Eve
        Save that in a booke whech Genesis thei calle?
        (I sey it onys wrete and red it on a eve;   *in writing; read; evening*
        Yet is that book not of oure beleve
545   Receyved as yet; me thinkyth it must nede,   *must be*
        Because he tellyth the begynnyng and the dede   *it tells*

        "Of oure olde faderes.) Who schuld eke know
        The worthy conquestys of elderys that were here
        If bokes teld hem not only be rowe?   *rehearse; one after another*
550   We can forgete that we dyd this yere!   *what*
        Wherfore oure bookes tell to us ful clere
        Swech manere thinges as we had forgete.
        Youre opynyon, therfore, sere, now must ye lette,   *sir; abandon*

        "For Goddys lawe, ne mannys, schuld not be know
555   Ne were oure bokes, this dare I savely say.   *Without our books; safely*
        Oure preestes arn fayn to loke hem be row   *eager; systematically*
        Ageyn a feest, ageyn an holyday,   *In preparation for*
        Whan thei wyll preche of any swech aray,   *conditions*
        Eythere of Jubiter or Neptune, his brothyr.
560   Leve we than this matere and carp of summe othyr.   *speak*

        "Blame not swech thing that stant in full grete stede!   *great respect*
        Curse not my mayster, for than wyll I be wrothe.   *angry*
        It semyth you bettir for to bydde youre bedde   *You would do better to say your prayers*

Than to sey swech wordes. (Eke it is ful lothe

565　To me to sey thus, but only for myn othe[1]

　　Whech that I made to meynteyn al maner thing　　*govern*

　　Whech longe to our goddis and to her offring.)"

Chapter 9

　　Than spake a lord thei called Ser Hercules,

　　The Prince of Paphon, of that gret cuntré.　　*Paphos (in Cyprus)*

570　Every man sat stille and held his pees

　　To here the speche, the tale whech that he　　*hear*

　　Began to telle, for his auctorité

　　Was thoo ful gret in special for his age.　　*especially*

　　His wordes were acordyng to his visage.　　*matched his appearance*

575　Thus he began: "It is bettir, my lady dere,

　　In swech a caas whan it mote nedis be doo,　　*When something must be done*

　　To do it at onys than for to lyve in dwere　　*perplexity*

　　And for to abyde eythir yer or too.

　　Take ye no heed? Consyder ye not ther-too,

580　How Ovyde seyde and wrote it in his booke:　　*What*

　　'Whan thing is newe bewar betyme and looke　　*soon*

　　"'For to amende it, for medecyn comyth ovyr late　　*too late*

　　Whan that the man his ded and hens i-goo　　*is dead; gone hence*

　　And with his frendes born oute at the gate'?　　*carried*

585　Youre londes, lady, if ye take heed ther-too,

　　Ly fer asunder, for fro this cuntré, loo,　　*apart; indeed*

　　Whech we be inne rith onto Famagost

　　Is many a myle. How schuld ye with your host

　　"Ryde sweche a way? And if that ye schuld sayle,　　*sail*

590　It wold yow fese the salt watter row.　　*scare; rough*

　　Youre hert wold drede, withoutyn ony fayle;

　　That I sey now, me thinkyth it for youre prow.　　*benefit*

　　The lond of Cipre that I cam thorow now

---

[1] Lines 564–65: *And I hate / Having to say this; I do so only because of my oath*

Is eke ful ferre. It mote nedes be a man
595   Whech schal, wil, and eke that may and can,

"Do al this labour both in flesch and gost,   *body and spirit*
Ryde and seyle, labour to se his lande,
Sumtyme here, sumtyme at Famagost.
Thus shal he governe the lond, the see, the sand.
600   Than may ye have youre bokes in youre hand
And stody youre fille; it shal not greve us.
Me thinkyth sewyrly that ye shul wil thus: *surely; wish*

"Ye shul desyre to be more at youre ese,
To weld youre leysere as ye desyre to have.   *manage; leisure time*
605   There is mech thing that doth you oft displese
Whech shuld not than.[1] Therfor, if ye wil save   *preserve*
Youre owne astate and thus no lenger wave   *rank; waver*
Both too and fro, doth be oure counsayle.
In tyme comyng it may yow mech avayle."   *benefit you much*

Chapter 10

610   "Gramercy, sere, of youre goode counsayle,"   *Thank you, sir*
Thus seyd the qween, "if ye be as ye were,   *i.e., if you have not changed*
Youre myth and cunnyng may us mech avayle,   *might*
And, as me thinkith, no man schal us dere.   *challenge us*
On Paphon or Cipre shal there be no were   *war*
615   Whil that ye lyve — herof I drede ryth nowth!
Now, wold God so, it were ful dere iboute

"Upon my body, in case that it stood soo
Thorow all my lond as it in Cipre stant![2]
I mith than stody, than myth I tend ther-to,   *might*
620   And al my wil therof now I want.   *do as I wish, as I now cannot*
Ye shuld plese God if ye wold set and plant

---

[1] Lines 605–06: *I.e., Were you to marry, you would not have so many annoying duties*

[2] Lines 616–18: *If only God would allow that at whatever cost — / Upon my body — things ran as smoothly / Throughout my land as they do in Cyprus*

Youre knythly maneres in yong men that be here,   *knightly*
To lern hem just, I wolde wele qwite youre hyere.   *joust; reward; labors*

"Of that gret godd ek whech governeth all batayle —
625   Mars I mene — whos knyght ye hafe be founde,   *been found [to be]*
Ye schall haf worchep, thow ye hafe non avayle,   *success*
To tech hem holde the schaftes that be rounde.
With youre praysyng my tale schuld more abunde   *I would praise you further*
But that we schuld noght preyse men in presence.   *to their faces*
630   Than in youre londe I lak not now the absence   *do not feel the absence*

"Of my lorde my fadyr; it is noght gretly aspyed   *detected*
His deth with yow. I sette cas ferthermore
That if I were, as ye wolde, now newe alyede —   *newly allied*
Weddyd I mene — what schuld than youre sore   *how; grievances*
635   Therby be esed? That man is not yet bore,
Were he nevyr so wys, manfull, or stronge,
Of hert fell, of body broode and longe,   *fierce*

"That myght at onys be in all these places
Whech ye spak of ryght now in youre tale.
640   Thow he had plenteuously all the grete graces
Whech kepe a man fro byttyr peynes bale   *suffering bitter pains*
And save him harmles, as withinne the wale   *preserve; gunwale (plank)*
Of a strong schyppe a man is bore alofte,
Yet myght he noght, rode he nevyr so softe,

645   "Be in too places at onys. For ryght as a stone   *just as*
Whan he is layd in his naturall place   *it; its*
May not that tyme be founde but there alone   *but only there*
Where he was leyd, ryght so in this cas
O man may not be in dyverse place
650   And that at ones, fore be oure phylosophye
It is condempned as for an heresye.

"Therfore, ryght thus we conclude oure clause:
Every body hath his naturall rest   *habitats*
Aftyr his kende or aftyr his pryvy cause   *nature; individual reasons*
655   Whech that the goddes ryght evene as hem lest   *just as it pleases them*

76

Have departed. To opyne thus than holde I best: *To conclude [an argument]*
He that is here, he is here and noowhere ellys.
Example, lo, I mene, whosoevyr that dwelles

"At grete Alysaundyr, he dwelleth not in Famagost.
660   Than must every man nedys himself remeve   *remove*
And cary his men thorowowte all the coost,   *coast*
Ete at noone, rest him eke at eve,
Here and there as his jornay wyll preve.   *turn out*
Ryght so may I, thow I a woman be.
665   Than in your argument me thynkyth no difficulté."

Chapter 11

The Duk of Damaske was wroth with this answere.   *angry*
He stoode up tho and thus he gan to sey,
"In my yong age ryght thus dyd I lere:
The pupyll must nedys onto the kyng obeye,
670   Love him and drede him evyr tyll thei deye,
For thei are bounde full sore thus to do,
And we wyll evyr hertly bowe ther-too.

"So is a kyng swore eke ful depe   *sworn also very deeply*
To love his pupyll, be thei heye or lowe,
675   Ryght and trowth amonge hem alle to kepe   *truth*
So that noo wrong schuld hem ovyrthrowe.
Thus are ye swore, madame; ye it knowe
Bettyr than I what is to breke an othe.
Reson may not, ne schall not, make yow wrothe.   *angry*

680   "Youre othe was this, if ye remembyr yow welle,
To ordeyn so for londe, for man and town,   *govern*
That alle these thingys at every tyme and seele   *occasion*
Schuld be redressed, be it up or down,
For that thei longe alle onto youre crown.   *are all subject to*
685   This othe may ye not save non other wey   *preserve*
But if ye wyll onto oure wyll obeye

"For to be weddyd onto summe worthy man.
'Where is no lorde there is no lawe,' men say.
Now, be my trowth, in no wey think I can   *truly*
690   That ony woman if there come a fray
Schuld sese us sone, and specyaly a may.   *subdue; immediately; maiden*
Ye bere us down with youre philosophye,
But at the last ye must bowe hardylye."   *surely*

Chapter 12

"Sere," seyd the qwene, "ye make now swech a skyll   *claim*
695   Ryght in your tale whech ye enforsed now   *set forth*
That I wold thus, and that it were my wylle,
That ye no governauns had. And I sewyre yow   *assure*
I thowte it nevyre; it were not to my prow,
For thow I schuld noye alle oure oost,
700   Thys wote I well, it schuld touche me moste.[1]

"I kepe and schall myn othe whech I made —   *oath*
Tyll that I deye I schall it nevyr breke.
Ye may wel carpe and in your langage wade,   *speak; wallow*
New wordes reherse and new resones speke
705   Whech were rehersyd and have her answers eke.   *their*
Me lyst not for to remembre swech thyng ageyn,   *be reminded*
But thus mech, sere, to yow dare I seyn:

"As for my fadyr, he left yow in rest and pes
And in noo debate, ne lykely for to be.   *conflict*
710   If there ryse ony, ye may youreself it ses   *cease*
And but ye do ye be ontrewe to me,   *unless*
Not to me oonly but to the magesté
Of my crown and gylty for to deye.
Avyse yow bettyr whan that ye lyst to seye."

---

[1] Lines 698–700: *It would not be to my advantage, / For though it (failure to govern) would vex everyone here, / I know very well that it would affect me most*

Chapter 13

715	A gret clerk thoo stod up be himselve	
	That was ful scharp in wytte as I wene.	
	In this matere he thowte thoo for to delve	*dig*
	A lytyll deppere; therfor unto the qwene	*A little deeper*
	Thus he spake: "These lordes all bedene,	*together*
720	Thei can not, lady, aspye as yet youre art,	*comprehend*
	Who pregnantly ye can kepe youre part.	*cogently; hold your own*

	"Ye arn lerned and so be thei nowte;	*not at all*
	It is less wondyr thow thei concluded be.	*overcome*
	But evyr wondyr I gretly in my thowte,	
725	Ye sett no more be that hye degré —	
	Grettest of all, I mene the regalté.	*royalty*
	Who schuld preys it but ye? I supposyd,	*appreciate*
	Aftyr the name with whech ye are losed,	*In keeping with; honored*

	"That ye wold enhaunse this ilk degré	*promote*
730	Most of all women. What eylyth now your wytte?	*ails*
	I am in poynt to leve it is noght ye.	*inclined; believe*
	This matere, lady, onto myn hert it sytte	
	So sore, iwys, me thynkyth it will it kytte.	*cut*
	Ye drynk so sore, I trowe, of poetrye	*so ardently, I daresay*
735	And most in specyale of him, Valerye,	*especially*

	"Whech wold, it semyth, that no man wedded schulde be:	*Who wishes*
	He counseled so to on Ruffyn, ye know it welle.	*to a certain Rufinus*
	'Ya ovyrwelle, what nede is for me	*But indeed,*
	For to rehers the sorow, the langoure everydelle,	*every bit*
740	Whech that longyth unto that fykil whelle	
	Of spousalye,' as wrytyth this hold clerke,	*marriage; old*
	Valerye, the moost in this forsayd werke.	*most of all; aforesaid*

	"But thow in the pore be often swech myschauns,	*though*
	It is not thus in swech grete magesté	

745	With whech we wolde yow, lady, now avauns.[1]	
	And evyr contrarye onto oure wylle are ye.	
	Thynk ye not what ye seyd wole late, pardé?	*just recently*
	Ye spake not long sythe and seyd ryght even thus:	
	Ye wold, ye seyd, have on to governe us.	*someone*
750	"What schuld he be but he were a kyng?	
	There may no man governe this grete reem	
	But swech a man that is able in all thing	*in every way*
	To wedd you, and for my lord your em	*because; uncle*
	May not wed you, neyther in whech ne drem,	*awake nor asleep*
755	Therfore he may not here as in this place	
	Bere noo crown, for it stant in your grace	*it is up to you*
	"Who schall it bere; it longeth onto your ryght.	*it is your right to decide*
	Syth ye have graunted than that we schall have	*Since*
	A governoure to sett us in good plyth,	*condition*
760	Than have ye graunted all that evyr we crave;	
	And fro this purpos efte ye turn and wave	*again*
	And sey ye wyll no husbonde have as yitte.	*yet*
	Beholdeth now wysely if so be that your wytte	
	"Be stedefastly i-sett evyr upon o poynt.	
765	Me thynkyth nay, ye changen too and froo:	
	Now wyll ye, now are ye in another joynte,	*direction*
	And than wyll ye not. Who schuld we come ther-too	
	To know youre purpos whan ye vary soo?	
	Let us know pleynly, lady, what ye mene!	
770	We be youre men; thinkyth ye be oure qwene."	*bear in mind that you*

Chapter 14

	"Sere," seyd the qwene, "ye be lordes fele	*many*
	And wyse also. What nedyth yow thus to care	*Why; worry*
	Whan ye be yung, lusty, and in good hele?	*health*

---

[1] Lines 743–45: *But though such bad fortune [in marriage] is often found among the poor, / It is not thus among such great royalty / As those with whom we now wish to promote you*

	Eke your countres beth as now not bare	*are*
775	Neyther of corn, of men, ne of welfare.	
	But to yow, syr, I wondir mych more than ye,	*I am much more amazed*
	For ye sey in this matere ye hafe merveyle of me;	

	"And where ye sey that I wold now disseyve	*deceive*
	With my termes, my lordes, whech I love,	*arguments*
780	I pray yow hertly that ye wyll noght conceyve	*heartily; imagine*
	Of me swech thing. For truly, it wold not prove.	*prove true*
	Swech japes to make were not to behove,	*jests; befitting*
	Neythyr to me ne to non other wyght.	*person*
	To be a dysseyvoure, it is a grett despyte.	*deceiver; really despicable*

785	"Ye sayd eftsone that I dyspyse a kyng,	*earlier*
	Eke that astate I trede all undyr fote.	*office (i.e., kingship)*
	Thow I be not enclyned to your askyng	*Although*
	As for to be weddyd whan I schall, Godd wote,	
	Yet am I come bothe of that stok and rote —	*stock; root (i.e., royalty)*
790	I may not hyde it for it is know so wyde —	*so well known*
	Bothe on my faderes and on my moderes syde.	

	"Schuld I than dyspyse that hye degré	
	Whech that is ordeynd be Goddys providens,	
	Whech is eke come be descense to me?	*has been passed on to me*
795	Godd forbede in me that gret offens,	
	Or that I were founde in swech neclygens.	
	I wote full weele a kyng is all above,	
	Ovyr his ligys, bothe in fere and love,	*subjects*

	"And thei be to him, as it were, botraces	*buttresses*
800	To schove and holde fast and stedefastly,	*prop up*
	To meyten ryght ageyn all wrong traces.	*maintain; paths*
	A kyngis myght full small is, hardyly,	*certainly*
	Withoute swech help, ye wote as weel as I.	
	But that ye lyst to seye as for youre part,	
805	Than semeth it, sere, that I use treuly myn art	*correctly*

"And not pretende in no manere terme
Non othyr sentens than the terme schuld have[1]
But use my langage stabyly and ferme.   *in a fixed and stable manner*
Myn entent is swech, so Godd me save,
810   And evyr schall be, I trow, nevyr to wave   *trust; waver*
Fro that purpos whylys that I am here.
This is my mynde, if ye wyll it here.

"Ye list also me efte to reprove   *again*
For I grauntid yow to have a governoure;
815   Therfore ye sey fully I gave you leve   *permission*
To have a kyng, lord of town and toure.   *fortress*
Lett be youre sophym! Your termes are but soure,   *sophistry*
For thow ye bryng forth alle your hool bunch   *whole*
Ye schall not mak an elne of a unch.   *ell (about 45 inches); inch*

820   "I sett cas a man hath gove to you a best: *suppose*
It folowyth not ther-of that he gave yow an ox
He may as weell paye the more as the lest,
He may chese to geve yow a hors or a fox.
Your termes come owte of that sotyll box   *subtle*
825   Of Aristoteles *Elenkes*, made in swych wyse   *such a way*
Who so that lerneth hem, he schall seme wyse.   *learns*

"So grauntid I to yow to have youre choys fre,
To chese a duke whech that schuld lede yow,
Not for to have no governauns upon me,
830   But to my byddyng he must lowte and bowe.   *kneel*
All this entent yet eft I new alowe: *repeat*
Thus schull ye have your wylle and I schall have myne,
For of myn answere, sere, here is the fyne."   *conclusion*

Chapter 15

"Madame," quod the Erle thoo of Lymasones,   *Earl of Limousin*
835   "Alle these lordes that now here sitte

[1] Lines 806–07: *And in not one of my words do I misrepresent, / With a meaning other than the word should have*

	Wondyr full sore of your grete resones.	*impressive reasoning*
	Thei wayle, eke, that ye have swech a wytte.	*complain*
	Youre wordes are scharpe — thei can bynde and kytte —	*cut*
	But had ye ben as other women are	
840	Than schuld ye a ferde as other women fare.	*have fared*

"Youre scole wyll schath us, iwys, we skape it nowte.   *learning; harm; escape*
We hoped of you to have had summe grete empryse,   *noble act*
But all is turned nothing as we thowte.[1]
In many materes men may be ovyre wyse.   *too wise*
845   Youre conceytes, madame, set hem in summe syse.   *views; moderate them*
For love of Godd, whech is oure governoure,   *who*
Accepte oure wyttes and leve sumewhat of youre.

"We may weel doo rith as ye sayn,   *exactly*
Chese us now a ledere, if that we list,
850   Whech schall be to us in manere of a chevetayn.   *chieftain*
But in this lond it was yet nevyr wyst;   *it is unheard of*
He myght be swech, paraventure, that he schuld fro your fyst
Drawe mech of youre lande evyn unto him.
Avyse yow ryght weele; this matere is full dym.   *Think carefully; very uncertain*

855   "Eke thow we peyned us alle him to plese,
He schuld noght lyke us, certeyn, lyvyng yow;[2]
Oure hertes schuld not have no rest ne no ese
But he were lorde, ryght as ye be lady now.   *just*
It is full harde ageyn wylle to bowe.   *to submit willingly*
860   He cowde not be chose eke among ony of us,
And hard it is to leve in langoure thus."

Chapter 16

Than answeryd schortely that fayre, swete may: *maiden*
"Sere erl," sche sayde, "ye may full wele tryst   *trust*
There is but o poynt to whech I sey nay,

---

[1] *But nothing has turned out as we expected*

[2] Lines 855–56: *Also, even if we labored to please him, / He would not please us, with you alive*

865   And my cawse is this: I have yet no list   *purpose*
    That ony man my maydynhod schuld twyst   *take my virginity*
    But if I knew bettir what that he were.
    Thus say I now and thus sayde I ere: *before*

    "I wyll abyde tyll bettir tyme may come,
870   A yere or two tyll that I elder be,
    For to wedde yet me thynk it full sone,   *still; too soon*
    And to youre governawns thus I demene me.   *submit myself*
    If ye lyst not to have on, I graunt you two or thre   *one [regent]*
    Whych men may governe withowtyn envye.
875   I profyr yow reson whatsoevyr ye crye."   *no matter what you argue*

Chapter 17

    Than spak the Amyrell of gret Alisaundre.   *Admiral*
    Thus he gan sey, ryght in this manere:
    "Youre wordis to your wysdam are but slaundre,   *are a disgrace to your wisdom*
    Thus thynk your frendis all that sytte here.
880   Loke that ye throw not now all in the mere,   *throw everything into the sea*
    Loke that ye lese not now your gret namyd lose   *lose; reputation*
    Whan that ye may so heyly it endoos.   *increase it so highly*

    "How honour ye youre owne grete astate!   *Look how you honor; rank*
    Why hate ye now that ilk lady must have?   *what each lady*
885   Wherfore have ye swech thing in hate   *despise such a thing (marriage)*
    That may youre londes and eke yourself save?
    If ye were not my lady, I wold wene ye rave,   *suppose*
    For yf all these conceytes had come of wyt   *opinions*
    Mo folk than ye wold have usyd it!   *held them*

890   "Men seyn, madame, that he maddyth more   *is crazier*
    That doth lich no man, and is more oute of herre   *like; off-hinge*
    Than is a foole that can not se before,   *look ahead*
    Ne can not knowe the best fro the werre.   *worst*
    Be ye ware betyme that ye no lengere erre.   *before it is too late*
895   Schape not youreself ne youre lond to schend;   *Drive; ruin*
    Thynk now betyme what shal be the ende!

"Ye wote that I am keper of this grete cité,
And in this same cité, as now standyth it soo,
There is many a man and many dyverse degré,
900   Both Cristen and hethen frely com ther-too.
I woote not sumtyme what is best to doo.   *know*
I dwelle here soo in swech maner drede,   *such a state of dread*
I knowe not my frend whan I have nede.

"I se also here anothir grete myscheffe   *danger*
905   In you, madame, and ye lyst to here: *if it pleases you to listen*
Ye be to every man both deynty and leffe,   *esteemed; beloved*
And ye no man cownt not at a pere.   *pear (i.e., deem worthless)*
It wyll not prove, swech solen daungere.   *succeed; singular resistance*
Thinke on othir that have abyden long,   *waited (i.e., put off love)*
910   And at the last thei have walkyd wrong."   *have chosen the wrong path*

Chapter 18

"And dede thei so," seyd this noble qwene,   *Although*
"So shal I not wyth grace of God above.
My wyttes, I telle you, nothing besy been   *have not been occupied*
In swech matere, neythir to lust ne to love.
915   Fy on tho hertes that evyr on swech thing hove!   *dwell*
Dred yow not of me in this matere:
Beth not aferd tyl ye more thing here.

"And as for youre puple that amonges you dwelle,
Have ye not powere and ful auctoryté
920   To put out hem whech beth of hert so felle,   *malicious*
Or hem that use falshed or sotylté   *treachery*
Be whech oure rewme happyly harmed myth be?   *perhaps*
Syth that ye may, why do ye not youre dede?   *duty*
Thei that lett yow are worthy to be dede!   *hinder; dead*

925   "Ye are a man large and grete of bones:
Yf youre hert be as youre grete body is,
Ye ar ful lyckly to do more note at onys   *good; alone*
Than othir three men. A schame for soth it is   *in truth*
That swech a man schuld fere ony of his   *fear any of his subjects*

930   Whan that he may correct hem himselve —
      I wold wene ye alone shuld oppresse twelve!"   *overpower*

Chapter 19

      An othir duke gan than to approche.
      Ser Clamadoure thei calle his ryth name,
      A worthi man and Duke of Antioche,
935   The qwenes cosyn, a lord of ful grete fame.
      "Thei that lerned you ar ful mech to blame,   *who taught*
      As in my conceyt," thus seyd he to the qwene,   *In my opinion*
      "For of swech wytt and of swech cunnyng ye been,   *cleverness*

      "It passith oure wittis; there is no more to say.   *surpasses*
940   Lych to an egle ye flye us all above,
      Yete in as mech as ye be yet a may   *maiden*
      And eke a qwene, it fallyth to youre behove   *behoves you*
      To fostre hem whech you drede and love.   *To take care of those who*
      Despise hem nowt thow that thei be dulle —   *even though; stupid*
945   Nout lich to you, for ye be in the fulle,   *replete [with wisdom]*

      "As I suppose. I pray God, as for me,
      Grow ye no hiere — youre wyt is hye inow.   *higher*
      Than thow oure wytt be not in swech degré,
      Yet oure good wyll must ye nedes alow —   *admit*
950   What shal men ellys wryte and sey of yow,
      That ye dysdeyne the pore creature
      And hauns youre witt out of all mesure.   *exaggerate*

      "What thing letteth yow that ye wil not us leve?   *keeps you from believing us*
      And be we youre men and youre servauntis alle,   *Since*
955   Youre counsayl, lady, whech shal yow not greve,   *council; distress*
      Ye shuld tel us, for it may so falle
      That the bettir end that mater schale
      Be browt to, for the mo wyse hedes there be
      In ony matere, the bettir is it, as thinkyth mee."

Chapter 20

960	"Cosyn," sche seyd, "ye preyse sore a kyng,	*arduously*
	But I wold wete of you the cause qwy	*why*
	That o man above many shall have governing,	
	To byd and comaund, send both fer and nye.	
	What is the cause that he hath swech maystry	
965	Ovyr all men and no man hath ovyr him —	
	He his lord of lond, of body, and of lym?	*is; limb*

	"In elde tyme, for stryff and for debate	
	Amongys the puple that reygned to and froo,[1]	
	And for to staunch bothe envye and hate,	
970	For to have reule, thei were compellyd ther-too	*To restore order*
	To chese a leedere hem for to governe thoo.	
	This was the cause why thei chose a kyng:	
	Thei schuld ellys a streve for many a thyng,	*have striven*

	"For whan there is not ellys but pere and pere,	
975	There is non as than wyll do for othyr:	
	On seyth here, another seyth it schall be there.[2]	
	This stryffe, it fallyth betwyx brother and brother;	
	Ageyn the son sumtyme stryvyth the modyr.	
	Than were thei chose ryght for this entent:	
980	To bryng in reule thing that was wrong went.	*into order*

	"Summe were chose for wysdam and for wytt,	
	Summe for strenght, summe for humanyté.	*compassion*
	That I sey treuth, cronycles wytness it.	*testify to it*
	So than a kyng as in auctorité	*in terms of*
985	Excellyth his puple, for there be as wyse as he	*though there are [people]*
	Oft tyme seyn ryth withinne his londe.	
	Than may ye se that all this servyle bonde	

---

[1] Lines 967–68: *In past times, on account of the strife and conflict / That reigned everywhere among the people*

[2] Lines 974–76: *Because, when all are equal (peers), / There is no one who will do anything for anyone else: / One person argues for one opinion, another argues for the opposite*

	"Came oute of fredam; the puple was sumetyme fre	*once*
	And had noo lord, but ych man reuled himselfe.	
990	Thus cam thei than oute of her liberté:	
	Be her fre choys, ten of hem or twelve	*By their*
	Were draw awey; thei schuld no lengere delve	*dig*
	Ne do no laboure but reule the cuntré abowte;	*around them*
	And to her heed hemself yet must thei lowte.	*head; bow*

	"But for ye wyll allgate know myn hert,	*in any case*
	What that I thynk, I tell you platt and pleyn:	*plainly and simply*
	There schall nevyr man, be he nevyr so smert	
	Ne eke so strong, wynne me — that is to seyn,	
	Have me to spowse — I wyll no lengere feyn,	*dissemble*
1000	But if he be so strong himself alone	
	That he be able to fyght with all his fone.	*foes*

	"Thys is the ende and this my wyll now is;	*final word*
	Let us no more as in this matere speke.	
	So God my soule bryng onto his blys,	*unto*
1005	This covenaund made ne schall I nevyr breke.	*covenant*
	Ye may well carp, stryve, clatyr, and creke;	*talk, argue, clatter; creak*
	Whan all is doo, this schall be the ende.	
	Your wordys therfore lett hem falle fro mende."	*i.e., be forgotten*

Chapter 21

	Than was there woo and waylyng eke enowe.	*woe; enough*
1010	Thei morned alle and made mekyl mone	*much moaning*
	Whan that thei sey where-to the matere drowe.	*matter was concluded*
	Carefull wytys were thei than ilkone.	*Unhappy creatures; each one*
	The qween hir modyr gan to syghe and grone.	
	Sche seyd, "Doghtyr, this is noght your avayle;	*advantage*
1015	Put not your purpos in swych grete perayle.[1]	

| | "Your dotyng dayes, I trow, now be come! | *days of dotage; believe* |
| | What wold ye hafe? Wote ye what ye say? | |

---

[1] *Do not set your mind on a plan of such great peril*

88

Thorowoute this worlde, in Grece ne in Rome,
Is no swych man that this thyng do may,   *who may do this thing*
1020   Schuld kepe a londe of so gret aray,   *manage; complicated affairs*
And he alone. What wene ye for to hafe?   *all by himself*
It is impossible that ye desyre and crafe!   *what; crave*

"Avyse yow bettyr and take another day
Tyll that your wytte is chaunged and your thowte.
1025   Is your wysdam now turned to swech aray   *such a condition*
For to desyre swych thing as is nowte?   *nonexistent*
Cursyd be thei that yow here-to browte
Onto this errour, to do as no man dothe,
That every poynt thei varye fro the sothe."   *In every detail; truth*

Chapter 22

1030   "Madame," sche seyd, "this thing whech I schall doo,
I not who sett it in myn hert, treuly: *know not*
It is so fast I may not fle ther-froo;   *fixed so firmly*
It clevyth so sore it wyll not slyde forby;   *clings; slide by*
Wheythyr I goo, sytte, knele, or elles ly,
1035   For noo counseyll I may it not forsake,
Ne for noo crafte awey I can it schake."

Chapter 23

Than wept the qween and was in care and woo,   *i.e., Katherine's mother*
And to the lordes sche sayd, "All is i-lorn!   *lost*
What schall we say? What schall we speke or doo?
1040   I wayle the tyme that evyr sche was born;   *bewail*
Hir hert is harde and tow as is the thorn;   *tough*
Hir wytte is sett so hye I wot not where.
There is no man that may hir here answere!

"What sey ye cosyn, lord and duk of Tyre?
1045   What comyth herof? Can ye owte ferther say?   *anything*

For as wyth me, dunne is in the myre.[1]
Sche hath me stoyned and browte me to abay: *stunned; to bay*
Sche wyll not wedde; sche wyll be styll a may.
It schall cause my deth but mech sonere, loo,   *sooner, indeed*
1050 Because I leve thus in swech care and woo!"

Chapter 24

Than roos this lord, em to the qween,   *uncle; i.e., Katherine*
Gaufron he hyght. He was hir omagere   *subject*
And Duke of Tyre. Mech thing had he seen;
He had passed, eke, many a grete daungere.   *overcome*
1055 He was the next of hir kynrod there;
He myght more boldly sey all his entent.
"Madame," he seyd, "a thing that was nevyr ment,

"What ayles yow that ye desyre so sore
(And ye so yung and wys woman alsoo)
1060 A thing that lawe forbedyth evyrmore?
(Nature eke wyll geve no leve ther-too!)   *will not consent*
This ye desyre, ye wyll not twynn ther-froo.   *depart*
What is youre wyll — I wolde wyte what ye mene —
Wyll ye youre bodye fro alle men kepe clene?   *pure*

1065 "What boote was it to us that ye were born   *benefit*
If that ye wyll not do ryght as thei dede —   *did*
I mene youre fadyr and modyr yow beforn?   *before you*
Ye had not come ne sote now in this stede   *would not have; sat; place*
Had not your modyr with mech care and drede
1070 Browt yow forth and to this lyght yow bore.
Folow ye the steppys of hem that went before!

"Ye do wrong ellys onto tho chyldryn alle   *those*
Whech ye are lykly to bryng forthe and bere.
What desese and what myschefe may falle   *distress; trouble; befall*
1075 But if ye do thus I trow youreself wot nere: *you have no idea*

---

[1] *As far as I am concerned, the horse is stuck in the mire (i.e., I am at a loss)*

To put all this thyng oute of drede and fere
And that this synne in yow schuld not be sene,   *so that*
A kynges doghtyr to dey bothe mayd and qween,   *die*

"I counsell yow thus and ye receyve it wold,   *if you would accept it*
1080   To fle this chauns of feyned chastité,   *venture; affected*
Hewe not so hye but if ye may it holde,   *Climb*
Desyre no thyng that may not goten be.   *be gotten*
Lerneth this lessoun if that ye lyst of me: *from me*
Sche is not born, me thynkyth, that myght wynne
1085   To grype a degré so grete as ye begynne."   *grasp*

Chapter 25

"Uncle," sche seyd, "and that were me full lothe   *I would hate*
To clyme so hye that I myght not come down,
For, as I wene, that matere wold greve us bothe
And lese oure londe be cyté and eke be town,   *lose*
1090   It were destruccyoun eke to oure crown,
God He lede us that we come not there   *God grant*
To ley oure worchep so lowe undyr brere.   *briars*

"But for ye say to me it schuld be joye
To hafe a lord schuld governe both yow and me,
1095   I sey yow nay, it schulde be but a noye   *an annoyance*
Onto myn hert. For if it were so that he
Were lovyng and gentyll and all his hert on me
That he lovyd me and I him best of alle,
What sorow hope ye onto myn hert schuld falle   *do you expect*

1100   "If that he deyd or ellys were slayn in felde   *died*
And I forgo that thing that I loved best?
It myght fall also, thow it hap but selde,   *turn out; happen; seldom*
That this love betwyx us too myth brest   *burst*
And part asundyr; this were a full hard rest   *rough resting place*
1105   Onto oure hert! Therfore to put alle oute of dowte:
I wyll not entere whil I may kepe me owte.   *enter; stay out*

"What, counsell ye me swech game to begynne
Whech is not stedfast in lowe ne in astate?   *commoners; nobility*
In all her gladeness, sorow is evyr withinne,
1110   And with her plesaunce eft medeleth debate.   *pleasures; mixes*
Therfore that lyfe I despyce and hate
That hath noo sewyrté but evyr is variable;   *security*
I wold hafe lyffe and love that evyr is stable."

Chapter 26

"O mercy Godd," seyd the gret Baldake,
1115   He was thoo lord and prince of Palestyne,
"There may no man my lady grype ne take;   *grip; overcome*
Hir craft is swech we may hir not enclyne.   *cunning; persuade*
There is no philosophyre ne ek noo divine   *prophet*
Whech sche dredyth — hir termys be so wyse.
1120   Whatevyr we say, sche gevyth of it no pryce.   *she thinks it worth nothing*

"I sey yow, madame, as it is seyd before,
We want a leedere, if we owte schuld doo.   *need; anything*
Bethynk yourself: fro tyme that ye were bore
To Gorgalus tyme thre hundred yere and moo
1125   It is, certeyn, and yet stod it nevyr soo
As it stant now, madame, in no lond of youre.
Of thing that ye rejoye we schall hafe langoure!"   *distress*

Chapter 27

"What wold ye hafe," seyd this noble qween,
"Have ye not gove to me bothe crown and londe?
1130   I am your lady; my subjectis all ye been: *you all are my subjects*
I wot full wele what longyth to the bonde   *contract*
Of regalté whech I hold in myn honde.   *royalty*
For every werk, sothely, it stant in too:
In good councell and eke in werkyng alsoo.[1]

---

[1] Lines 1133–34: *Every action, truly, has two parts: / Planning the deed, and actually carrying it out*

1135	"The wytt and councell, syre, that schall be oure —
	We schall telle how we wyll hafe it wrowte —
	And all the labour and werke, that schall be youre.

1135   "The wytt and councell, syre, that schall be oure —
        We schall telle how we wyll hafe it wrowte —
        And all the labour and werke, that schall be youre.
        Youre grete lordchype ye schul nogt have for nowte: *not have for nothing*
        The lond of Palestyne, it was nevyr to yow boute;   *bought by you*
1140   It was gove youre elderes yow before
        To serve my crown and ther-to be ye swore."

Chapter 28

        Than spake anothyr, lord of Nychopolye;   *Nicopolis*
        He seyd wordys whech sempt full wyse .   *seemed*
        His name was called thoo Syre Eugeny.
1145   To the qween he spake than ryght on this wyse: *exactly in this way*
        "The estate of regalté is of swych a pryce   *value*
        Ther may no man sothly to it atteyne   *truly; attain it*
        But if he hath both powere and wytte, certeyne.

        "Therfor, sey I yett that we nedys muste
1150   Be rewled be on whech that hath these too,   *these two [qualities]*
        Bothe wytt in sadnesse and powere eke in lust,[1]
        And elles oure reule sone wyll breke in two.
        As other londys are reuled, let us be reulyd soo;
        Let us suppose thei be as wyse as we,
1155   For thus he wrytyth, the astronomere Tholomé,   *Ptolemy*

        "'Who-so wyll not doo as his neyboure werk
        Ne wyll not be ware be hem whan thei do amys,   *learn from their mistakes*
        Of him schul other men bothe carp and berke
        And sey, "Beholde this man, lo, he it is,
1160   Wheythyr he do weel or wheyther he do amys,
        He wyll none exaumple of other men i-take;
        Exaumple to othyr mene he schall be for that sake.

        "'"All othir mene schul be ware be him,   *warned*
        For thei schul se and fele in hemselve

---

[1] *Both wisdom when serious and power in obtaining his will*

1165	That his werkys were bothe derk and dyme."'	*dark and dim (i.e., misguided)*
	Therfore, madame, what schuld I lengere delve	*why*
	In this matere? Me thynkyth ten or twelve	
	Schuld geve exaumple rathere than schall oone.	*provide examples*
	Ye have my mocyoun, for my tale is doone."	*I have said my piece*

Chapter 29

1170	The qween full sadly answerd to this lord:	*gravely*
	"I wold wyte," sche seyd, "of yow whyll ye be here	*know; from you*
	And alle, I trowe, togyder mote acorde,	*agree*
	If that I dede this tyme at youre prayere,	*as you request*
	To leve my wyll and put me in daungere,	*someone else's power*
1175	I sett cas the man whech that I schall chese	*Suppose (Imagine the proposition)*
	To be youre lord, that he have non of these —	
	"That is to sey neythyr wytte ne strength.	
	What sey ye now? Who schall reule yow than	
	Youre londys that ly so fer in brede and length?	
1180	The febyll may nott, the fool eke ne can	
	Demene swych thing; than wyll ye curs and bane	*Govern; curse; lament*
	That evyr were ye subjectys to swech a foole	*fool*
	And to youre hert it wolde be full grete dole.	*grief*
	"Ye schuld be fayn, than, for to reule him,	*Then you would want*
1185	To councell and rede that he do not amys.	*advise*
	This were noo worchepe to me ne to my kyn!	*honor*
	And sekyrly a full grete cause it is	*certainly*
	That I wedde nowte, for owte of joye and blis	
	Schuld I than passe and make myselve a thralle;	*servant*
1190	Held me excused, for sykyrly I ne schalle!	*Hold*
	"For syth ye sey that I am now so wys,	
	Than have I o thing whech longeth to regalté.	
	There is no man but if he be ovyr nys	
	But if he wyll sey and held with me	
1195	That it is bettyr whan it non other wyll be	

To chese the on than for to want bothe.[1]
Chese ye now; we be no lengere wrothe."

Chapter 30

	Yet gan to knele eft befor the qween,	*likewise*
	Bothe maystir and Duke of Athenes, that cyté;	*scholar*
1200	Mayster he was in scole and long had been,	
	And duke i-chose be the puple thoo was he,	
	For her choys there as than was fre,	
	To have what man whech hem liked to heed.	*as ruler*
	Thus in his tale began he in that steed:	*place*

1205	"We supposyd, lady, evyr onto this tyme,	
	That ye had come of that gentyll bloode	
	Of your modyr descendyd down be lyne,	*lineage*
	And of your fadyr that was ful gentyll and good,	
	But oure opynyoun is chaunged and oure moode,	
1210	For as it semyth ye are nothing of kyne,	*no kin to them*
	And if ye were, ye coude not cese ne blyne	*cease nor*

	"To folow the steppes of your elderys before,	*before you*
	As grayn reall growyn oute of her grounde,	*royal grain*
	For nature wolde, thow ye the revers had swore,	*opposite*
1215	That ye were lych hem, certeyn, in every stownde.	*respect*
	And in oure philosophye, I hope, thus it is founde	*I believe*
	That naturaly the braunch oute of the rote	*from the root*
	Schall tak his savour, be it soure or swote.	*flavor; sweet*

	"Ferthermore, yet sey oure bokys thus:	
1220	That every lych his lych he schall desyre.	*like seeks like*
	Be all these menes, it semeth than to us,	*For all these reasons*
	Eyther ye cam nevyr duly to this empyre,	*rightfully*
	Or ellys your hert dyspysyth joye as myre!	*as if it were mire*

---

[1] Lines 1193–96: *No man, unless he is really stupid, / Will do otherwise than agree with me and say / That it is better, when there is no alternative, / To take the one thing (wisdom) / Than to lack both (wisdom and strength)*

	I can no more — I speke oncurteslye.	*uncourteously*
1225	I may not chese, I am so vexed trulye."	*I cannot help it*

Chapter 31

	Onto the duk thus answerd thoo the qween:	
	"Ye make a resoun of ful gret apparens;	*an argument that looks good*
	Ye schew full wele where that ye hafe been,	
	In the grete nest of bysy dylygens,	
1230	Where stody and wytt is in experiens —	*put to use*
	I mene Athenes, of wysdam it beryth the key;	*bears*
	Who will oute lerne, lat him take thedyr the wey.	*learn anything; go there*

	"But nevyrthelasse, thow that ye be endewyd	
	With wordly wysdam and can all thing pleynly	*know everything*
1235	So that ye may with no sophym be pursewyd,	*sophistry; answered*
	Yet to your motyff answere thus may I	*argument*
	And voyd youre resoun well and pregnantly,	*cogently*
	If ye wyll here and take entent to me,	*pay attention*
	For if men take heed, oft tyme thei may se	

	"Owte of a tre growyng dyverse frute,	
1240	And that same tre that sumetyme bare the grene,	
	Now bereth he reed or whyte of dyverse sute.[1]	
	Be this example pleynly thus I mene:	
	My modyr is and so am I a qween,	
1245	In this we acord, and that I am a may,	*agree; maiden*
	In that we dyverse, I can not ther-to sey nay.	*differ*

	"It semeth me that lych a griff am I,	*graft*
	I-planted be God upon an elde stoke	*stock*
	Of anothir kynde, anothyr savour hardyly,	*altogether*
1250	And evene as be miracle the elde blok	*just as; stump*
	Whech is clovyn in foure with many a knok	

---

[1] Lines 1241–42: *And the very tree that once bore green (unripe fruit) / Now bears red or white fruits of different sorts*

Schall rathere folow the gryff than the gryff him,
So faryth it be me and be my eldere kyn: *goes it with me*

"Thei schul rathere consent to leve all sole,   *live all alone*
1255   As I do now, than schall I folow hem,
For certeynly I kepe not of that scole
Where that her joye is but lych a drem.
Farwell fadyr, farwell modyr, and eem: *uncle*
Whan that her counsell is not profitable,
1260   I take swych lyffe, I hope, is ferm and stabyll."

Chapter 32

Whan thei had sayd all that evyr thei coude,
Thei went asundir and parted for a space,   *time*
Comound her wyttys styll and nothing lowde,   *Pooled their wits*
Evyr hopyng and lokyng aftyr grace   *some concession*
1265   Of this same mayde, if thei it myght purchase.   *obtain*
And at a day sette, thei cam togedyr ageyn   *appointed*
To have an answere of hir, plat and pleyn.   *plain and simple*

Thei chose a clerke to telle hir alders tale,   *to speak for all of them*
Whech was full wys and of full grete cunnyng.   *Who; very*
1270   For very stody his vysage was full pale;   *From so much studying*
Alle his delyte and joye was in lernyng.
Be alle her consent, he had enformyd a thyng
Whech he wyll uttyr if he may owte spede,[1]
And all is lost but sche ther-to take hede.

1275   "Foure thinges," he seyde, "madame, be in yow,
Whech schuld excite yow wedded for to be.
If ye comaunde, I wyll declare hem nowe:
The fyrst of hem is that grete dygnyté
Of your bloode ryall; I trow that there non be   *believe*

---

[1] Lines 1272–73: *By common consent, he had composed an argument / Which, if he has any luck, he will present*

1280   In all this world whech is so hye alyed.   *i.e., nobly born*
        The secunde also may be sone aspyed,   *readily apparent*

        "For it is open to every mannes eye,
        I mene your beuté, God mote it preserve.
        There lyvyth no man that evyr fayrere syye —   *saw a fairer one*
1285   Evyr lest it tyll tyme that ye sterve!   *May it last; die*
        That blessed lady whech we clepe Mynerve,   *Minerva*
        Sche hath gove yow the thryd that I of sayde,   *I spoke of*
        Whech is cunnyng—it is so on yow layde

        "It may not fall fro yow be no weye.
1290   And eke the fourt is the gret rychesse
        Whech that ye welde — I can not tell ne seye,   *wield; count*
        For, as I suppose, no man may hem gesse.   *guess*
        Suffyr me, lady, my resones to expresse
        So that thei may be onto yow plesaunce,   *please you*
1295   And eke your puple, I hope, it schuld avaunce.   *benefit*

        "The fyrst of alle, as I seyd before,
        Is youre bloode, your reall stok and lyne   *royal stock and lineage*
        Owte of whech ye were begote and bore.
        This schuld your hert bothe drawe and enclyne
1300   For to spede oure purpos well and fyne.   *to support*
        Wote ye nott welle of what lordes ye came?
        Kyng Alysaundyr that all this worlde wan

        "Was of your kyn, and so was that noble kyng
        Whech made this cyté, Babel, I mene, be name.
1305   Eke many another that here in her lyvyng
        Were enhaunshed hyely with gret fame.   *exalted highly*
        Take heed herto, for Goddys sake, madame:
        Syth thei weddyd were and ech on had a make,   *mate*
        Doth ye the same for youre kynrod sake!

1310   "On the other syde, of your bryth beuté,   *For my next point, about your shining beauty*
        Thus dare I say and I dare stand therby:
        There is no man that evyr with eye yet see   *saw*
        Swech anothyr as ye be hardyly.   *Another woman like you*

I flatyr not; I am non of thoo, sewyrly —
i.e., flatterers; surely

1315 It is not presyd in noo book that I rede.
I.e., Flattery; praised

Than sey I thus, that Nature, withoute drede,
without a doubt

"Whan sche wyll peynt, there can no man do bettyr,

For sche schapyth parfytely all that evyr sche dothe;
shapes

Sche is undyr Godd made be patent lettyr

1320 His vycere generall, if I schall sey sothe,[1]

To geve mankynd bothe nase, eye, and tothe,

Of what schape that hir lykyth to geve,
whatever; that it pleases her

And of hir werk, no man hir to repreve.
reprove

"Sche hath gove, lady, ryght onto your persone

1325 Youre bryght colour and fayre schap eke withalle
besides

To this entent: ye schuld not leve alone
For this reason; live

But with charyté departe this gyfte ye schall;
disperse

But ye do thus, ye may sone have a fall,
Unless

For sche may take thing that sche gafe, certeyn,
take back things

1330 And doth allday fro hem that are dysdeyn,
every day; ungrateful

"Whech can not thank hir of hir hye grace.
Who

Therfore, madame, taketh heed herto I pray:

Lese not your holde, lese not your purchase,
assets

Lete mekenesse dwelle with swych a fresch may,
within; young

1335 Than schall we sykyrly of yow syng and say
truly

That all is well, ryght as we wold it have.

Ferthermore, so Godd my sowle mote save,

"I trow thow Nature had coupled in o persone
if; combined

All hir gyftis, as if sche wyll sche kan,
as she can do if she wishes

1340 Than trowe I welle ye have hem all alone.

Of youre charyté, than, take to yow summe man:

Lete him have parte of swech thing as ye han.

Swech goodely gyftis wold not evyr be hyd —

If Nature were here, the same sche wold byd!

---

[1] Lines 1319–20: *To tell the truth, she was appointed, by patent letter, / To be God's viceroy*

1345 "And for the thyrd poynt in whech I yow commende,
Whych is your wysdam and your gret lernyng:
Youre wyttys are swech there can no man amende
Youre conceytes hye, for if ye had a kyng   *lofty thoughts*
He myght ful well trost in your cunnyng
1350 Thow he himself had not as ye have,
And, as me thinkyth, your soule can ye not save

"But if ye comoun this gyfte to other mene: *share*
It is not gove yow to have it all alone!   *You are not meant to hoard it*
The Fyrst Mevere, as oure bokes us ken,   *First Mover; teach*
1355 Whech syttyth above the sterrys in His trone,   *Who*
He gevyth summe man more wysdam be his one   *by himself*
Than have twenti only for this entent: *for this reason alone*
That he to other schall comoun that Godd him sent.   *share with others*

"Take heed, herto, for perellis that may falle
1360 If ye dysplese that Mevere whych sitt above:
His gyftis fro yow draw awey He schall.
That I spek now, I sey it of very love,   *for love of you*
And, as me thinkyth, mech to youre behove.   *for your own good*
The fourt poynt of theyse and last of alle
1365 Is the rychesse whech is onto yow falle.

"Ye be so rych the world wondyrth of it.
What schall ye do with alle this welth alone?
I sey of this as I seyd of youre wytt:
Thei were i-graunted of Godd to youre persone
1370 That ye schuld part all this welth and woone;   *share; property*
That schall ye best do if ye take a kyng.
Here is my tale, here is myn askyng."   *request*

Chapter 33

Than answerd sone that swete gracyous wyght,   *person*
And to this mayster sche seyd thus ageyn:
1375 "Youre commendacyoun whech ye dyd endyth,   *compose*
If it be soth as ye sayd, plat and pleyn,
Schall cause me, there is no more to seyn,

To plese that Lord with all hert and mynde,   *i.e., the First Mover*
That in His gyftis hath be to me so kynde

1380   "And sent me graces whech othir women want.
        Ye seyd efte for that I am so fayre   *because*
        And eke so wys and rych as ye warant,   *affirm*
        Therfore me must purpos to have a ayre,   *plan; heir*
        To chese an husbond, good and debonayre.   *gracious*
1385   Avyse yow, syre, what that ye have sayde:
        We wyll not lyght lowere than ye us layde.[1]

        "Ye have sett oure loos above so hye   *honor*
        We pase all women that now formed are.   *surpass; who now exist*
        And on youre grounde ageyn I thus replye: *on your own terms*
1390   I wold know to me who that worthy ware.   *is worthy of me*
        This is your argument, this is your owne lare,   *instruction*
        That I am worthyest lyvyng of all women,
        Than must I hafe the worthyest of all men:

        "It folowyth full evene ryght of your tale,[2]
1395   If ye take heed. I pray yow, where dwellyth he,
        So wyse, so fayre, so rych, withouten bale,   *beyond measure*
        And of swech lynage born as we be?
        But if ye fynde swech on, ye may leve me,   *Unless; such a man; believe*
        I wyll non haf; therfore, loke well aboute —
1400   The more ye plete, the more ye stand in doute.   *argue*

        "But ye wyll wyte allgate what I desyre;   *nonetheless know*
        I schall dyscryve myn husbond whom I wyll hafe.   *describe*
        Above all lordes he must be withoute pere,   *peer*
        Whom he wyll to spylle or elles to save;   *Able to kill or spare whomever he wishes*
1405   He must be stable and nevyr turn ne wave
        Fro noo purpos that he set him on.   *set himself to*
        But he be swech, husbond schall he be none

---

[1] *I will not settle for less than you rated me*

[2] *It is the logical conclusion of your arguments*

"As onto us, whom ye hafe so commended.
He must be wyse alsoo that he knowe alle,   *so that*
1410   Every thing, that it may be amendyd
And reryd ageyn or it fully falle.[1]
If there be swech on, receyve him sone we schall,   *immediately*
And ellys, sekyr, we wyll have husbond none.
Loke well aboute if ye can fynd swych on!

1415   "Ferthermore, yet must he have swech myght
That him nedyth no help of no creature
But he himself be suffycyent to do the ryght
And evyr his myght demened with mesure.   *managed; moderation*
If that ye wyll swech on me ensure,   *guarantee*
1420   I wyll him hafe; I schall nevyr sey nay.
Herkenyth also more what I wyll say:

"I wold eke that he schuld be so rych
That him neded not of othir mennys goode.
No lorde in erthe I wold have him lych.
1425   I desyre eke he schuld be so large of goode,   *generous*
Fre of hert, and manfull eke of moode,   *temperament*
That what man onys asked him any thing,
He schuld hem graunte more than her askyng.

"He must be fayre also, he whom I desyre,
1430   So fayre and amyable that he must pase me,   *surpass*
For syth he schall to me be lord and syre,
It is good resoun that his schynyng ble
Pase hir coloure whech schall his servaunt be[2]
And onto his lordchype bothe servaunt, spouse, and wyffe.
1435   Ferthermore, yet schall this lordes lyffe

---

[1] Lines 1410–11: *Know how to set right everything [that might go wrong] / Before it completely collapses (goes completely wrong)*

[2] Lines 1432–33: *It is reasonable that his shining face / Should surpass the brightness of her who is his servant*

"Be eterne — elles all this is nowte,   *worth nothing*
All that is sayd, but he have this —
For syth he schall with so gret labour be sowte,   *sought*
As me semeth, the game went sore amys   *sorely*
1440   Whan all were well and all in joye and blys
Sodenly to fayle and falle fro swech welth.
Therfor, I tell yow, I dysyre that his helthe,

"His age, his strength, that all these fayl nevyr
But evermore lest, for sorow that it wold make   *cause*
1445   To me, whech tyme that we schuld dyssevyr,   *part*
For other lord wold I nevyrmore take,
But wepe and morne all in clothys blake.
Therfor ye schull me warant he schall not deye,   *guarantee*
This lord to whom ye wold me newe alye.   *ally me*

1450   "And than consent I to all that evyr ye crave —
Elles nowt. Wene ye that I wold fare
As many other do, and have as thei have,
Lych to my modyr, the sorow, the wo, the care,
Whech sche had whan thei departed ware,   *parted*
1455   My lord, my fadyr, and eke my lady, asundyr?   *apart*
That I fle this, me thinkyth it is no wondyr!"

Chapter 34

Whan sche had seyd these wordes all alowde
And uttyrd hir conceyte pleynly to hem alle,
There was no man as than that him kepe cowde
1460   Fro wepyng; teres full sore thei gun down falle.
Hir modyr fel down as rownd as any balle —   *quickly*
For very sorow sche swounyd in that place,   *swooned*
For now sche seeth there is non othyr grace.   *hope*

Sche was lyft up and comforted new agayn,
1465   And at the last, whan sche had caut wynde,   *caught her breath*
"Alas," sche seyd, "sorow hath me nye slayn!
Where schall we seke? Where schall we swych on fynde?
My dowtyr, I trowe, hath not well hir mynde —

Sche wote not what sche seyth, sche is so made!   *knows; mad*
1470 Who may it be? Where may swech on be hadde

"As sche desyryth? It is not, pardé, possible.
Ther is non swech, than schall sche nevyr have non!"
"Nevyr deye, nevyr seke? He must be impassible!   *immortal*
We may well see sche scornyth us echon.   *each one of us*
1475 Go we fast hens, let hir have it aloon.
Worchep and rychesse, sche schall ful soone lese;
No defaute in us for we may not chese":   *No fault of ours*

Thus wayled the lordes as thei sote bedeen,   *sat together*
Cursyng hir maysterys, cursyng hir bokes alle.   *her teachers*
1480 "Alas," thei seyd, "that evyr any qween
Thus schuld be comered! Oure worchep is down falle.   *encumbered*
God send nevyr rem kyng that wereth a calle.[1]
We pray Godd that he nevyr woman make
So gret a mayster as sche is, for oure sake."   *scholar*

1485 Thus with wo, mych care, and grucchyng,   *complaining*
Thei parte asoundyr, ech man onto his home.
Thei goo, or ryde, or sayle, at her lykyng,
For with the qween wroth thei are echon.
Sche is now left for hem to dwell alon:
1490 Sche may stody, rede, reherse, and wryght.
Thus is the parlement fynchyd and every wyght   *finished*

Is in drede and leveth with hert suspens,   *in suspense*
Lokyng alwey aftyr new chaungyng.
Alle her wyttes and all her grete expens
1495 Are now but lost. And here schall be the endyng
Of this same boke, whech tretyth of the pletyng   *debate*
Betwyx this qween and all hir lychemen.   *vassals*
God send us parte of hir prayere. Amen.

---

[1] *May God never send any realm a king who wears a caul (woman's cap)*

Book 3

[Katherine's conversion and mystical marriage to Christ]

Prologue

    Sith no man may here in this lyffe present
    Doo no good dede but he enspyred be   *unless*
    Of that Goste whech fro the omnipotent
    Fader of hevyn and fro the Sune so fre   *freely*
5   Is sent to us, ryght so beleve now we
    That it is best that we oure laboure commende
    Onto this Gost if we wyll have goode ende.

    For I have tolde yow schortly as I can
    The byrth, the kynrod, the nobyllhed of this mayde;   *nobility*
10   The gret disputyng of lordes, who it began;
    And eke hir answere, what sche to hem sayde.
    This have I pleynly now befor yow layde
    In swech ryme as I coude best devyse.
    Schall nevyr man lese no laboure ne no servyse

15   Whech that he doth onto this noble qwene.[1]
    And now hens forwarde schall be my laboure
    To tell of hir be ordre and bedeen,   *forthwith*
    How sche was wonne to Crist, oure savyoure,
    How mervelously he entred to hir toure —   *tower*
20   I mene daun Adryan, the munke whech oure feyth   *brother; monk*
    Fyrst to hir tawte, as this cronycle seyth.

    And if ye dowte, ye reders of this lyffe,
    Wheyther it be soth, ye may well undyrstande   *true*

---

[1] Lines 14–15: *Any labor or service done for this noble queen (Katherine) will not be wasted*

Mech thing hath be do whech hath be ful ryve   *well known*

25   And is not wrotyn ne cam nevyr to oure hande,

Mech thing eke hyd in many dyverse lande.

Evene so was this lyffe, as I seyd in the prologe before,

Kept all in cage aboute, it was not bore.   *brought forth*

Now schall it walk wydere than evyr it dede

30   In preysyng and honour of this martir Katerine.

Hir lyff, hir feyth, hir passyoun schall nevyr be dede   *i.e., lost to the world*

Whyll that I leve. I wold ful fayn enclyne

Hir holy prayere to be my medycyne

And eke my tryacle ageyns the venym foule   *medicine*

35   Whech that the devyll hath throwyn on my soule.

I dresse me now streyt onto this werk;   *apply myself directly*

Thow blyssyd may, comfort thou me in this.   *maiden*

Because thou were so lerned and swech a clerk,   *scholar*

Clerkes must love thee — resoun forsoth it is.   *it stands to reason*

40   Who wyll oute lerne, trost to me, iwys,   *anything; trust me*

He dothe mech the bettyr if he trost in this may —

Thus I beleve and have do many a day.

Chapter 1

There was an hermyth, as elde bokes telle,   *hermit*

A munke, a man of ful hye grace and fame.   *monk*

45   Be the see thei sey sett was thoo his celle.   *located*

Adryane I rede that it was his name.

His knelyng had made his knes full ny lame.   *nearly*

A prest he was eke, sothely as I fynde.

He had a chapell in whech he song and dynde,   *dined*

50   Slepe and welk, for other hous had he non.   *Slept; walked*

This man knew the counsell of this mayde   *inner thoughts*

Fyrst of alle, for Athanas, of whom long agon

We spoke befor, was not than arayde

Ne eke anoynted with baptym, ne assayde   *baptism*

55   With Godyis scorge, for he was turned be hir —   *converted by [Katherine]*

And sche convertyd be miracle, as ye schul here.   *was converted*

	This man was ordeynd lych, I undyrstande,	*chosen*
	To seynt Joseph, oure Lady to lede and gyde,	*guide*
	For evene as Joseph into Egypte lande	
60	Went with oure Ladye, evermore be hir syde,	
	So was this ermyte than in that tyde	*hermit; time*
	A bodyly leder to this gostly werke	
	Whech tyme that Cryst this noble mayd schulde merk	*mark*

	With His crosse to make hir strong and stabyll	
65	Ageyns the flesch, ageyns the affluens	*abundance*
	Of wordly delyte, and make hir to Him abyll	*capable of being*
	Bothe spouse and wyffe, whech feestly dylygens	*holy*
	Was wroght so wondyrly it paseth experiens	
	Of wordly men. Wherfore I am agast	*worldly; afraid*
70	To speke therof, knowyng it passeth the gnast	

	Of my cunnyng,[1] but that I leve in hope	
	That thorow the prayere of hir and Adryane	
	I schall have myght and strength eke to grope	*explore*
	This holy matere, to telle forth of this man,	
75	How that he lyvyd and how he vytail wan,	*acquired food*
	For onto town wolde he nevyr aproche,	
	But tyllyd his londe heye upon a roche.	*tilled; rock*

	Sumetyme of schyppes that ryden there fastby	*from; nearby*
	Had he comfort of mete and eke of drynke.	*food*
80	Sexty yere this lyffe he led sothely,	
	That nevyr went he awey fro that brynke.	*shore*
	Thus party with elmesse, party with his swynke,	*partly with alms; work*
	Alle blyssydly in abstinens and prayere,	
	This lyffe led he, this ermyte or this frere —	*hermit; friar*

85	For frere was name than to all Crysten men	
	Comoun, I rede, and ermytys were thei called	
	That dwelt fro town mylys sex or ten,	*miles*
	Were thei growen, were thei bare or balled.	*hairy; bare-headed; bald*

---

[1] Lines 70–71: *it lies beyond my little spark / Of wit*

> Because thei were eke all soole i-walled, *alone cloistered*
> 90 Sume men called hem munkys, withowte drede, *monks*
> For these wordes munke and soole are on, as we rede.[1]

Chapter 2

> Whan this ermyte was fall stope in age *hermit; stooped with*
> And myght not byd his bedys as he was wont, *say his prayers*
> Than wold he goo forthe a grete passage *distance*
> 95 Ryght be the see on stones scharp and blunte,
> And evyr his body wold he chyde and runte: *scold*
> "What eylyth thee now? Why art thu so sone oute *ails; indisposed*
> Of holy prayere, of werkes that be devoute?

> "Now God," he seyd, "that sytthest hey in trone,
> 100 Forgeve it me that I do not so weele
> As I was wone. My body is cause alone *used to*
> And not my soule — ful sykyrly this I feele.
> I may not wake ne fast nevyr a dele; *hold vigil or fast at all*
> I can no more all this — defaute is myne. *the fault*
> 105 If any goodenes have I, Lord, that is Thine.

> "Demene not me, Lorde, aftyr my febyll myght *Judge; according to*
> But aftyr my wylle, that evyr desyreth in-on *steadfastly*
> With blessed dedes to be alowed in the syght *sight*
> Of Thi mercy. For thow my myght be gon, *though; strength*
> 110 Yet is my soule as stable as any ston,
> And evyr schal be, as I can best devyse,
> In Thi drede and eke in Thi servyse." *In awe of you*

> Unnethys had he ended his oryson, *Scarcely; prayer*
> He saw a syght, a mervelous tho he thowte, *then*
> 115 For as he walkyd the strondes up and down, *shores*
> He fond a thing whech he had long i-south, *sought*
> A blessed syght onto his eye was browte: *sight*

---

[1] *For these words, monk and solitary, mean the same thing, as we read*

	A qween, he sey, of vysage and stature	*queen [Mary]; saw; appearance; height*
	Passyng full mech alle erdely creature.	*Surpassing by far*
120	All hir aray acordyng eke ther-too—	*appropriate to [her state]*
	So bryght a corown, so bryte clothys eke,	
	He wot not what him is best to do.	
	He is not febyll, he is no lengere seke;	
	His blode is come ageyn onto his cheke,	
125	His eyne have caute of new comfort a lyght,	*eyes*
	His body is youthyd, he thinketh himself ful lygth.	*made young*

Than gan this ermyte stalk ny and nye *closer and closer*
To se this syght, this selcowth new thing. *marvellous*
"O benedicité!" he seyd, "mech merveyle have I *Blessed be God!*
130 That this lady fresch and fayre and yyng
Is come so sodenly hydyr in this morownyng —
And schyppe ne boote ne can I now here see, *boat*
Neyther on lond ne fletyng on the see." *floating*

Thus merveylyng betwyx joye and drede,
135 A ful softe pase onto hir ward he went, *Very slowly toward her*
For as him thowt sche also to him yede. *came*
But sche spake fyrst with full meke entent:
"Brothyr," sche sayde, "the Lord omnipotent
Whech made the hevyn, the watyr, and the londe,
140 He save yow evyr and blysse yow with His honde." *May he*

The ermyte than onto oure Lady sayde,
"Gramercy madame! And He kepe yow alsoo
Fro all myshap that ye be not afrayde
Of noo dysese but evyr withowten woo —
145 I pray to Godd ye mote be on of thoo
Whech that schall dwelle with Him in His blys,
Where may no joye ne no solace mys." *be lacking*

"Good syre," seyd sche, "I wolde yow pray full fayn
To do a message fro me unto a whyte[1]

150   Whech that I love and trost. Ye may hir sayn   *tell*
So doth my Sone, for werkys that be ryght   *My Son does too; because of*
Whech that sche usyth, that mayde fayre and bryght.   *she practices*
And ye syre oure messangere I wold ye were,
Oure wyll and oure wordes to this lady for to bere."

155   "O, mercy Godd," seyd thoo this Adryan,   *then*
"What, wold ye now I schuld forsak my celle,
Forsake my servyse, and to be youre man?
I have made covenaunt evyre here to dwelle
Whyl that me lestys brethe, flesch, and felle,   *While I still have; skin*

160   Tyl Jesu wyll fecch me that was maydenys Sone.   *maiden's Son*
Spek not ther-of, for it may not be done!"

Chapter 3

Than sayd that mayde ageyn onto him,   *i.e., Mary; in response*
"Art thu avysed what thu hast seyd to me?   *Do you realize*
Thu prayed full late, whyll the nyte was dyme,   *night was dark*

165   That God Himself nothing wrothe schuld be
With thin age ne wyth thi febylté.
Thu prayed eke His modyr — I herd it loo —
Sche schuld be mene ryght betwyx yow too.   *intermediary*

"I am sche to whom that thu so ofte

170   With pytous voys hast cryed bothe day and nyght   *night*
That I schuld help thi dulnes for to softe.   *relieve your sluggishness*
Therfor, I wyll thu force thee with thi myghte   *force yourself*
To be my messangere and eke my gostly knyth   *messenger; spiritual knight*
Onto that lady whom I love full wele —

175   Yet hath sche of me knowyng nevyr a deele.   *Though she knows nothing of me*

"Therfore, busk thee to Alysaundyr for to goo,   *prepare*
Onto that cyté whech men called sumetyme

---

[1] Lines 148–49: *I wish greatly to ask you / To take a message from me to a person*

	Grete Babell — there be swych no moo	*there is no greater*
	In all this world, thus seyth every pylgryme.	
180	What schuld I lengere tary in my ryme:	
	Thou schalt fynde there a qween full reall	*royal*
	And onto hir bodyly speke thu schall.	*in person*

"Sey ryght thus: 'The Lady bothe modyr and mayde
Gretyth hir well, and that in goodely wyse,
185   Ryth be me, for sche both comaunde and prayde   *Through me*
That I schuld doo to hir this goode servyse.'
Thus schall thu sey, ryth as I devyse.   *exactly*
Sche schall make straunge and be astoyned sore;   *act surprised*
Leve not this message for that cause nevyr the more.   *Abandon; errand*

190   "It is not goo now but a lytyl whyle   *just a little while ago*
Syth that this lady was with hir counsayle,
In whech there was ordeynyd many a wyle,
And many a mene, and spent mych travayle,
To do hir wedde, but it myght not avayle,[1]
195   For I myselve have ordeynd hir a lorde   *chosen a husband for her*
To whom sche schall in clennesse well acorde.   *purity*

"Eke that thu schuld the more deynté have   *pleasure*
To do this message and all this grete laboure,
I wyll thee telle pleynly — I wyll not wave,
200   I wyll not varye — but the lynage, the honoure,
The vertu, the occupacioun, of this swete floure,
Thou schalt it knowe be informacyoun of me,   *information I provide*
Bothe hir goodenes, hir cunnyng, and hir degré.

"Fyrst of alle, thu whyte sche is a qween —   *you [shall] know*
205   A rych, a reall, a wys, and eke a fayre,
For in this worlde swech no moo there been.   *none like her*
Sche hath no chylde, ne sche hath non ayre,   *heir*
For if sche leve, sche schall love bettyr the hayre   *believes; hair shirt*

---

[1] Lines 192–94: *During which time many strategies / And methods were used, and much labor was spent, / To make her marry, but it could not succeed*

Than any reynes aftyr that sche be drawe   *fine linen*
210   Onto my servyse and to my Sones lawe.

"Sche is also in sothenesse a ryth grete clerke,
And eke a sotyll in alle the Sevyn Scyens —   *suble one; Seven Liberal Arts*
That schewyd sche welle bothe with word and werke,   *deed*
In the parlement where was grete expens
215   Of wordly rychesse, and eke grete dylygens
Of wordly wytte, to make hir wedded be,
But thei sped not. A heyere lord of degré   *succeeded; higher ranking*

"Schal be hir spouse, whom sche yet not knowyth.
Sche must forbere fyrst mech thing, certayn.   *give up*
220   I mene, the rychesse in whech sche now flowyth,   *abounds*
For of povert schall sche be as fayn
As evyr sche was of rychesse, soth to sayn,
Or of ony welth or ony grete honour.
I schall be to hir a comfortour

225   "In all hir nede. Whan that sche schall fyght
Ageyns the heresye of philosophye,
Of all her resones sche schal rek but lyght.   *count as nothing*
Thow thei her sophymes sotyly multyplye,   *sophisms*
Sche schall asoyle hem and ageyn replye   *assail*
230   So myghtly that thei schul lese her art   *their skills*
And sche schall drawe hem to be in Goddis part,   *on God's side*

"For aftyr me, I tell thee sykyrlye,
There was nevyr swech another lady lyvande   *living*
That withowte ensaumple cowde leve parfytely,   *precedents*
235   As sche hath now newly take on hande,
So holy a lyffe. Therfore, thu undyrstande
Sche schall have eke as gloryous a hende   *end*
As evyr had woman that lyved here in kende."   *as a human*

Chapter 4

Whan that oure Lady had seyd all this thing,
240   This ermyte fell to grounde plat and pleyn.   *flat*

112

He was aferd and ravesched in swownyng,
And sche full mekely lyft him up ageyn.
"Be not aferd," sche gan thoo to him seyn.
And he answerd, "Gramercy, now, madame!
245   Forgyfe me now in that I was to blame

"That I knew not Crystis modir dere,
But all wytles, rekles, and boystous   *stupid, thoughtless, and blustering*
Was I, Lady, full late in myn answere.   *recently*
Ye may well se my wytte is komerous!   *cumbersome*
250   Your comyng was to me so mervelous,
My wytt was goo than I sey yow veryly,   *gone when I saw*
My Lordes moder, myn advocate, my Mary —

"And I hir servaunt and evyre hath be and cast!   *always; intended to be*
Allas, allas! And it is wrete full pleyn,
255   A hard thing, of whech I am agast:
Who wyll not know schall be forgete certeyn.
This is my thowght, my Lady sovereyn:
Because that I so recles was full late,   *reckless; just now*
That youre love schuld now turn to hate.

260   "Therfore, youre grace with pytous voys I pray,
To punch and snybe yourself as ye lest.   *punish; rebuke; as you yourself*
And I am redy evermore, nyght and day,
To be obedyent ryght at your request,
To do your message so as I can best —
265   But sewyrly this gret cyté large   *honestly*
Of whech ye spoke whan ye dyd me charge,

"I know it noght, ne eke the wey ther-to;
I have not herd but lytyll of it certayn.
But as ye wyll, ryght so mote I do:
270   To fulfyll youre byddyng myn hert is ful fayn;
Thow I for werynesse dey or elles be slayn,   *die; killed*
I schall go thedyr. Yet hafe I full mech care   *worry*
Of wylsom weyis or that I come thare.   *hazardous paths*

"For, as I wene, many a wyldyrnesse
275   Is in that wey and many a wyked beest!
Yet schall I forward hastly now me dresse —   *move right along*
I trost on yow, that ye schull at the leest
Ordeyn for me that I be noght areest,   *hindered*
But undyr your wyng and your proteccyoun   *But rather that*
280   May be this vyage and this progressyoun."   *voyage*

Chapter 5

Than seyd the qween onto him ageyn,
"Well may thu blys that Lord that boute us alle,   *bless; redeemed*
That He be thee wold send or elles seyn   *through you; say*
This reall matere and eke ther-to thee calle.
285   Go now thi wey: thu may not stumble ne falle
Whan swech a ledere is to thee a gyde.   *guide*
But whan thu comst within thoo gatis wyde,

"Whomevyr thu mete, if he spek to thee,
Spek not ageyn in no manere wyse.   *Do not make any reply*
290   I tell thee why: the hye noble secre   *mystery*
To whych thu schall do laboure and servyse,
If unworthy herd it, thei myght it dyspyse.
Eke thiself, thi mouth must thu spere   *spare*
And kepe thi wordys only for this matere.

295   "So schall thou goo thorow that grete cyté
Tyll that thu come onto the paleys reall
Whech that he made — Costus, the kyng so fre —
Both dych and hylle, doungon, toure, and wall.   *moat*
Many a knyth and many a sqwyere thu schall
300   Fynd there and se the gates for to kepe.   *guarding the gates*
Be not aferde; my Son schall thee kepe

"Fro all her manace and all her grete daungere.   *their*
Blesse thee well, and eke my Sones name   *Bless yourself*

Ryght in thi forhed loke thu crouch and bere,[1]
305   Than no man schall have powere thee to blame,
Ne eke to lett thee tyll thu come at that dame,   *stop*
And where sche dwellyth now wyll I thee say:
Thu schall goo forthe and passe all that aray   *company*

"Tyll that thu see wallys fayre and newe,
310   And at a posterne smalle of forme and of schap   *gate; size and shape*
Onto that same, loke that thu fast sewe.   *follow*
There nedyth thee noght neyther ryng ne rap —   *you need not*
The gate schall ope lyghtly at a swap.   *tap*
Thu schalt entere and fynd that swet may,
315   Whech schall to hir be full grete afray,   *[your entrance] will alarm her*

"For sche schall wondyr how that ony man
Myght entere to hir into that pryvy place.
Hir booke, hir stody schall sche leve ryght than   *set aside*
And loke on thee with full sobyr face.
320   Have thu no fere in no manere cace   *in any case*
Of hir qwestyons ne of hir apposayle: *interrogation*
I schall enforce thee soo thu may not fayle   *strengthen*

"To geve hir answere to every questyoun.
So sayd my Sone to His aposteles twelve,
325   'Whan ye stand,' He seyd, 'befor the dome   *judgment*
Of many tyrauntys, and ye alone youreselve,
Thow thei yow calle Lollard, whych, or elve,   *Lollard, witch, or elf*
Beth not dysmayd — I schall gyve yow answere.'
There can no man swech langage now yow lere —   *teach*

330   "Ryght so schall thu have in thi langage
Swech wonder termes that sche schall stoyned be.   *astonished*
Cryst schall endewe thin eld rekeles age   *endow; feeble-minded*
With eloquens whech full mervelous — trost me —
Schall be to thee, and most specyaly sche   *in particular*

---

[1] Lines 303–04: *Mark and display my Son's sign (i.e., the Cross) on your forehead*

335   Schall lyste ful sore aftyr this new doctrine.   *listen closely to*
         Alle hir wyttys therto wyll sche enclyne —

         "No wondyr it is, for my Sone in sothenesse
         Hath chose hir specyaly above all othir lyvande   *living people*
         For hir vertew and for hir grete clennesse.   *purity*
340   He wyll wedd hir in schort tyme comande.   *coming*
         Thu schall be messangere and tak this werk on hande:
         Thu schall brynge hir evene unto this place,
         Thiselve alone, withowtyn othyr solace.   *comfort*

         "Thys same tokne schall thu to hir bere,
345   For if sche enqwyre who thee thedyr sent,
         The same lord, sey ageyn to hir,
         Whom that sche chees syttyng in parlement,
         For whech choys sche was full nye i-schent   *nearly ruined*
         Of hir lordes, so as thei than durst.   *dared*
350   Sche toke the bettyr and forsok the wurst.

         "Withinne hir stody thus schall thu hir fynde.
         Be not aferd of hir sotell cunnyng —   *subtle*
         Thu schall not fayle of answere to the kynde   *on a par with*
         Of all hir wytte and all hir stodying.
355   Go now forth fast and hedyr sone hir bryng:
         Gyrde thee sore and tuk up well thi lappe;   *Prepare assiduously; tuck in your robe*
         Tak with thee thi staffe and eke thi cappe!"

Chapter 6

         Thus goth this ermyte forth ryght in his way,   *on his way*
         Trostyng on gydes swech as long to hevene,
360   For thow he non aungellys thoo herd ne say,   *saw*
         Withoute dowte her ledyng browte him evene   *guidance*
         Onto this cyté long or it was evyne —   *long before evening*
         Nowt that same day, but aftyr a full long whyle,
         Whan he had go and rune full many a myle.

365	Thus wyll God with ful onlykly thing,	
	As to the world, werk whan that Him leest:[1]	
	He chesyth sumetyme onto His hye werkyng	*for his lofty missions*
	Full febyll and sekely and awey can kest	*cast*
	The strong and wyse — Poule seyth this best	*Paul*
370	In his epistoles, who that wyll hem rede —	
	Ryght thus dede he here, withouten drede.	

Ful onlikly was this man to this message
But that God chese him of his goodenesse;
He is now goo forth in his vyage,
375 Be hyllys and pleyn, felde and wyldyrnesse.   *open field*
He is now come where as this emperesse
Satte in hir gardeyn, stodying than ful sore.
Sodenly enterd set he is hir before.   *He suddenly found himself*

Ful sore astoyned were thei than, both twoo,   *astonished*
380 The on for mervayle of hir hye beauté,   *one*
The other was marred, if we schuld sey soo,   *dumbfounded*
That sche a man so sodeynly there gan se
Befor hir knele now ryght in hir secré.   *private quarters*
As if ye wyll this conceyt here more pleyn   *thought*
385 The ermyte in his wytte was astoyned certeyn,

For he fond hir than lenyng on a booke   *poring over*
In sad stodye, ful solitarye, all alone,   *serious*
And often among to hevene gan sche look;   *at frequent intervals*
But swych beuté sey this man nevyr none
390 As now he sethe in this same persone —
Save oure Lady, blessed mot sche be —   *bless her!*
So bryght and scynyng was thoo hir fayre ble.   *shining; countenance*

"A mervelous Godd," thowth he in his mynde,
"Wend I nevyr a seyn swech creature lyvyng!   *I never expected to have seen*
395 I trow in erde as in womannes kynde   *no earthly woman*

---

[1] Lines 365–66: *Thus God will work, when He pleases, / With what looks to the world like a very unlikely instrument*

Is non so bryght, so beuteuous in all thing!
Blessed be Jesu, that hye hevyn kyng,
That me sent hedyr to se this creature,
For aftyr oure Lady sche passeth withoute mesure

400   "Alle othir women." And with this thouth anon
Sche lokyd on him and was astoyned sore
How that he myght ovyr thoo wallys of ston,
This olde man, clyme — or ellys if he wore
Crope thorow the gate than mervelyth sche more   *Sneaked through the gate*
405   Syth that hirself had be there last,
For sche bare the key and sperd it wondyr fast.   *locked*

With this same stoynyng hir bloode gan to renne   *surprise*
Mech more freschere than it was before:
In cheke and forhed newly doth it brenne;   *burn*
410   And if sche fayre and bryght were before,
It is amendyd a hundred parte more,   *She was a hundred times more so*
As to his syght. This olde ermyte lame,   *In his eyes*
He knelyth down and seyth, "All heyll, madame!"

Chapter 7

Sche ryght thus ageyn onto him sayde,
415   "Good syre, tell me how may this be,
For of youre persone be we sore dysmayde
That we so sodenly yow in oure presens see,
I-come thus alone withowte othir menee.   *company*
This ask we fyrst, for sekyr wete we must.   *certain know*
420   Wheythir this is truthe or apparens, it schall be wust   *illusion; known*

"What manere mane myght make yow so maisterlye   *enable you*
To clyme oure wallys whech are so hye.
I trow be enchauntment or be nygromancye   *necromancy*
Are ye entyrd now here before oure yye!   *eyes*
425   We wyll wete this thing, be ye nevyr soo slye:
Who gave yow hardynesse for to be so bolde
Withowte oure leve to entre to owre holde?   *permission; stronghold*

"For of all the lordes and knytys that we have
Is non so hardy, but we gefe him leve —   *unless*
430   But if he wyll reklesly his lyff lave —   *forfeit his life*
Onys to entre neythir morow ne eve
Oure privy secré. Therfor is it repreve   *private quarters; discredit*
Onto your age to tak swech thing on yow.
It wyll not fall happyly onto youre prow.   *turn out well for you*

435   "Therfore, now, tell me schortly in a clause,
Who gave yow boldenesse to do this grete folye?
Sekyr may ye be, we wyll wete the cause   *You may be sure*
And every mene thorow whech ye were hardy.   *means*
Peraventure if treson be found in oure meny   *If, by chance; household*
440   This schall ye telle or ye fro us wende —   *before you; depart*
Ye gete of us elles no ryght fayre ende!"

Chapter 8

Be this was the erymyte comforted ageyn,
For with bolde spech he gave this answere,
And with manly voys thus gan he seyn:
445   "Sche that me sent is grettere, if ye wyll lere,
Than ony lady in erde that dwellyth here,
And eke the lest that longyth to hir boure   *least of her personal servants*
Is more of astate than kyng or emperoure.   *of higher rank*

"Eke for ye ween that ye be so fayre,   *though you believe*
450   So rych in welth, as it is seyd certeyn,
Yet may ye not to hir beauté repayre,   *compare*
Ne nevyr ye schal, sothly dar I sayn —
Bothe hir and yow with eyne haf I seyn.   *eyes*
I may thee more boldely mak this commendyng:
455   Sche paseth yow, certeyn, in all maner thing,   *surpasses*

"Eke hir grete powere that is spred so fere.
Sche may doo what that evyr sche lyst,
For be yon gate whech ye dyd spere,   *fasten*
Sche browte me in, sekyr, or I it wyst.   *truly, before; realized*
460   If sche be wrothe, no man skapyth hir fyst;   *escapes*

Therfore, avyse yow, lady, what ye wyll sey,   *consider*
Lest that my Lady turne fro yow awey."

Chapter 9

 Than gan the qween merveyle of this word
 More than sche dyd evyr hir lyve before
465 Of ony mater. Cryst had made His horde   *hoarding place*
 Or this ermyte cam and leyd His grete tresoure
 Ryght in hir hert, emprended full sore,   *impressed*
 For thow He sent the ermyte as his messangere,
 Or the ermyte cam, Crist Himself was there,

470 Ryght as Gabriell whan he fro hevene was sent
 Onto oure Lady to do that hye message.   *convey*
 Into Nazareth in forme of o man he went,
 Fayre and fresch and yong eke of age,
 But ere that he cam onto this maydes cage,   *dwelling*
475 Cryst was there, as we in bokes rede.
 Ryth so dyd He here, if we wyll take hede.

 But thow God were come as than to hir hert, *had by then come*
 It was fer as yet fro hir knowlechyng.
 Therfore, with wordes that were full smert,   *sharp*
480 Sche turneth ageyn onto the same thing
 Whech we left ere, and thus in apposyng *From which we digressed before; arguing*
 Sche thus procedyth, seyng to this man,
 "How may youre Lady be so worthy woman

 "As ye commende now in your tale to me,
485 Of hir hye worchepe and also of hir wytte?   *honor*
 The worthyest of all women we wene that we be — *believe*
 We herd nevyr of non worthyere yytte!   *yet*
 Where lyghte hir londe? We wold fayn know itte. *is located*
 Who is hir lorde — or wheyther is sche lordelees?
490 Ye telle us thingys whech we holde but lees! *lies (i.e., give little credit to)*

 "Wheythyr is that dame lyvyng in spousayle *marriage*
 Or levyth sche sool as we do now?

If sche be weddyd, sykyrly sche may fayle
Mych of hir wyll, for sche mote nedys bowe
495 Onto hir lord, loke he nevyr so row;   *rough*
And if sche lyve be hirself alone,
Than may sche make full oft mech mone,   *many complaints*

"Ryght for vexacyoun of hir lordes aboute —   *On account of*
This know we well; we are used ther-to!
500 Therfor, goodeman, put us oute of doute:
Tell us the sothe, be it joye or woo,
Whech that this lady most is used too,
And we wyll thank and rewarde yow eke
With swech plenté that it schall yow leke!"   *please you*

Chapter 10

505 "Iwys, madame," seyd this ermyte thoo,
"The grete lordscheppe of my Lady sovereyn   *domain*
Is spredd ovyr hevyn and ovyr erd ther-too
And ovyr the see eke, sothely to seyn.
There comyth noo sune, no dewys, ne no reyn   *dew; rain*
510 But be comaundment of hir Lord and hir desyre —
Swech is hir myght and allso hir powere.

"Hir ladyschepe eke therto is so strong   *i.e., power/authority*
And evyr so stedfast that it may not fayle.
There may no man treuly do hir wrong,
515 For thow thei doo, thei lese her travayle.   *if they try, they waste their effort*
There may no myght ageyn hir myght avayle.
Hir Lord and sche, thei lyve in full grete pees,
With many mylyons of men and mekyll prees.   *a great crowd*

"He is hir Lord and eke to Him sche is
520 Moder and noryse, yet is sche a mayde.   *nurse*
Lord and Sone bothe togedyr, iwys,
This longyth to Him, and yet eft, as I sayde,
Levyth my tale and beth nothing dysmayde,   *Believe*
For sche is modyr and also clene virgyne;
525 This schall ye know aftyr well and fyne."   *understand very well later*

121

Chapter 11

"Sere," seyd the qween, "now merveyle I ful sore,
For ye preche of this hye degré
Of this same lady, for ye seyd this more,
Sche passyth all othir in very felycité
530   Whech that be here now or evyrmore schall be.
Than wondyr we sore that sche sent us here
So evyll arayd, so sympyll a messangere,   *Such a badly clothed*

"For to hir astate it had be full convenient   *appropriate*
To send moo men and not send on alone,
535   Where sche so many hath at hir comaundment!
Eke, as me thinkyth, to swech a grete persone
Schuld long all servauntis that are in hir wone   *retinue*
To clothe more clenly for worchyp of hir hous,
For, syre, your clothyng semeth not ryght precyous."   *refined*

Chapter 12

540   "Madame," seyd he, "if ye wold me leve,   *give me permission*
I wold tell yow pleynly the cause and why
To mak me messangere dyd this Lady meve,   *chose to make*
For thow that sche hafe many mylyons of meny,   *attendants*
Sche is in hert nevyr the hyere hardyly,
545   And swech as sche is are hir servauntes, lo,
For all that love hir thei must do ryght so.   *i.e., follow her example*

"Ye wote well, madame, for mych thing ye know,
That gostly aray passeth in sovereyn wyse   *clothing; in the highest way*
Bodyly dysgysyng, in hye and in lowe;
550   The sete of verteu is sett in swych asyse,   *position*
Even as thei witnesse, clerkes that be wyse,
That treuth is fayrere be many degrees   *more fair*
Than evyr was Eleyn the fayre lady of Grees.   *Helen*

"Therfore, that Lady that me to yow now sent
555   Desyreth more gostly inwardly aray
Than golden clothys spred on bodyes gent.   *genteel*

And ferthermore — yet boldly dar I say —
Sche hath before hir in hir paleys ay
Many a thowsand wyth faces bryght and schene   *shining*
560   Swech as in erde yet nevyr were sene.

"Sche sayde to me, that hye, noble qweene,
That my servyce plesyd hir so weele
That sche wold send me with this aray mene   *humble clothing*
To sey hir wyll onto yow every dele.   *convey all her will to you*
565   And be this processe may ye see and feel,   *argument*
If ye wyll this ladyes frendchyp now wynne
Fro wordly delyte mote ye part and twynne,   *separate yourself*

"For erdely welthys sett my Lady at nowte,   *considers worthless*
Therfore hir servauntis schull not have.
570   Whoso hir love holy mote be her thowte,   *Those who love her must by their*
With devoute lyvyng her sowles to save.
The more thei forsake here, the more may thei crave   *request*
Whan that thei come there her Lady is,   *where*
To hir regyoun where thei dwell in blys.

575   "But, lady, to the purpos now wyll we goo:
Thys blessed qween a tokne dyd me take   *give*
Whan sche me sent youre reverens onto.
Thus sayd sche than, 'My messangere I thee make
Onto yon maydyn. Sche may it not forsake
580   The tokne I take thee, so enprended it is   *impressed*
Onto hir hert sche can it not mys.'

"Thys is the tokne: that ye, syttyng in parlement
With princes, dukes, and erles in fere,   *together*
This was your answere and this your entent —
585   Ye wold no lorde ne kyng have but if he were
So strong, so myghty, that he had nevyr fere,   *fear*
So fayre, so gentyll, that no man were him lych,
So endwyd with good that no man were so rych.

"Thys was at that tyme, lady, your desyre:
590   That this lorde whech that ye wold have

123

Schuld lyve evermore; nevyr with watyr ne fyre
Be dreynt ne brent, but evyr hymselfe save.   *drowned; safe*
Ye wold be with him evyr and nevyr fro him wave —   *stray*
This was your wyll and fullfyllyd schall it be.
595   My Lady sent yow bode, if ye wyll folow me,   *sent word*

"For this same Lord whech with my lady is,
He hathe alle these more pleynteuously, I telle,
Than ony man in this world may think, iwys,
For of alle vertues He is the very welle.
600   Come ye forth with me, hom to my celle,
And if ye fynde my wordes be unstable,
Anothir day arest me be youre constable!

"Ye schull have hir Lord and hir Sone eke —
A gracyous lynage that may noght mys,   *fail*
605   A merveylous kynrode to lerne if ye leke:
He is hir Lorde, sche His modyr is;
He is hir Sone and sche mayde iwys;
He made hir, sche bare Him in hir wombe;
The synnes of the world He clensyth, this Lombe."   *Lamb [of God]*

Chapter 13

610   Than was this mayden sore marred in mynde,   *shocked*
Men myght se in hir coloure, in cheke and in pytte,   *(see note)*
So ran hir bloode, so changed hir kynde,   *visage*
For nevyr was sche or now put in this wytte.
Sche is in swech a trauns, wheyther sche stant or sytte
615   Sche wote not hirselve; sche is in swech cas,   *such a state*
For to sey a soth, sche wote not where sche was.   *to tell the truth; knew*

Betwyx too thingys so is sche newly falle,
Whech sche schall leve or whech sche schall take.   *leave*
If sche leve hir lawe whych hir lordes alle
620   Hold at this tyme and now it forsake,
Falle to a newe for a straunge lordes sake,
Sche seeth not what perell in this matere is.   *peril*
But for the ermyte spake of this Lordes blys,

His wordes have enclyned now ful sore hir thowte
625 That sche schall have a thing long desyred.
Alle hir goddys and hir goode set sche at nowte,
So sore is hir hert with this love i-fyred,
It schall no more, sche cast, with the world be myred. *determined; polluted*
Therfore to the ermyte eft sche gan thus sey,
630 "All your informacyoun I bere well awey, *receive well*

"Save that of o thing grete merveyle I bere:
Ye seyd me ryght now whan ye told your talle
That this grete Lady, if I wolde lere,
Bare a noble chyld withouten any bale,
635 And yet sche is a mayden at asay and sale — *upon inspection*
This same matere is ageyn kynde. *nature*
What, wene ye sere, that I were so blynde

"That I cowde not undyrstand of generacyoun *procreation*
The prevy weyes? Thow I non exersye *experience*
640 Hafe had in my lyffe of swech occupacioun —
Ne nevyr wyll have, be that hye justyse
Whech ye to me now newly gan devyse — *to relate*
Yet know I wele, and ilk man it knowyth,
Who wyll have a chylde, seed sumetyme he sowyth!"

Chapter 14

645 "Wythouten seed, lady, or withoutyn synne
May God make a man, and so He dede or now: *create*
For if we at Adam or at Eve begyne,
It is full pleyn for to schew onto yow.
For whan that same Adam slept in a swow, *swoon*
650 Oure Lord owte of his syde than made Eve.
Than be this ensaumple pleynly may ye preve, *conclude*

"Sith that He made a virgyne of a man,
He was of powere eke for to make
A man of a virgyne — thus He werk can,
655 This gracyous Lorde whech ye to make *as your mate*
Chosen in your parlement. Yet, for your sake,

125

Another demonstracyoun in this same matere
I wyll to yow schewe, if ye wyll it here:

"There may no man, if we take good hede,
660   Preve be any resoun how all thing began —
Speke we now of creatures and leve the Godhede.   *set aside*
The sune and the mone, the bryght and the wan,
Of her begynnyng there can nowe no man
Have no remembrauns ne tell in what plyght   *circumstances*
665   That thei were made, eythere day or nyght.

"Than syth no man may of these erdely werkis
Tell the pryvy cause, no wondyr is certeyn
That thei of feyth schull tell ony merkys,[1]
For feyth is not provable, as clerkys seyn.
670   Therfore oure wyttes must be ful beyn   *inclined*
To leve swech thingys that we can not prove:
Lete argumentys walk, thei are not to oure behove."   *Forget arguments; profit*

Chapter 15

"What aylyd that Lord that all myght hadde,   *possessed the almighty Lord*
In oure frele nature Him for to clothe,   *frail*
675   To leve the bettyr and thus take the badde —
Or ellys at His lykyng to kepe styll bothe?
Was He with mankynde evyr or now wrothe?   *before now angry*
Was He evyr offendyd? We wolde wete fayn
What ye to this matere now can us sayn."

Chapter 16

680   "For myschef, madame, that man fell in   *misfortune*
Whan Adam the appyll ete in paradys
Wold this Lord in erde lowly take His ine,   *abode*
Not levyng that place full of delys,   *delight*

---

[1] Lines 666–68: *Since no one may explain the hidden origin of these earthly works, / It is no wonder that they (the earthly works) / Should reveal themselves through faith*

But bothe here and there at His devys   *devising*
685   He dwelt, as we leve, oure soules to leche.   *heal*
This semyth to yow full wondyrfull speche.

"And that same Lord as nobyll marchaunt
His blood for oure synne on crosse wold spylle.
Of that same deth we may make avaunt: *boast*
690   It waschyth from us alle that we dede ille.
Of oure feyth, lady, this is the grettest bylle: *article*
That Cryst His bloode payed for oure synnes alle.
Best of all marchauntis, therfore, we Him calle."

Chapter 17

"How may ye couple now that ye have sayd?   *reconcile*
695   He is Lord of all — eyre, watyr, and londe —   *air*
Lyvyng in pees with His modyr and mayde.
Her-too thus ye adde that He is so bonde   *bound*
That He suffrede to be slayn with wykkyd honde —   *allowed himself to be*
How can ye acord that this gret possessyoun   *agree*
700   Schuld long onto Him and eke this strong passyoun?

"How may that Lord lyvyn evyr and ay   *eternally*
Whan He is coupled of contraries too?   *composed*
For of man and Godd His persone, as ye say,
Hath take resultauns.[1] And yet sey ye moo:
705   He is bothe eterne and temporall, loo.
Lok if youre spech be now no heresye —   *is not heretical*
This wote I weel, that it offendyth phylosophye!"

Chapter 18

"To these questyouns thus I answere:
For it paseth Nature and all hir scole,   *surpasses; teachings*
710   Nature fayleth whan we feyth lere;
For oure beleve standyth so sole

---

[1] Lines 703–04: *His person, as you say, / Has resulted from the union of man and God*

With these argumentis whech are full of dole   *deceit*
Wyll sche not medelle be no manere preve —
There were no mede than in oure beleve.   *Then believing would have no merit*

715   "Therfor, lady, if ye wyll, lerne this thing;
Ye schall mech bettyr whan ye your groundys have,   *have grasped the basics*
For of oo poynt I geve yow full warnyng:
Ye can nevyr grace of youre Lorde crave,
Ne youre soule eke schul ye nevyr save,
720   But if ye forsake forevyr your elde beleve,
And trow swech thing as ye can not preve.

"How knew ye that Costus, kyng of this londe,
Was fadyr onto yow? And what evydens have ye
That ye were bounden sumetyme with a bonde,
725   Armes, bodye, bak, legges, and kne,
Layde thus in cradyll, as chyldyr are, pardé?
Of all these thingys can we make no preve,
Wherfore full mekely we must hem beleve.

"So schall we beleve all manere thing
730   Whech that oure Lord comaundeth onto us,
For that same Lorde that all hath in weldyng —   *rules all*
Oure blessed God, oure savyoure Jesus —
Whan that He byddyth that we schall do thus,
Suffyseth us as than to be obedyent,
735   For but if we be, I holde us but schent!   *ruined*

"Yet, for ye argue be your demonstracyoun
That this same doctrine schuld be contrarius,   *contradictory*
Because that I seyd in my declaracyoun
Who that blessed lord whech is full delicyous —   *delightful*
740   I mene Jesu, oure Savyoure, of all most vertuous —
That He schuld be God and man eke in fere,   *at the same time*
Of this same doctryne example may ye lere.

"And for ye dowte eke of this coupelyng,   *because*
That we two natures in Cryst sey and preche,
745   I wyll preve this be your own felyng,   *senses*

128

And ye yourselve your owne selve schall teche —
Myn arbytroure I make your owne tung and speche.
For withinne yourselve, if ye take heede,
Two natures haf ye, withouten any drede,

750   "Whech contrarye be. I preve it be this skyll,   *argument*
For that the on desyreth, the other wyll nouth;
Contrarye than be thei, these too, in wyll,
In desyre, in werkyng, in appetyte, in thowth.
Ryght so in that Lorde that us alle hath bouth   *bought*
755   Bethe too kyndes and wylles eke too,   *two natures and two wills*
Bothe in oo persone, oure feyth seyth ryght soo.

"Now wyll we declare onto youre reverens
How God is eterne and withouten ende.
For if ye loke wysely, that same sentens   *doctrine*
760   Schul ye have in youre bokes that trete of kende.   *metaphysics*
Thei determyn thus, if ye have mende: *recall*
All thing that is made begynnyng must have.
And for thei fro that heresye schuld hem save   *in order to avoid heresy*

"Whech two begynnynges puttyth in kynde,
765   Therfor on hafe thei chose and thus thei Him calle
The Fyrst Mevere, if I have mynde,   *First Mover; understand*
Of whech mevere other causes alle
Her oryginall spryng both have and schall,
All that have ben and evermore schul be —
770   Of youre owyn bokes this is the decré."

Chapter 19

Whan Adryan the ermyte these wordes had herde,
Assoyled alle these questyons and many moo,   *Resolved*
Onto the lady thus he last answerde:
"Madame," he seyth, "if ye wyll now goo
775   And walk forth with me, non but we two,
This Lord schall ye see, this Lady schall ye speke,   *converse with*
Howses schall ye have there schull nevyr breke."   *collapse*

These wordes went so depe sche left bokes alle,
So astoyned sche was, sche wot not veryly
780 Wheyther sche schall this ermyte a man now calle
Or ellys an aungell come down fro hye,
For his clothys to his wordes are full onlykly: *unsuited*
An olde man and hore, clade in clothys bare,   *hoary; worn*
A wyse man, a well avysed, and a ware;   *prudent*

785 A man lych a begger whan men him see,
A man lych a doctoure whan thei him here.   *theologian*
Few wordes and wyse and full of sentens had he,
He semyth not so wyse be aray ne chere   *physical appearance*
As this lady hath prevyd in dyvers manere.   *many ways*
790 Wherfore aftyr his counsele certeyn sche wyll do,   *she will take his advice*
No man schall lett hir for sche wyll soo,

For anoon as the ermyte buskyd him to fare   *prepared to depart*
Forth in his jornay, sche folowyth apace.
All lordes and knytes that in the castell ware,   *were*
795 Thei herd not, thei sey not, of all this solace,   *joy*
Ne thorowoute the cyté as thei gun trace,   *went*
Was no man aspyed hem, but as invisible
Thei passed forby. Ryght so seyth oure byble

Of the men of Sodom aboute Lothis hous,   *Lot's*
800 How thei neyther dores ne gates myght fynde.
Godd smet hem thoo with a sekenes mervelous —   *struck; sickness*
It is called acrisia, it maketh men seme blynde
As for a tyme, for sykyr all her mynde   *Temporarily*
Schall be so astoyned that thei schull not see
805 Thing that in her hand up hap than bee.   *happens to be*

So was all the cyté astoyned ryght than,
Be Goddes providens, fully as we wene.
Lete hem curse now, let hem chyde and banne: *complain; swear*
No man knowyth now whedyr is the qweene.
810 Thus goo thei forth, walkyng bedeene,   *together*
Tyll thei come to the stronde where that his hous —   *shore*
This ermyte, I mene, this man mervelous —

130

	Was won for to stande, but all is agoo.	*Used to stand; gone*
	There is no home — all is wylldyrnesse.	
815	He wayled, he loked, he went too and froo;	
	He cast the cuntré, but he coude not gesse —	*searched; figure it out*
	Thus is he lefte in care and hevynesse.	
	"Good Lord," he seyth, "with me do what Thou lest,	
	But as Thou hyght me, comfort my gest."	*promised*

820	In how long tyme or in how many dayes	
	That thei fro Alysaunder went to his celle,	*It took them to go*
	It is full harde to telle, for sewyrly tho wayes	
	Were so mervelous we can not with hem melle.	*concern ourselves with*
	Therfor of this matere no more wyll I telle.	
825	But He made hem myghty this jornay to take	
	That be the aungell led Abacuc to the lake.	*Habakkuk; lions' den (see note)*

	Thus mornyth this man, thus turneth he aboute;	*mourns*
	He lokyth every coost sekyng his celle,	
	He is falle now sodeynly in full grete doute,	
830	For all his sorow, sothely for to telle,	*to tell the truth*
	Was for this lady, where sche schall dwelle.	
	Thus seyd he to hymselve, "Sche schall ween I were	*think I am*
	A fals deceyvoure, a ontrewe messangere."	

Chapter 20

	The qween aspyed be the ermytes face	
835	For very vexacyoun how he chaunged moode.	*frustration*
	"Good syre," sche seyd, "I pray yow of youre grace,	
	Have we any tydynges othyr but goode?	
	That ye are turmentyd, I se be youre bloode.	
	Telle me what doute that ye stand now inne?	
840	Councell ha ye non but me, more ne the myne."	*have; neither more or less*

	"Madame," he seyd, "here left I myn hous	
	Whan I went for yow as I was sent,	
	And now the cuntré to me is mervelous.	*unfamiliar*
	Alle is agoo, i-drenchyd or i-brent!	*washed away*
845	I must seke a new hous, for myn elde is schent.	

| | I had nevyr thowth myn herborow to chaunge; | *dwelling* |
| | Now mote I nedys, and that schall be straunge." | *I must do so* |

	Tho sayd the qween to the man ageyn,	
	"That Lady that sent yow for to fech me,	
850	Sche is so gentyll, so trew as ye sayn,	*If she is as noble*
	Sche wyll not suffyr us in this adversyté	*permit*
	To be lost or devoured in this straunge cuntré.	
	Trost we upon hir and hir gentylnesse,	*graciousness*
	For in good hope lyghte sumtyme sykyrnesse."	*Sometimes our security resides in faith*

855	"Now evyr be ye wele," seyd the ermyte,	*Bless you!*
	"Ye hafe set your trost hyere than myselve.	
	Thow ye be entered into the feyth but a lyte,	*just initiated*
	Ye wyll pace in schort tyme other ten or twelve!	*soon overtake*
	Beth not aferde of best ne of elve,	*beast; elf*
860	For that same Lady whos Son ye choos,	
	Sche schall us save, I leve soo douteles.	*believe*

	"But all my thowth is now for my celle:	
	Schall I now grubbe and mak all newe ageyn?	*labor*
	Schall I now delve and make me a welle?	
865	My myght is i-goo, sothely for to seyn;	*gone*
	To chaunge my dwellyng was I nevyr fayn.	
	This is my grucchyng, lady, this is my care.	*complaint*
	But for your comfort well mote ye fare."	*You should be cared for*

	Godd suffered this man to falle thus in trauns,	
870	That he schuld not hymselfe magnyfye	*become self magnified*
	Of so grete sytys and of swech dalyauns	*sights; interaction*
	Whech that he had with oure Ladye.	
	It is the use of oure Lord to lede men hye	*practice*
	Fro full low degré, as David fro the schepe	
875	Was led to the kyngdam, if we take kepe.	*pay attention*

Chapter 21

In all this feere whech the ermyte hadde,
Evyr was this qween comfortour to his age:

The more he hevy was, the more was sche gladde, *unhappy*
And evyr with full goodely, full trosty langage *confident*
880 Sche seyd on-to him, "Lete youre hevynesse swage, *unhappiness abate*
Lete it be lost that lost now wyll be.
But trewly I telle, a solempne thing I se *sublime*

"Evene yondyr above, sere. Se ye nowth? *Do you not see it?*
The woundyrfull wallys schynnyng as sune,
885 Swech another thing was nevyr wrowte — *made on earth*
There was nevyr swech thing in erde begune!
The stones are bryght, the roves are not dun. *buildings (roofs); dim*
Loke up, man, meryly, se ye noght yon syght — *joyously*
The castell yondyr whech schynyth so bryght?"

890 The ermyte behelde but he sey nowth, *looked; saw nothing*
Neyther wall ne gates, and tho sorow gan he make. *then*
"Lady," he seyde, "in blessed tyme were ye browte
Onto this grounde youre spouse for to take.
He hath do now more for your sake
895 Than I hafe felt all my lyffe levande. *experienced in my lifetime*
Ye be more worthy, as I undyrstande."

Tho wept he full sore, and sone than he say *saw*
That same vysyoun, but sore astoyned he was:
His chapell was turned all in other way, *transformed*
900 For this whech he sethe is bryghtere than glas —
The othir was elde, all growyn with gras. *overgrown*
His elde hous was lytyll, this new is large.
Than gafe he the mayden a full grete charge.

Thus seyd he to hir, "Madame, now goo ye
905 Onto yon castell, on-to yon toure. *tower*
Trostyth no lengere of the ledyng of me, *Rely no longer on my guidance*
For I am not worthy to prese to that boure. *press on; dwelling*
God graunt that I may be youre successoure,
That I may sumetyme come to that place,
910 If ye may, I pray yow, aske me that grace." *request that favor for me*

Than went the mayden forth be hir one,   *by herself*
Desyryng sore to se this goodely place,
But Adryan folowyd whan sche was gone.
Oute of hir hardynesse he gan him purchace *courage; acquire*
915 Onto his comfort now a new solace.
But whan thei were come at the gatys wyde,
There where thei receyved on every syde

With swech manere persones of face and of clothyng
We can not speke it. I trow thei told it nowte, *express; revealed*
920 For thei that are lyfte to swech mysty thing, *lifted up; mysterious*
Thei telle what thei sey whan thei were thedyr broute,
But thei cannot expresse her wyll ne her thowte
In whech thei hade that manere solace[1] —
It is anothyr langage that longyth to that place.

925 But these too persones, as many other moo,
Were lyft up in soule swech sytes for to see.
Seynt Poule hymselve was on of thoo   *Paul*
That was thus i-raveched, yet dowted he   *transported*
Wheythyr his body or nowte were in that secree. *partook in that mystery*
930 But this doute I not, that the body of this mayde
Was in that temple where sche was arayde   *adorned*

With holy baptem and anoynted eke   *baptism*
With holy crisme, as oure Lord wolde.
No man may be baptyzed, if we treuly speke,
935 But thei have a body, be thei yong or olde — *Unless*
Thus sey the elde bokes, therof are we bolde. *we have confidence*
God may do whatevyr Him lyst
And dothe mech thing whech is not wyst.   *known*

Thus are thei receyvyd in the fyrst warde, *outer entrance*
940 But aftyr mech bettyr and of worthyere men
Whan sche to the secunde cam, whech savoured as narde — *smelled like nard*

---

[1] Lines 921–23: *They tell what they saw when they were brought there, / But they cannot convey the feelings and thoughts / They had when they were experiencing that joy*

Nay mech swettyr. There met sche mo than ten —
Of hundredes, I mene — but non can sche ken.   *recognize*
Thei were other maner persones than sche had seyn,   *seen*
945 But all these in fere onto hir gan seyn,   *together; say*

"Wolcom, syster, onto this holy place!
Wolcom to oure Lorde, whech hath yow chose
For to be His spouse ryght of His grace!
Wolcome of clennesse very swete rose;   *rose sweet in purity*
950 For youre virginité, wythowte ony glose,   *truthfully*
Schal we receyve yow." And thus forth thei hir lede,
These gostly folkys in wondyrfull wede,   *apparel*

Tyl thei to the temple cam. But there was a syght:
There came kynges, there cam emperoures,
955 There cam a meny with habytes so bryght,   *company; clothes*
It is not possible to erdely successoures   *followers*
To expresse thoo fresch, thoo gay coloures!   *describe*
Sche sey hem than in her goodely aray;
We leve in hope to se hem anothyr day.   *live; i.e., after our death*

960 Thei led hir thoo forthe a full softe pace   *at a leisurely pace*
Onto the barres of the temple gate.
Hir wolcomyng at that tyme swech thoo it was:
"Wolcom oure syster, wolcom oure mate!   *comrade*
As ye be now were we full late,   *once*
965 For sumtyme had we bothe flesch, fell, and bonys, *skin*
As ye hafe now, had we all ones!"

Upon her habytes certen tokenes thei bere —   *emblems*
Sum man oo tokyn, sume man another bare
Aftyr the passyones whech thei suffred here.   *According to; i.e., on earth*
970 So were thei merked with tokenes full bare;   *emblems; exposed*
Thoo toknes were sett there, ryght to declare
That men had thei be and with grete distresse   *they had been humans*
Oute of this herde com to that holynesse.   *earth*

But whan this lady to the dore was browte,
975 Sche loked in, hir leders louted alle;   *guides bowed*

135

Sche herd there melodye, as to hir thowte,   *in her opinion*
Sche herd nevyr swych. Therfore is sche falle
Down all in trauns — there was nevyr man ne schalle
That may susteyn in body swech hevynly blysse,   *Who*
980   For who schall it susteyn must dye fyrst iwys.

Oute of hir traunce whan sche was wakyd,   *awakened*
Sche folowyd forth than to that noble place.
Than sey sche oure Lord whech all thing makyd,
Whech had called hir to that noble grace,
985   Sittyng full reall — but upon His face
Durst sche not loke, for no manere thing,   *on no account*
So was sche aferde at hir fyrst comyng.

Than wyst sche wele it was more than man
That sche had sowte and now sche hath it founde,
990   For with all the wytt that sche gadyr can
Dare sche noght fixe hir eye in this stounde   *at this time*
But evyr sche in poynt is to falle onto the grounde —   *about to*
Hir body is cause. It must be claryfyed,   *made morally pure*
And all the carnalyté fully puryfyed,

995   Or sche swech thinges eythere fele or grope.   *examine*
Thus is this maynesse all in hevynesse
Left and leyd in manere of wan hope,
For that same Lord whech of His goodenesse
Lyst for to chese hir as a specyal spousesse
1000   Now is so straunge — sche may noght hafe that grace   *unfamiliar*
To come sumewhat nyher and se His face.

Chapter 22

Tho cam oure Ladye and left hir up sone.   *lifted her up at once*
Thus sayd sche to hir: "Be of good comforte.
Youre hevynes is pased, ye hafe youre bone;   *your request is granted*
1005   All this grete hevynesse schall turn to dysporte.   *joy*
I sent aftyr yow that ye schuld resorte   *make your way*
Onto this howsolde, for ye schall hafe this grace: *household*
Next me aforn all women to be in this place.

"Therfore come forthe now, for I wyll yow lede
1010   Ryght to my Sone, onto that magesté."
Both maydes in fere thus forthe thei yede.   *went*
But this noble Adriane, at that tyme where was he?
Myn auctour telleth noght, but sekyr may ye be,
He had blysse enowe assygned to his parte,   *was happy enough*
1015   He had so mech he was lothe to departe!   *reluctant to leave*

Thus are these ladyes even onto the trone
Of oure Lord allmyghty walked forthe apace.
Withouten othyr company, thei went thoo aloone.
Peraventure other folk stood not in that grace;   *As it happens*
1020   So ny that magesté, so ny Goddys face,
To approche at that tyme it was a specyalté   *privilege*
Ordeyned of purpos at this solemnyté.   *especially for this ceremony*

Oure Lady had the wordes whan sche cam there:
"Sone," sche seyth, "and makere of all maner thing,
1025   I hafe browte a mayde here in full grete fere;   *reverence*
The spouse whech Thu lovyst, here I hir bryng.
Sche desyryth that Thu schalt now with a ryng
Despouse hir to Thiself for evyrmore —   *Espouse*
This is hir desyre and hath be full yore."   *for a long time*

1030   Oure Lord spake ageyn mysty wordes too,   *in response mysterious*
Whech that this mayde full hevy thoo made:
"Modyr," He seyth, "ye know yourself, loo,
The cause that this company in joyes thus wade   *go*
Is the look of Myselfe whech dothe hem glade;   *the sight of Me; gladden*
1035   For thei that hafe that, thei nede noo othyr thing.
But thei that schul hafe this gracyous syght lestyng   *enduring*

"Full clene must thei be in body and in gooste,
Wasched fro all synnes that be fowle and derk;
Of swech hafe I here — ye see a grete hoste
1040   Clensyd with My blode and merkyd with My merk.
All this was My laboure and My bysy werk   *i.e., their redemption*
Whan I in erde was to bye mankynde,   *redeem*
Whech that I fynde full oft to Me onkynde.   *ungrateful*

"Therfor, modyr, thus I answere onto yow:

1045 This mayde may not hafe as now that grace   *as of now*

Whech that ye aske for hir sake now,

I mene the vysyon, the syght of My face.

Lete hir goo clense hir, lete hir goo purchase   *obtain*

The holy baptem, than hath sche My merke.   *baptism; will have*

1050 Bryng hir than to Me and I schall hir merke

"With swech a tokne that nevyr mayde but ye   *no maiden but you*

Had it so specyaly. Lete this thing be doo.   *done*

A prest hafe ye redy, and a man, pardé,   *on hand*

Bothe in flesch and goost; lete him goo thertoo.

1055 Performe he schall this werk with his handys too;

Myn aungellis wyll I noght occupye with this dede —

It longyth to mankynd, withouten drede.   *no doubt*

"And yet thow We myght of Oure hye powere

Graunte onto aungellis this specialtee,   *privilege*

1060 That thei schuld baptize men in erde here,   *earth*

Yet wyll We noght that thei occupyed schuld bee

With swych manere offyce as to humanyté

Longyth and schal longe as for most ryght —   *more properly*

Go now and baptize that noble wyght!"   *person*

1065 Than spake oure Ladye to swage hir hevynesse,   *assuage*

"Beth not discomfortyd in no manere weye

With my Sones wordes, for in sykyrnesse

Ye must to His byddyng ful buxumly obeye.   *graciously*

It is a goodely usage, sothely to seye,

1070 Who schal be weddyd onto duke or kynge

Befor hir weddyng to hafe a bathynge   *take a bath*

"For to mak hir swete, for to make hir clene,

Ellys myght sche renne in ful grete offens.   *incur his displeasure*

Be this example onto yow I mene   *I mean to say*

1075 Do ye youre devere, do youre dylygens   *duty; make every effort*

For to plese youre Lorde. Anon goo we hens

Into yon chapell to your baptistery —

Aftyr your waschyng, ye schal be full mery!"

Chapter 23

Thus are thei walked, the mayden and the qween,

1080   Into this chapell on the mynstere syde.   *attached to the temple*

There fond thei redy a funt, as I wene,   *font*

With watyr and with crisme in a vessell wyde.   *chrism*

Adriane is called fro the puple asyde,

For he must do all this holy servyse,

1085   Lych as oure Lady the manere schall devyse.   *As our Lady instructs*

Thus seyd sche to him, "Go do now this dede —

It longyth to thin ordre Cristen folk to make.   *i.e., the priesthood*

Aray thee anone in swech manere wede   *garments*

Whech I myself here thee now take.   *present to you*

1090   This mayde schal be bathyd for hir loves sake

In this cold watyr, and Crysten schal sche be.

My Lord, my Son, thus comaundyth He.

"I myselfe schal of hir clothes strepe   *undress her*

And make hir all naked, redy to this thing.

1095   Hir name Kateryne styll schal thu clepe,   *Continue to call her Katherine*

Ryght for this cause and for this tokenyng:

That thei whech knew hir ethir eld or yyng

Schul hafe an evydens sche is styll the same   *proof*

Whech sche was befor. Therfor styll hir name

1100   "Schal sche thus kepe, in confirmacyoun

That all thing is trewe whech we do here.[1]

No wyles wrowte are, ne no collusyoun;   *tricks; connivance*

We wyll noght suffyr that in no manere."

Tho was Kateryn spoyled, but blynd was the frere,   *stripped*

1105   Bothe in hir spoylyng and in hir bapteme.   *during; undressing*

Of that solempne fest this was the theme: *pronouncement*

"I baptize thee here in the blessed name

Of the Fadyr and the Sone and the Holy Gost,

---

[1] Lines 1100–01: *to confirm / That everything we perform here is authentic*

In presens and wytenes of oure reverent dame, *witness*
1110 Modyr unto Cryst, of all women moste, *greatest*
Godmodyr onto thee, and that may thu boost. *boast*
Lok thu beleve, dowtyr, as I seyd to thee:
That oo God there is and persones thre.

"Beleve eke in bapteme and in Holy Kyrk; *Church*
1115 Beleve in the passyoun of oure Lord Jesu;
Beleve that the miracles whech He dede werk
Were withoute deceyte, stable and trewe;
Beleve that of a virgyne His manhode grew,
And sche undefouled. For sche is present, *undefiled*
1120 Sche can bere wyttenesse of this testament."

Kateryne answeryd onto these articles alle:
"I beleve hem, sere, as ye rehers bedene. *just as you say them*
Therfor on knes as I now down falle,
In this same funte, whech ye may not sene, *font*
1125 Baptize me, par charité, and make me clene, *please*
For this is the wyll of the soveren Lorde above,
And my wyll is it eke ryght for His love." *on account of*

Thus was sche baptized, and in this manere
Confermed eke, and renewed hir name.
1130 Oure Lady hirselfe servaunte was here; *took off*
Sche dede of the clothes of this swete dame. *film*
All this ilk tyme there was a hame *eyes*
Of blyndenes before this ermytes yye,
For of all this werk nothing he syye.

1135 But sone aftyr this sacrament is doo, *was performed*
His lyght receyvyd he newly ageyn. *sight*
The myrth, the joye that the man made thoo
We can not esyly expresse now ne seyn.
Ful sekyrly wende he nevyr eft a seyn — *he thought he would never see again*
1140 Now thanketh he Godd, of His hye grace,
That evyr he cam into that holy place.

	Oure Lady comaunded to daun Adryan	*brother*
	That all this thing whech he herd and sey doo,	*saw done*
	With all his besinesse, ryght so as he can,	
1145	To wryght it pleynly whan he may tend thertoo.	*have the chance*
	And as sche bad, full sekyrly he dyd soo,	
	This noble ermyte, for onto oure ere	*ears*
	How schuld it come ellys? How schuld we it lere?	

Chapter 24

	Now is oure Lady forth with this mayde	
1150	Into the temple entred ageyn.	
	Yet in hir going thus swetly sche sayde,	
	"Dowtyr myn, Kateryne, loke ye be glad and feyn,	*Daughter*
	For youre desyre schul ye have, certeyn,	
	Ere ye goo hens — beleve this sykyrly."	
1155	Swech wordes talked thei, walkyng sobyrly.	

	Now be thei come evene before the trone	
	Of oure Lord God, the mayde and the qwene.	
	Oure lady had the wordes hirself alone —	
	Swech was the ordre of hir tale, I weene.	*This is what she said, I think*
1160	"O kyng of kynges, blyssed mote Thu beene!	
	I have browte here the doghtyr of clennesse,	*purity*
	Prayng Thee, Lorde, with alle humbylnesse	

	"That Thou schew now the blysse of Thi face	
	Onto Thi spouse, onto Thi creature.	
1165	Evene as Thu grauntyd that grete grace	
	To kepe hir virginité in clenly trappure,	*in a pure state*
	So graunte hir now that hye portrature	*picture*
	Of Thi blyssyd ymage to se and beholde,	
	For than are sche and I mech to Thee beholde."	*greatly indebted to You*

	Oure Lorde answerde onto His modyr ful fayre:	
1170	"Whatsoevyr ye wyll, modyr, it must be doo;	
	All heven and herde to yow must repayre	*earth; appeal*
	For help whan hem nedyth to refresch her woo.	*relieve their sorrow*
	I graunte your petycyoun, I wyll it be soo."	

1175	Than fell that qween down plat to the grounde,	*flat*
	Hir corown sche toke of that was ful rownde,	*off*
	Sche leyd it befor Him and thus sche spake:	
	"Lord of all creatures that be lyvande,	
	Nothing that I aske of Thi grace I lake,	*lack*
1180	Evyr be Thu honowred in hevyn and in lande.	
	I myselfe am werk of Thi hande;	
	Thow I Thi modyr be, Thi servaunt am I.	
	Thi grace I thank, for Thi mercy I crye!"	*I am grateful for*
	Oure Lord bad hir ryse and sche rose sone.	
1185	Sche was corowned ageyn or thei were ware.	*realized*
	Tho men myght see what is to done	*Thus; must be done*
	Of ony creature whan thei come thare;	
	This same exaumple sat thoo full sare	*weighed heavily*
	On Kateryns hert; sche fell down anoone,	
1190	Plat on the grounde, styll as the stoone.	
	Thus seyd sche, in schort, for to tell pleyn:	
	"I se wele, Lorde, that of all maner thing	
	Thou art makere of erde, eyre, and the reyn —	*air; rain*
	All be obedyent to Thi comandyng.	
1195	Mercy I crave, Lord, at my begynnyng —	*to start with*
	Have I Thi mercy, I desyre not ellys,	
	For I have lernyd of mercy here the welle is."	*the well of mercy is here*
	Sche was lyft up be oure Lorde Hymselfe.	
	Thus seyd He to hir: "Wolcom, doutyr, to Me."	
1200	Aboute hir stode vyrgynes ten or twelve,	
	Wondyrly arayed and full of bewté.	
	Oure Lady had called hem onto that deuté,	*duty*
	To comfort this mayde and do hir servyse.	
	Tho spak this Lorde, this hye justyse:	
1205	"Ask what ye wyll, Kateryne, ye schul it have	
	Of Me at this tyme to your wolcomyng.	
	Syth ye forsake bothe castell and cave	
	For love of Me and for My byddyng,	

	I will graunte yow youre hertis desyryng,	
1210	For I am that same whom ye in parlement	*the one*
	Ageyn all youre lordes and comouns consent	*the will of lords and commons*

"Chosen onto spowse. Who leke ye now? · *What do you think?*
Wyll ye now have Me for evyrmore?"
With these swete wordes sche fel in swow · *swoon*
1215 Plat onto the grounde, the good Lorde before. · *Flat*
But whan He hir wyttes ageyn gan restore, · *to her senses*
Thus spake sche than onto that kyng:
"O Soveren, makere of all manere thing,

"Of angell, of man, of best, and of tre,
1220 If I were worthy onto Your hye presence
For to be couplede with solemnyté,
Than wold I desyre of Your excellens,
That Ye forgefe me all manere offens — · *everything I have done wrong*
Make me Your servaunt and not Youre wyffe;
1225 I am not worthy to so hye a lyffe!"

"Yys," seyd oure Lorde, "My modyr wyll here · *wishes*
That I schall wed yow — so wyll I, saun fayle. · *without fail*
Therfor I ask yow, youre wyll for to lere. · *learn*
If ye consent onto this spousayle, · *marriage*
1230 With many joyes I wyl you newly rayle. · *adorn*
Consent ye Kateryne? What sey ye nowe?"
"Lord," sche seyd, "thoo I wyll as wilt thow. · *in that case*

"I forsake here, Lorde, for Thi love,
Crown and londe, castell and town,
1235 Gold and sylvyr, bothe hows and rofe, · *roof*
Brochys and ryngys, mantell and gown.
Suffyr me no more, Lord, for to fall down
In delectacyoun of wordly thingys. · *On account of my love for*
Kepe me Thiselfe, Lorde, kyng of all kyngys.

1240 "All that evyr I hafe, that wote I wele,
I hafe it of Thee, Lord — of whom hafe I elles?
My spech, my thowt, my mende — every dele —

My bones, my body, my flesch, and my felles!   *skin*
Now as in Thee of plenté be the welles,   *Now, as the wells of plenty are in You*
1245   Suffyr me nevyr for to part Thee froo,
For fro Thi presens kepe I nevyr to goo."   *seek*

Than spak oure Lorde ryght on this wyse:
"Long was it ordeynde befor this tyme
That ye schuld come onto Oure servyse.
1250   Above all othir I wyll that ye clyme —
Save only My modyr, schortly to ryme,   *rhyme*
Ye schal be next joyned to My presence,
Ryght for your chastyté and youre obediens.

"For thow all thoo maydenes that kepe hem clene   *Although; themselves*
1255   For My sake and for My plesaunce
Be wyves unto Me all bedene,
Yet is there to yow schape a hyere chaunce.   *prepared for you; higher fortune*
Befor hem all schal ye go in the daunce,   *dance*
Next My modyr, ryght for this cause:
1260   For ye forsoke, to say schortly in clause,   *to put it bluntly*

"Emperour, kyng, and duke, for My sake.
I receyve yow, therfore, be a specyalté.   *in a special way*
My wyffe forevyr here I yow make
Because of your constans in virginité.   *commitment to*
1265   And a new conflycte in schort tyme schul ye
Begyne for My sake, but drede yow noght.   *Enter into*
Whoso offend yow, ful dere it schal be bowte!"   *will pay dearly*

Tho spak oure Lady ryght in this manere:
"Syth that this spousayle mote nedys be doo,
1270   This same mayde, Lord, geve I Thee here.
A mayde geveth a mayde; Thu servyd me soo,   *did the same for me*
Whan Thu commendyd Jon me untoo
Where that Thu hyng on the blody tre.   *hanged*
Here is the ryng, Lord, and here is sche."

1275   Oure Lord tok that ryng in His honde;
He put it on the fyngere of this clene virgyne.

"This is a tokne," He seyd, "of that bonde
Whech ye youreselfe, as on of Myne,
Lyst now youre wyll to My wyl enclyne.
1280   This tokne eke beryth wytnesse full ryffe   *apparent*
That here I tak yow for My weddyd wyffe."

Certeyn men that had seyn this ryng,
As myn auctour seyth, thei told it pleyn.   *described it clearly*
Thei seyde that it is a fayre gravyn thing
1285   Oute of a ston whech, as thei eke seyn,
It is clepyd a calcedony. Lych a clowde of reyn
Or ellys lych the watyr, swech his coloure is.
His vertues are touchyd many, iwys;   *Its many virtues; discussed*

The auctoures sey that he is gracyous   *brings fortune*
1290   To the berer of him if that he wyll trete   *bearer; be involved in*
Of ony materes whech that be perlyous;
He schall have fortune down for to bete
All the bate and stryffe in toun or in strete;   *debate*
He is vertuous eke to geve men a tast   *an inclination*
1295   For to kepe hir body bothe clene and chast.

Tho began a song in heven all abowte,
The wondyrfull notes that evyr man myght here,
Wordes sounded thei to the notes full devoute,
Full well acordyng to her song there.
1300   The song that thei sungyn, if ye wyll lere,
Was this same *Sponsus amat sponsam,*
The overt thertoo, "*Salvator visitat illam.*"   *prologue*

So semeth it well this song in heven began
Amonge aungellis and seyntes in blysse;
1305   Well may it than be sunge of mane   *by humans*
Here in this vale of wrecchydenesse.   *i.e., this earthly life*
This chyrch must folow for sothe, I gesse,   *i.e., the church on earth*
The chyrch above in all that it may.
Thus endeth the weddyng of this may.   *maiden*

Chapter 25

1310	Tho lest oure Lorde His leve to take	*wished to take leave*
	Of His new spouse as for a space.	*for a while*
	That same hand whech all thing dede make,	
	He lyfte on hye, and of His goode grace	
	He blessed this swete, bothe hede and face.	
1315	"Farwell," he seyth, "My wyffe ful dere;	
	Lete no dyscomfort yow noy ne fere.	*disturb; frighten*

"Thow that ye lese your londe, youre welth,
Thynk it is bettyr that I yow geve;   *what I give you is better*
Thow sekenes come in stede of helth,
1320   Kepe ye youre counstans in trewe beleve.
And thee, Adryane, make I My refe   *reeve*
As in this matere: thu schall hir teche
Of Myn incarnacyon the manere speche;   *how to speak of*

"Teche hir the feyth eke of the Trinité,
1325   The Fadyr, the Sone, and the Holy Gost;
Teche hir of the Godhede the unyté;
Truly teche hir, withouten boste.   *pride*
Of all this cuntré, I trost thee now moste.
Therfor, do truly my comaundment —
1330   But if thu do, thu may sone be schent!

"Thys werk, this lessoun, truly to performe,
Eyt dayes wyll I sche dwell with thee.   *Eight*
My modyr schall I sende hir to enforme
Aftyr that tyme, with solemnyté,
1335   Of many other thinges touchyng hir and Me.
But Kateryne, wyffe, this schall I yow geve,
Above all women that now erdely leve,   *live on earth*

"Myn aungellis schul honour yow with a servyse,
In tokne that we be wedded in fere.   *together*
1340   There was nevyr sey yet swech funeral offyse
Of no seynt that in erde deyed here.
This schal I do for youre love dere.

Farewel now, and think 'not longe.'"
Thus pased oure Lorde with myrthe and song,   *departed*

1345 And all thoo creatures fayre and bryght,
Alle are i-passed; the temple eke is goo,
So is that chapell, that funt, and that lyght,
Of all this thing thei se now no moo
But Adryanes celle, where that thei too
1350 Are left alone among trees olde.
But than was it reuth for to beholde,   *a pity to see*

To se this swete, how sche than felle
Down in a swow, as ded thoo sche lay.   *swoon; as if she were dead*
Adriane now is runne to his welle;
1355 With watyr he comyth and grete afray.   *anxiety*
"Awake, madame," he gan thoo to say,
"Allas that evyr ye come in this place!"
He rubbyd hir chekys, the nose, and the face;

He wept, he prayed, he cryed ful sore
1360 To sche awoke, sat up and spake.   *Until*
Adryane sayde to hir, "Lady dey no more —
For and ye do hens schal I me pak!   *unless you do*
Alle manere comfort here we do lak
That schuld yow rere; therfore I charge yow   *sustain*
1365 Fall no more in swech manere swow.

"Thynkyth thow your love as for a tyme   *that although*
Hath left yow here, yet hath He nowth
Forsak yow, lady, but as a pylgryme
He wyl ye be in dede and in thouth.   *thought*
1370 I wote full wele ye nevyr mech rowth   *delighted*
Of no wordly ne erdely plesauns;
It may yow nothing so hyly avauns   *can never promote you as highly*

"As may that Lorde to whom that ye be
Wedded now newly. For Goddys sake,
1375 Comfort yourselve and think how that ye
This same blesse sumetyme schul i-take

147

In swech manere sewyrnesse that schal nevyr slake.   *never end*
Therfore beth glade and loke on your ryng —
It wyll remembyr yow youre gloryous weddyng."   *remind you of*

Chapter 26

1380 "But now must ye, myn own lady dere,
      Youre beleve undyrstand, ful sykyr and pleyn.
      Youre swete spouse bad I schuld it yow lere,
      Whom ye in flesch now full late seyn,   *seen just now*
      In whech He soked and also was slayn,   *suckled*
1385 But of His Goddehed, whech is grownd of all,
      Feythfully the treuth tell now I schall.

      "Thys must ye beleve, as I told yow ere,
      Whan ye were baptized, if ye hafe mynde —
      Sette your hert therto and bysyly it lere:
1390 Oure Lord Godd is of swech a kynde
      That sykyrly, as I of Him wretyn fynde,
      He is on in substauns and in nature,
      Thre eke in persones I yow ensure.

      "O God, o Lorde, o maker, o magesté:
1395 The Fadyr and the Sone and the Holy Goost,
      Thre persones in o Godhede, thus beleve ye,
      Of whech non is smallere, ne non is most.
      All are of evene powere in every cost,   *respect*
      For the pluralyté of persones is no prejudyse   *does not contradict*
1400 Onto the unyté of Godhed, in no manere wyse.

      "And yet He that is the Fadyr is not the Sone,
      Ne the Sone the Gost, withouten fayle;
      O wyll hafe Thei in all that is done,   *One will*
      O myght, o powere, o lyght, o counsayle:
1405 This lessoun must ye hyde in your entrayle   *keep in your heart*
      Ful sadly, madame, for it is oure grounde,   *foundation*
      On whech to beleve ful sore are we bounde.   *obliged*

"Dystynctyoun in persones, in nature unité,
This is oure scole — it must be oure besynesse.   *doctrine; we must accept it*
1410   The Fadere geveth to the Sone, thus beleve we,
All substauns of deité and He hath nevyr the lesse.
The Fadyr begetyth the holy Sone, in blesse   *bliss*
The Sone is begotyn, the Goost fro Hem too
Procedyth, the thryd persone, thus belefe we loo.

1415   "To the Fadyr longyth myght, to the Sone cunnyng,
Godeness to the Goost: thus couplede be Thei, I gesse,
And yet must we sey for ony manere thing
O myght, o cunnyng, and eke o goodenesse,
That the Fadyr is allmyghty, the Sone hath nevyr the lesse.
1420   Thow the Sone have cunnyng the Goost hath the same,
Goodenesse have Thei alle, wete ye wel, madame."

Swech manere dalyauns had these folk than   *discussions*
All thoo eyte dayes in hye communicacyoun.   *eight*
Mech more thing was seyd than — more than I can
1425   Reherse at this tyme. Suffyseth yow this lessoun,
For all thoo holy wordes of swech exhortacyoun
May bettyr be thowth than thei may be spoke —
Swech langage in synfull tunge is but brok.   *broken*

Chapter 27

At the eyte dayes ende, as was promission,   *promised*
1430   Comth oure Lady with lyght down fro hevene;
Chaunged sodenly is thoo that mansyon,   *dwelling place*
For it semyth now brytere than the levene.   *lightning*
Aungellys were there mo than sex or sevyne —
It longeth onto hem to do her dew servyse   *due*
1435   To the emperesse of hevyn, modyr to the hye justyse.   *i.e., Christ*

Many other ladyes come thoo with the qwene —
With Mary, I mene — so ded Jon Baptyst.
There were eke vyrgines full fele, as I wene.   *a great many*
He was there eke, Jon the evangelyst;

1440 Who had be there of joye he myght a wyst.[1]
   Oure Lady hirselfe onto this blyssed mayde
   Swech manere wordes at that tyme sayde:

   "Dowtyr to me, wyffe onto my Sone,
   My Sone gretyth yow with His good blessyng.
1445 As He behestyd yow, now am I come   *promised*
   To tell yow the manere of youre endyng.   *i.e., death*
   A tyraunt — a wers was nevyr levyng — *a worse one never lived*
   Schal distroye youre regne and your body sle.   *slay*
   We wyll not ye repent yow, we wyll not ye fle.   *recant*

1450 "Abydyth styll, ryght in youre owyn place.
   Boldly stryve ageyn his tyrannye.   *oppose*
   My Sone wyll endew yow with swech grace
   Was nevyr no woman honoured so hye.
   But fyrst mote ye sufyr schame and vylonye,
1455 Losse of your godys, in your body passyoun,   *torment*
   Deth at the last — this is the conclusyoun.

   "I must goo now onto my Sone ageyn,
   Ye to your owne courte schall repaire.   *return*
   All this tyme thei mysse yow not, dare I seyn.
1460 Farewele my dowtyr, farewel ye fayre! *worthy one; fair one*
   Whyl ye with my Sone were in the ayre
   A qween leche to yow all that tyme kept *who looked just like you*
   Youre grete astate: sche ete and slept,

   "Spake and comaunded, bothe dempt and wrote —   *judged*
1465 All this dyde sche ryght in your stede.   *place*
   There was no man withinne that mote   *castle*
   That cowde aspye in hir womanhede
   Ony manere differens, sat sche or yede. *whether she sat or walked*
   My Sone ordeyned this for youre sake.
1470 Whan ye are ded and your corown take,

---

[1] *Anyone who had been present would have experienced joy*

"Than schall ye know swech pryvy thingys —
How thei ar doo and in what manere.
Yet of another matere I geve yow warnyngys:
The qween your modyr, the whych dyd yow bere,
1475 Is i-pasyd and ded, leyd low on bere.
But beth not dyscomfortyd — now wyll I be
Modyr onto yow, my Sones wyffe, pardé.   *by God*

"Too yere in your place and sumwhat more
Schull ye dwell or this Maxencius
1480 Come for to spoyle your tresore —   *destroy*
Of that same rychesse be ye not desyrous.
Kepyth your chambyr with levyng vertuous,   *Keep to your chamber*
With prayre, fastyng, and almes dede;   *alms-giving*
Geve to the pore folk bothe mete and wede.   *clothing*

1485 "Aftyr this tyme be pased and i-goo
Than schall this tyraunt mak sone a hende   *an end*
Of yow, doutyr, and of many moo.
This lesson I wyll that ye emprende,   *memorize*
Now and evyr set it in youre mende.
1490 Farewel, now fyrst I wyll yow kysse,
I go to my Sone, to evyrlestyng blysse."

Thus is oure Lady sodenly i-goo
As now fro this qween. Sche is home, eke,
Unto Alysaundyr — myn auctour seyth soo.
1495 Thei that wyll rede him, thei may it seke.
Wheyther sche cam thedyr in day or in weke
I wote noght now, but there now sche is.
Was non all that tyme that dede hir mys   *during; missed*

For that tyme whech sche was oute;
1500 Thus was it ordeynyd be oure sovereyn Lorde.
This same book whech we hafe be long aboute
We wyll now ende, if ye therto acorde.
God send us alle of unité acorde
To plese Him oonly above all mene.
1505 Therto sey we alle with oo voys, Amen.

Book 4

[Katherine challenges Maxentius and debates the fifty philosophers]

Prologue

These erdely dwellers whech lyve now here
Are lykened to bees whech dwell in hyve,
Or ellys to dranes, if that ye lyst to lere.   *drones*
It faryth with men ryght thus in her lyve:
5   Summe wyll labour and summe wyll nevyr thryve.
Dyverse conceytes there be, and diverse eke degrees.
The goode laboureres are likened to the bees,

Specyaly thei that oute of Goddys lawe
Of dyvers partyes[1], syttyng on the floures,
10   Lerne and teche, bothe soke and drawe,   *suck*
Of goode exaumples of holy predecessoures
Swete conceytes, wel famed savoures: *tastes*
Alle these be bees whech to the housolde bryng
Alle her stuffe and alle her gaderyng.

15   Othir there be whech are not profitable: *useful*
Thei ete and drynk, devowre eke and wast;
Thei labour noght but if it be at table,
For onto werk have thei no grete hast.   *they are in no hurry to work*
Fylle wele her bely and geve hem goode repast,
20   Than wyll thei slepe sekyr with the best.
We sey not of hem but "dranes lofe well rest."   *can only say of them; love*

Yet to goostly laboure dranes wyll not drawe   *drones will not engage in spiritual toil*
For that in her thoughtis thei have noon delectacyoun

---

[1] Lines 8–9: *From different portions of God's law*

In the heryng yet of Goddys lawe.
25 Thei not encresse ne promote her stacyoun,
For thei hemselve to goostly occupacyoun
Wyll not draw at no mannes reqwest.
Suffyseth hem her full bely and rest.

Thus semeth it to me that Holy Scripture is
30 In manere of a felde with flowres fayre arayde,   *like a field*
And Holy Kyrk is benethe iwys.   *Church*
Sche is the hyve with many stormes afrayed;   *assaulted*
The vertuous bees in this hyve have portrayed   *fashioned*
Her dyverse celles of hony and of wax.
35 What all this menyth, if ye lyst to axe,   *ask*

Ye may it lerne. I sey the grete labour
That goode men have to rede exaumples olde,
It is to hem of solace newe socour   *comfort and fresh aid*
Her vertuous levyng stabyly to beholde
40 And eke to fyght with corage fresch and bolde
Ageyns this wordly deceyvable affluence,
Ageyne the fleschly slulkyd neclygens.   *lurking*

On of these bees was this same qweene,
The mayd Kateryne, whech with besynesse
45 Of every floure whech was fayre to seene
Sokyd oute hony of gret holynesse,
Bare it to hyve, and there sche gan it dresse —   *prepare*
For it wyll do servyse bothe to God and man.
That same lycoure whech sche gaderyd than,

50 This hony gadered sche fere and woundyr wyde:
In the lawe of nature laboured sche formest,   *foremost*
Where sche the vyces lerned to ley osyde   *aside*
And vertues to chese as a clenly nest,
To do to no man, dwelle he est or west,

55   Werre than he wolde he schuld onto hym do.[1]
      This ladye gadered in this felde ryght soo:

      In the wretyn lawe sche gadered eke mech thing,
      The ten comaundmentys to kepe treuly in mynde.
      There lerned sche the mervelous begynnyng
60   Bothe of the world and eke of mankynde;
      There lerned sche the lame and eke the blynde
      To fostyr and clothe, bothe helde and ying;   *old and young*
      This was hir laboure, this was hir gaderyng.

      In the lawe of grace soked sche swettere mete   *i.e., Christianity*
65   Of ryper floures: feyth, hope, and charyté.
      Sche bare hem, and there sche gan hem lete   *allow*
      Into this hyve, to Holy Chyrches secré —   *inner recesses*
      There ly thei yet as tresoure, trost thu me.
      Who that wyll laboure may fro that swetnes wryng
70   Mech bettyr than ony galey can bryng.   *galley*

      And forthe in this swetnesse wyll we now procede,
      Whech that sche gadered, this lady, here lyvande.   *while she was alive*
      God send us parte ryght as we have nede
      In vertuous lyvyng stably to stande
75   And for to come to that hevenly lande
      Where sche is now, for forthe to hir processe,   *story*
      Undyr hir socoure, streyt I wyll me dresse.

Chapter 1

      In the tyme of Costus, as oure bokys telle,
      Were thre emperoures in Rome cyté.
80   The fyrst was a man of hert full felle,
      Maximinus Galerius, ryght so hyght he.
      The secunde hyght Maximian, the threde, pardé,   *was called*
      Was namede at that tyme Dyocleciane —   *Diocletian*
      He was many a Crysten mannes bane.

---

[1] *Worse than one would want a person to do to him*

85 The fyrst emperour, Maximinus Galerye,
  Dwelt styll at Rome and kept there the pes;   *continually*
  The domes, the sacryfyces, dyd he thoo gye.   *judgments; direct*
  The other too men, withouten any lees, *without lying, i.e., to tell the truth*
  Were sent owte with ful grete prees   *force*
90 To brenne and sle, to take and to save —   *slay*
  This was offyce bothe to knyght and knave.   *charge*

  But these same too, for very werynesse,
  Left her honoure and resygned her ryght.
  Full grete excuse had thei in sekyrnesse:
95 Thei seyd her grete labour and her fyght
  Avayle hem ryght noght now it myght,   *cannot do them any good now*
  For the more thei dyd the more thei had to doo.
  Werfore in sykyrnesse thus thei too

  Resygned her ryght onto this same man,   *i.e., Maximinus Galerius*
100 And he undyr him made thre emperoures
  To help his empyre al that thei may or can
  In all batayles, in all scharp schowres,   *assaults*
  To wyne cytes, castelles, town, and towres.
  The fyrst hyght Maximinus, as seyth the gest;   *history*
105 He was assygned to governe all the Est.   *East*

  And to the secunde, whech hyght thoo Severe,   *Severus*
  Was eke assygned the kepyng of Lumbardye,   *Lombardy*
  Of Almayn, Tussy, the story seyth so here, *Germany; Tuscany*
  And many othir cuntres in that partye   *region*
110 Undyr his powere were tributarye.
  Eke of Brytayn, the londe in whech we dwelle,
  Was Constantyne mad lorde, sothe to telle.

  This fyrst emperour, Maximinus Galerius,
  For pryde and sorow and synfull lyffe
115 Was kylled in a batayle — the story seyth thus.
  He had defowled many a mayde and wyffe,   *defiled*
  And therfore, or he deyed oute of this stryffe,
  He stank on erde as evyr dyd carayn —   *carrion*
  Let him go walk in Salysbury playn!   *i.e., To hell with him*

120 Thoo toke the Romaynes the yong Maxens, *Maxentius*
Sone onto Maximyne that was in Est. *Maximinus*
Thei corowned him realy with grete expens,
With mych solemnyté and full grete fest. *ceremony*
The fame went oute to more and to lest
125 That he was emperour and his fadyr forsake. *has forsaken his father*
This made his fadyr, schort tale to make,

To leve his conqwest and com to Rome there.
But or he cam there his pryde was i-cast: *cast down*
In Cycile he deyd — ryght so dyde I lere *Sicily*
130 Of cronycles whech that I sey last. *consulted most recently*
There blew he owte his endyng blast, *dying breath*
And there lyghte he to abyde his chauns, *remains to await judgment*
Wheythyr it be to wepyng or ellys to dawns. *dancing (i.e., hell or heaven)*

Thys Severus eke that dwelt in Lumbardye *Lombardy*
135 Gadered up Almayne and all his myght, *Germany*
For with this eleccyoun had he grete envye;
Therfor bothe be day and eke be nyght
He laboureth be wrong and eke with ryght *by whatever means, right or wrong,*
To dystroye this Maxence, sothe for to sayn, *Maxentius*
140 That he myght reygne whan he were slayn.

But or he cam fully at this same Rome,
He was slayn of his sowdyoures be the weye. *killed en route by his own soldiers*
Than was there no more for to done
But Maxence reygneth, sothe for to seye,
145 As now alone; every man must obeye
If he wyll kepe his lyffe o lofte — *stay alive*
But if he do so, he slepe noght ellys softe. *soundly*

Thus regned this Maxence in Rome al alone.
No man speke to him whatevyr he wyll doo:
150 There was no mayde, no wyffe, ne no matrone,
But whan he sent thei must come him too
To suffyr his lust, to suffyr what he wyll doo.
What husbond lett it, he schuld anoon be dede — *hindered*
Upon his gate thei schuld sett his heede.

155	He turned the lawe; all went than be powere.	*overthrew*
	The pepyll cursyd the wombe that him had born.	
	Was no man durst in opyn langage there	*[who] dared*
	Onys sey to him, "Lord your lawe is lorn."	*ruined*
	Of all the senate sett he but a scorn.	
160	Pryde and powere had enhaunsed him soo	
	All that he coveyte, he wold haf it doo.	

Chapter 2

	Tho the Romaynes with a comoun consent	
	Letteres pryvyli of gret sentens ded wryght	*secretly, importance*
	And into Bretayn to Constantyn hem sent,	*them*
165	In whech thei prayd him, as he was a knyte,	*knight*
	That he come help hem ageyn this tyraunt to fyght;	
	Thei wold betray him, thei seyd, he schuld not spede.	*prosper*
	This was her ende: "Com help us at oure nede!"	*their*

	Anon this man ded gader a grete strenght,	*i.e., Constantine*
170	Bothe of this londe and of Fraunce there too,	*i.e., Britain*
	Evyr gan his ost encrese in brede and lenght	*army*
	Be every cuntré in whech he gan goo.	
	In Ytayle reyswd he up puple many moo	
	Than evyr ded Severe, ryth for this tyrannye	*Severus (see lines 134–36)*
175	Of this fals Maxence and for his leccherye.	

	He is at Rome. The hostys togedyr mette,	
	But Maxence trostyth oonly on the cyté there.	
	He is deceyvyd: alone thei him lette	*abandoned*
	With his howsholde in mech care and fere.	
180	Be this ensaumple wyse men may well lere	
	To trost in the puple, for thei wyll fayl at nede,	
	So ded thei here, so streyt fro him thei yede	*went*

	To Constantyn, that now came fro Brytayn.	
	Thus is he fledde, the same Maxencius,	
185	Deceyvyd ryghtfully thus be her trayn —	*their treachery*
	Ryght for his lyvyng, that was so vicyous.	
	He fledd to Pers and there as man vyctorous	*Persia*

Dede grete thingis and many strengthes wan.   *fortresses*
Soo as for lord, and for he was a man,   *because*

190 Thei crowned him there and called him king of Pers. *Persia*
   Thus hath Constantine wonne the feeld this day, *battlefield*
   The othir tyraunt is put al to the wers.
   Al this is told to this ende, sooth to say,
   To knowe how Maxcens with soo grete aray *company*
195 Cam to Alisaundre, swech maystries for to make, *presumptions*
   Whan he this lady ded arreste and take.

   For whan he was thus exalted in Pers,   *Persia*
   Thus set in astate, and in his faderes office, *honor*
   Tho wex he in condiciouns evyre wers and wers, *his morals grew ever worse*
200 And more enclined to synne and to vice.
   He sente oute letteres onto every justise,
   To serche the Cristene, to hange hem and to drawe,
   For truly, he seith, he wil destroye that lawe. *faith*

   These letteres come to Surry al aboute,   *Syria*
205 And he himself folwed aftir hem sone.
   The copy of hem I wil, withouten doute,
   Write here in English, me thinkith it is to done: *I think it appropriate*
   "The lord of lordis that dwellith undir the mone,
   Maxcens, the emperour of Pers, withouten pere,
210 Greteth weel oure lyges thurghoute oure empere. *subjects*

   "We wil ye wete oure faderes here beforn   *our ancestors*
   That worchiped goddis with her dew servise *the service entitled them*
   Were nevyre in batayle neythir convicte ne lorn, *vanquished nor abandoned*
   Sweche was the keepynge of goddis tho ben wise
215 Ovyr her puple. Therfore, we as justise
   And as a preest in religion of Saturne
   Wil that ye alle fro alle veyn lawes turne,

   "Most special fro Crist, whech heyng on tre,
   That no man be soo hardy Him for to name.
220 What maner God schuld He now be
   That was i-brout into swiche fame

To be hanged on a tre with so moche schame?
Therfore, noo man dwellynge now in oure lond
Schal be so hardy, neythir fre ne bond,

225 "To name Him oones or for to sette
His merke in the forhed, as is the usage   *i.e., a cross; forehead*
Of alle these Cristen. We wil hem lette   *prohibit*
Of alle her cerymonies and her pilgrimage —
If that thei forgete, thei schul have wage   *will be punished*
230 Swech as thei deserve, for to have   *Appropriately*
Lordschip ne richesse schal hem not save.

"Therfore, what man ony goddis honour
Othir than we doo now in oure sette,   *throne*
We wil that thei be take with officeris oure
235 And led to prison withouten ony lette.   *delay*
We wil ordeyn for hem swech a gette   *punishment*
Thei schul nevyre eft swech maystries make   *presumptions*
In all her lyve, and that we undirtake."   *guarantee*

This is the sentens of the letteres longe   *content*
240 Whech he sente oute onto al the Est,
Commaundynge lordis and knythes stronge
That thei come in hast, bothe more and leest,
And in most special onto that grete feest
Whech he wil make with ful grete store   *provision*
245 That ilke same day whech he was bore.   *same; born*

The messangeres arn goon bothe fer and wide
To bere these copyes into divers londe.   *i.e., the letters*
The emperour himself, he wil abide
Onto that tyme, as I undirstonde,
250 In grete Alisaundre, with ful myty honde,
In whech cité eke this noble qween soo dere
With a pryvy mené leved al in prayere.   *retinue*

To this cité cam king and soo ded qween,
Thedir cam lordis mo than I can telle:
255 The innes arn ful as hyves of been,   *bees*

159

There is now not elles but bye and selle,
In special mete and drynk, for there was nevyre welle
More plenteuous of water than was the cité of mete,   *food*
Soo were thei stored there, the marchauntis grete.   *provisioned; merchants*

260   Whanne alle were come whech schuld be there,
The Emperour thre poyntis dede tho declare,
Whech poyntis he seyde, withouten dwere,   *doubt*
Even as thei in sentens stoode platt and bare,   *as they were written*
He wold every man, what-so-evyre he ware
265   Or in what party he dwelt of his dominacyoun,   *Or where in the empire he lived*
Schuld kepe hem in peyn of dampnacyoun.

Chapter 3

The fyrst poynt was that Cristen all and summe   *i.e., any and all*
Must leve her feyth and that grete honoure
Whech that thei do to Cryste, Goddys Sunne,
270   Whom eke thei clepe now her salvatoure: *savior*
"His dyscyples into full grete errour
Have browte all men that wyll tend hem too,   *heed*
Ryght with the feyned miracles that thei doo.

"Therfore wyll we that thei now alle
275   To oure presence for to see and here
What manere decré that we geve schall.
Onto swech wycchys bothe fer and nere   *witches (heretics)*
We think for to mak oure lawe full clere,
And whan all are loked to chese the best,
280   This is the relygyoun that we hafe keste."   *decided on*

The secunde poynt whech he schewyd thoo
Was this: he seyd thei had rememberauns
How that of Rome not long agoo
He helde the honoure and all the governauns,
285   But betrayed he was with hem of Bretayn and Frauns,
Whech on Constantyne had browte in fere,   *assembled as a force*
A grete puple and a stately powere.

160

Thus had this traytour, he seyd, this Constantyne,
As a fals intrusore entred into his lande,   *usurper*
290   Wonne his cyté with gunnes and wyth myne,   *(see note)*
There mygth no walle ne noo toure thoo stande.
Thus bare Maxence the lordes on hande
Whech were with him at Alysaundre that tyde.   *time*
Wherfore, sekyrly, he seyth, he wyll ryde

295   Evene to Rome his ryght to conqwere,
To venge him on this tyraunt, on this Constantyne.
Wherfore, he prayed the lordes that be there
That thei schal be redy with bowes and engyne,   *siege engine*
For he wyll rewarde hem with gyftis good and fyne,
300   With rentys, londys, castelles, and toures eke.   *incomes*
If thei wynne Rome, rychesse nede hem not seke.

The thyrd poynt whech that he purposyd there,
Sittyng himself ryght in the parlement,
He seyde he wold renew, withouten dwere,
305   Alle thoo servyses and all that dew rent   *proper tribute*
Whech to the goddis was ordeynd be comon assent.
The goddis, he seyd, schuld be more propicious
If that her cerymonyes were renewyd thus.

A byschop stood up thoo, with mytere and with crose,   *crosier*
310   Swech as thei used thoo in her lawe.
There was cryede every man kepe close   *hold*
His mouthe and his tunge and herken to his sawe.   *listen to his speech*
Whan he had his brethe a lytyl whyll i-draw,
Thus spake he than, in maner of sermonyng:
315   "I wyll ye wetyn," he seyth, "that Jupiter that hye kyng   *know*

"Hath turned awey his good conservacye   *withdrawn his favor*
From all oure nacyon. I tell yow schortly why:
We have forsak him and fall in maumentrye.   *fallen into idolatry*
Many of us here, I drede me, are gyltye
320   In this same matere. Wherfor, Jupiter allmyghtye
And Saturn his fadyr, be pryvy apparicyon
In slepe, gove warnyng be very revelacyoun.

"Thei bode we schuld the puple teche to renewe
The held cerymonyes and the elde rytes   *ancient*
325   Whech oure fadres used or we anything knew,
And so used many lordes and many knytes.
Who geveth us helpe in pees or in fytys   *war*
But Jupiter alone? Helth evyr upon him,
Honour and servyse to him and to his kyn!

330   "No man may make so grete maystrye   *exert such power*
As Jupiter dothe whan he with hangyr qwakyth.   *anger*
The grete thundyr whech he maketh flye,
The orrible lytenyngys eke whych he makyth,
Alle these schew to us that what man him forsakyth,
335   He is ful lykly with venjaunce to be brente.   *vengeance*
Turn to him ageyn, therfore, lest ye be not schent;   *so that you not be lost*

"Leve all this newe thingys, kepe styll your olde.
What, schall Cryst among goddys put Him in place?
The schepperdys and plowmen in feld and in folde,
340   Thei wote ful well it stant not in mannys grace   *know*
Onto all the world salvacyon to purchase,
As sey this Crysten (for Cryst, as seyth her boke,
With His blode fro the world all synnes toke).

"He must be eterne that schall swech thingys doo,
345   That schall geve encrese to ilke generacyoun,
For to a godd of ryght this it longyth, loo,   *it pertains of right to a god*
To have in his nature evyrlestyng duracyoun.
Repelleth fro youre counsell this Crysten nacyoun —
This charge I yow in the goddys name —
350   Save your sowles and your bodyes fro blame."

This was the sentens of this grete sermoun
Whech that the byschopp at that tyme spake,
And this was eke his determinacyoun: *judgment*
That no man in that londe, but he wyll into the rak
355   And on that same ly with a broken bak,   *lie on the rack; back*
Be so hardy in no manere wyse
Speke ageyn the goddys or her servyse.   *their*

162

Chapter 4

The cyté of Alysaundre whech is full large,
It is now repleschyd, withoute and withinne,   *replete*
360   With lordes and ladyes; there was many a barge
At the princypale porte, for thei lay not thynne.   *they were packed in*
Welle is he at ese that may cacch an inne,   *find accomodations at an inn*
The puple was so grete, the pres was so strong.   *crowd was so dense*
There is now not elles but trumpyng and song,   *trumpet-playing*

365   For the nyte was come of that festful day
In whech Maxence was bore. Therfore he dyd crye
That every man there schall in his best aray
Sercle the cyté with noyse and mynstralsye.   *parade around; music*
He that schall slepe this nyght must be full slye   *careful*
370   That he be not perceyvyd for indygnacyoun
Whech he schall have for he went not his stacyoun.[1]

There was noyse of trumpys and noyse of men,
Mech more of bestys that deyd in her bloode,
For all that nyght, sekyrly ye may ful well ken,
375   The bocheres laboured as thei had be wode.   *butchers worked like madmen*
The waschyng of the carcays down in the flode,   *river*
Schewid the grete morder of the bestys slayn —
The water was as blody, saverly dare I sayn.   *confidently*

To the tempill thei goo the next day betyme,   *early*
380   The bischoppis have arayed hem to do the servyse.   *perform the service*
There was no matens seyd, servyse, ne pryme,
Thei had anodyr usage than I can devyse.[2]
Thus mech can I sey: the emperour as justyse   *judge*
Was sett upon hye that he myth all see,
385   Who the puple honoured that solempnité.

---

[1] Lines 370–01: *Because of the indignation / He would incur for not playing his part in the festivities*

[2] *I am not familiar with their religious practices*

Thei knelyd and thei cryed with marred devocioun,   *dazed*
All this beheld the emperour with sad yye,   *eyes*
For evermore hath he a fals suspecioun   *wicked*
That some are there whech will not sacryfye.
390   The fyrst god of all, whech stod most hye,
Was the bryth sunne with his hors and carte,   *horse*
Whech was i-grave of full sotyll art.   *very artfully carved*

Next was the mone, whech we clepe Diane,   *moon*
With hir wellis nyne and the maydenes eke.
395   Next here was Saturne, with his bittir bane,   *destruction*
With his sekyll in hand. Many men him seke,   *seek*
For non other cause but whan thei are seke,   *sick*
Thei wene than it were of his venjaunce,[1]
So cruell is his planete in his governaunce.

400   The auter next him was ful well arayed   *altar beside him*
On whech that Jubiter stode all on hye
With his wyfe Juno ful well i-porterayed.
Venus the fayre, sche stood next by,
With hir blynd sone Cupide, so wene I.
405   Thei calle him so that owe him servyse —
I owe him non, for maumentrye I despyse.   *idolatry*

Mech more thing was there not to purpos nowe,   *that I see no point describing*
But thus mech I telle: there were grete offeryngis.
Thei spared neythir hors, ox, bere, ne kowe,   *bear; cow*
410   But sle and sle, these were her cryingis.
The bischoppis and the prestys, thei do her thingis;   *their rituals*
The mynstrelles fayl not, for thei schul have wage;   *so they will be paid*
Every man makyth noyse aftir his age.

The elde seyd thei sey nevyr in her dayes
415   Swech anothir sacryfyce as this emperour
Hath renewed in her tempyll in many maner wayes:
"The grete goddes all, thei send him honour,

---

[1] *They attribute it (their sickness) to his vengeance*

Long lyffe and stable, make him a conqwerour."
The yong men daunsed joylyly on the ground —
420 There was revell among hem; lyghtly and round   *nimbly and boisterously*

Traced thei that tyme at that solempnité.   *Danced; celebration*
The noyse is herd aboute a myle on every syde.
Thus leve I hem in myrth these seres stoute;   *bold lords*
Thus ar thei occupyed in mechil pryde.
425 The emperour himselve lokyth on every syde
Who do most reverens to his goddes there.
This made the Crysten to have ful grete fere.   *fear*

Chapter 5

Oure noble mayde, oure holy devoute qwene
To whom this story longyth as now only,
430 This holy virgine Kateryne, hir I mene,
Was thoo in silens sittyng in hir stody,
All contemplatyff, sperde fro hir meny;   *apart from her attendants*
The wordly welthis are nowe fro hir shake,   *gone*
Aftir that tyme that Cryst hath hir thus take

435 To wyff or spouse, rede ryth as ye list.   *whichever you prefer*
This mayd was there and herd thoo this cry.   *clamor*
"O Jesu," seyd sche, "I wold now that I wist   *knew*
What that it menyth, the noyse that is so hy."
Knytys were walkyng, thre or foure fast by,
440 Waytyng upon hir. Thus to hem seyd sche:
"This grete noyse, seres, what may it be?"

"Iwis, madame," thoo seyd a elde servaunt,
"The emperour Maxence this day was he bore;
He hath comaunded to eld man and to faunt   *infant*
445 The elde rythes, the servises, to restore,   *ancient*
Whech to the goddes long and have do yore.   *by tradition are owed*
This is the cry, if ye will wet algate.   *if you really want to know*
No man of lyve, pore ne of astate,

"Is not so hardy this mater to disobeye —
450   Thei schal be dede that ageyns it speke.
Kepe stille youre closet; there is no more to sey.[1]
It is not oure powere his will for to breke.
Lete hem calle, lady, lete hem cry and creke.   *speak foolishly*
Suffisith you if ye may lyve in pees.
455   The man is comorous, withouten ony lees,   *undoubtedly oppressive*

"For he have made, if ye will leve me,   *believe*
A strong decré whech he will we kepe,
That all sectes of his sect now shull be.[2]
The childe anon as he gynnyth to crepe   *crawl*
460   Schal be tawth upon the goddes to clepe,
In peyne of deth the faderes shul him teche —
This herde I this day the grete bischop preche.

"Wherfore, madame, now is come that hour
That was thoo drede of youre frendys alle,
465   Whan that ye wold receyve no concelloure,
For no thing that men myght on you calle.
I am ful sory, for now are lyckly to falle
All tho myshappys whech were seyd before.
Avise you wele what ye wil do therfor."

470   Whan this mayd had herd these wordys alle,
Sche gan remembyr how oure Lady seyd
Whan sche passed fro hir, what schuld befalle.
Sche spake thus: "To yow I telle, my mayde,   *She (Mary)*
Ye schalle hereaftir be ful sore afrayde   *attacked*
475   Of a enmy both to my Son and me."
At hir leve takyng swech wordis seyd sche,

Oure blyssyd Lady Mary, to this qwene.
"Therfor," this qwene thought, "now is the hour
Whech sche behestyd, now is it wel i-sene,   *promised*

---

[1] *Stay quietly in your chambers; there is no alternative*

[2] *That people of all religions shall convert to his religion*

480 Ryth be the boldnes of this emperour
  Whech ageyn oure Makere and Creatour
  Thus boldly rysyth in destruccioun of His name
  Whos wyffe I am and servaunt to His dame."

  Thoo sche remembred what covenaunt that she made
485 Rith in hir baptim, whan she waschid was,
  Eke in hir weddyng with behestis ful sadde,   *solemn vows*
  That she schulde nevyr for more ne for las,
  Thow sche were throwe in hote caudron of brasse, *brass caldron*
  Forsake hir love whech she had only chose.   *only love*
490 Thoo wex she ruddy and fayre as a rose,

  Rith in remembrauns of that swete spousayle   *wedding*
  Whech that she caute be ledyng of Adriane. *had through Adrian's guidance*
  It is so emprended within hir entrayle
  Of wordly lustys there shall no fekill fane
495 Blow it awey[1]; neythir Juno, Venus, ne Diane
  Fro in hir hert this love thei shul not race.   *eradicate*
  Thus walkyd she forth softly than apace,

  Ful sore astoyned what is hir best to doo.   *uncertain*
  If she holde silens than is she not trewe
500 Of hir behestis, rith so thoute she, loo;   *vows*
  The fayre ryng whech was sumwhat blewe   *blue*
  Whech was eke gove hir at hir weddyng newe *recent wedding*
  Sche thoo behelde, and seyd thus be hir one: *said to herself*
  "Fy on the world, fy on crown and trone!

505 "I shal kepe that trewth whech that I made
  Onto my husbond, thow I shuld be dede.
  I shal the soner com to Him that me made,
  For in this worlde is nouth but slepe and brede.
  Allas that evyr ony lord or hede

---

[1] Lines 493–95: *[The memory of her marriage] is so impressed on her heart / That no fickle weathervane of worldly desires will / Blow it away*

510   Shuld thus boldly men dragge and drawe
        Ageyns all treughth, ageyns a rithful lawe!

        "Why sufferth my spouse now swech cursyd men
        To breke His chirchis, His servauntis for to kyll?
        O cause there is only, that wele I ken: *One*
515   His servauntis here shul not have her will;   *i.e., on earth*
        Who loveth this world, that love will him spill.   *ruin*
        Tribulacion is ordeyned for His servauntis here
        Whech to hevyn shul streyt fro the bere."[1]

Chapter 6

        Thus walketh she forth, sobyrly apace,
520   Thorowe hir pales; she hath forgote all thing.   *palace*
        Thei folowe hir eke, the servauntis of that place,
        Not many, but summe, for thei go to the kyng;   *i.e., Maxentius*
        Thei wote not eke what she in hir goyng
        Purposith to do, for betwix love and fere
525   Stakere the servauntis all that sche hath there.   *Waver*

        The tempill gates so full of puple now be,
        So ful repleschid no man may entere there.
        And evyr onto the porters thus sayd she,
        "Late us enter, late us oure erand bere
530   Onto the emperour, for and he wist what we were   *if he knew who we were*
        He wold not suffyr us no while stand without.
        We will him lerne sone, withouten doute,   *teach*

        "These solempnites bettir for to make,
        Not to no vanité, to no presumpcioun,
535   But to His worchip that all thing dede make."
        This was at that tyme hir peroracion.   *tirade*
        Thoo mette she lordes of ful straunge nacioun   *foreign land*
        Whech had performed her offeryngis and i-doo
        Forth to her innes thei dressyd hem to goo.   *prepared to return to their inns*

---

[1] *Who will proceed straight from their coffins to heaven*

540	The emperoures sone cam with these lordis in fere,	*accompanied these lords*
	But whan thei sey this lady so bryth and shene	
	Thei turned her jornay and with ful mere chere	*interrupted; solicitude*
	Thus spake thei all full godly to the qwene:	*graciously*
	"Madame," thei seyde, "the grete puple that ye sene	
545	Are com fro fer with grete devocion.	
	Blame hem noght, thow thei wold have don.[1]	

	"But we shall, lady, for youre reverence,	
	Turne with yow onto the tempill agayn.	
	We shall make space with strenght and resistence,	*clear a path*
550	That ye shall enter, schortly for to seyn."	
	With mace and manace thei made bare the pleyn,	*threats*
	Till she was entrede rith to the hye autere.	
	Than seyd she swech wordis lich as ye shull here.	*such*

	Thus she began and thus she spake to him:	
555	"Both kend and curtesie wold teche us this,	*nature*
	To honour thi crown because of thi kyn,	
	And yet for thi degré mech more iwis.	
	Alle these shulde excite us thee for to blys	*to bless you*
	And for to loute with reverens, ne were o thing	*venerate; except for one thing*
560	Whech thu hast do agayns the grete kyng,	

	"Lorde of all lordes, Jesu Crist I mene:	
	Thu takyst here fro Him His hye honour	
	And gevest it to maumentis, as is wele sene,	*idols*
	Whech may neythir help thee ne eke socour	
565	In non of thi causes, in no maner dolour.[2]	
	But if thu wold leve this cursid ydolatrye	
	And know thi God that sitt above ful hye,	

	"Whech made the sune, sterres, and the mone,	
	Than wold we honour thee with dew servyse,	
570	Knele down onto thee and oure homage ful sone	

---

[1] *Do not blame them for wanting to leave [and thus not escorting you back to the temple]*

[2] Lines 564–65: *Which may neither advance / Your causes nor alleviate your distress*

For to bryng onto thee as oure justyce.
But because ageyn Cryst thu makyst men to ryse
And worchip swech develles that be in helle,
Therfor, sothly, sire, I will thee telle,

575 "Oure servise will we for a tyme withdrawe
Rith fro thi persone till thou thee amende.
Turne fro this cursydnes, fro this wickyd lawe,
Knowe nowe thi makere that all thing can send,   *ordain*
Onto His byddyng loke thou condescende,   *Bow to His will*
580 Than shall thu have more prosperité
Than evyr thou had yete, trost upon me.

"These Cristen men here, whech are i-drawe
To offyr to thin idolis magré her hede,   *against their judgment*
Agens all reson ageyns all the lawe,
585 Thu thretist hem with turment and with dede,   *death*
With bath of picth and beverych of lede.   *pitch; beverage; lead*
I sorow for her sake; thei dare non othir doo.
If thei were stabill, thei shuld not werke so.

"Thi goddes are develes and thi prestis eke,
590 Deceyvores of the puple, rith for covetyse;
Thei wote as wele as I, thow men hem seke —   *entreat*
These maumentis, I mene — thei can not sitt ne ryse,   *idols*
Thei ete not, thei drynke not in no maner wyse.
Mouth without spech, fote that may not goo,
595 Handes eke have thei and may no werke doo.

"Wherfor, turne thin herte fro this illusion,
Knowe thi Godde that made the and all thing for thee,
Be not unkend in thi condicion,   *unnatural*
Ageyns thi makere, ageyn the Trinyté.
600 But if thu be amended, thu shall leve me,   *unless you reform*
Grete peynes God shall thee send,
Whech peynes shul nevyr have a ende."

170

Chapter 7

The emperour behelde hir wordis and hir chere,   *disposition*
Wondiryng sore how she durst be so bolde,
605   Befor swech puple, rith in his presens there,
And not consyderyng the fest whech he had holde,
For that same tale whech sche hath now tolde
Durst no man telle but if he wold be dede.   *Dared*
Hir fayre coloure betwix qwite and rede   *white*

610   Whech shone ful bryth he gan to beholde,
Astoyned with hir beuté, party with hir plesauns.[1]
Ful sobirly his harmes thoo gan he folde,   *folded his arms*
And thus he seyd with angry countenauns:
"Beware, good woman, of that grete venjauns
615   Whech oure goddes on her enmyes hath take.
Many a proude man ful low have thei shake.

"For but her mercy were more than her justice,
Ye shuld sone falle in that sory trappe
Whech thei have ordeynyd to thoo that hem despyce —
620   A woofull chaunce hafe thei and a sory happe.   *misfortune; bad outcome*
Beware, systyr, that thei yow noght clappe   *strike*
With her venjauns, ryght for youre blaspheme!
Ye speke of helle, ye speke also of hevyne,

"And thei may graunt yow bothe to your wage.   *whichever you deserve*
625   Kepe your tung clos, kepe your lyff on loft.   *stay alive*
Ne were the reverens of your grete lynage,
Ye schuld not this nyght slepe, I trow, ryght soft.
Ye were wel worthy to be lyft on lofte   *deserved to be hanged*
Ryght on a gybbet for your byttyr spech
630   With whech ye now ageyn oure goddis preche."

---

[1] *Astonished by her beauty [and] partly by what she wanted of him*

Chapter 8

     Thoo seyd the mayde with ful sad vysage: *solemn*
     "How be thei goddys, these maumentys that we see?   *are they gods; idols*
     Rede in your boke, loke in her lynage,
     Than schall thu know that erdely as we bee
635 Were thei sumtyme, for your Saturn, pardé,   *once*
     Was sumtyme kyng, as bokes telle, of Crete,
     And so was Jubiter, thus seyth youre poete.

     "Because thei myght not bothe in that lond acorde,   *get along*
     Jubiter, the sun, made Saturn, his fader, to fle
640 Ryght into Ytale, your bokes wyll it recorde,
     In whech tyme there thoo regned he   *then*
     Janus ye call with dobyll face, pardé,
     Because he lokyth to the elde yere and the new.
     Than is this soth, than is this tale trew,

645 "That men thei were and are noght eterne.
     How schuld thei be goddys whan thei were made?
     It longyth to a godde to be sempyterne![1]
     Ful falsly the puple ye deceyve and glade.   *comfort*
     He is a Godd that may nevyr fayle ne fade,
650 He is a Godd that mad all thing of nowte,
     He is a Godd of whom your goddys were wrowte."   *by whom; made*

Chapter 9

     The emperour thouth thoo bysyly in his mynde,   *then*
     In worchep and strenght of his beleve,
     Bothe with ensaumples of craft and of kynde,   *of power and of nature*
655 His secte wyll he trew and stable preve.
     "Mayde," he seyth, "I trow I shall you meve
     Fro that ground that ye have newly take.
     Lete youre wordis as for a while now slake,   *cease*

---

[1] Lines 646–47: *If they were themselves created, how can they be gods? / A god is supposed to be eternal*

"For I will preve now opynly first of alle

660   That youre sect, whech ye Cristen clepe,   *call*

May not stand, for it must nedis falle   *withstand scrutiny*

Right for the impossibiles whech therin ye hepe.   *impossibilities you attribute to it*

Alle that I sey now loke that ye sadly repe.   *take in*

How shulde a mayde in hir wombe bere

665   A child and she mayde as she was ere?   *and remain a virgin*

"This thing is contrarie, ye may se, to nature;

This thing is impossible onto scoles alle.

Remeveth youre hert, for I you ensure   *Change your mind*

In swech errour ye may so depe down falle

670   That thow ye aftir mercy cry and calle

We may not graunt you, because that oure lawe

Will condempne yow to be hange and drawe.

"Therfor chaunge youre feyth, I rede, and forsake   *advise*

Swech maner opiniones that ilke man o lyve   *living*

675   As for heresies evyr more hath take.

Ye sey a childis blode with woundis fyve

Shuld washe fro every man and every wyve,

From every childe her synnes echon —   *their*

These fonned conceytes reson have non."   *foolish*

Chapter 10

680   Unto these wordes whech sempt so wyse   *seemed*

Answerd the qwene with ful grete constauns: *constancy*

"Sere emperour," sche seyd, "I wolde devyse

To prove onto you with grete circumstauns —

But that the tyme lettith us of swech daliauns —   *prevents such an undertaking*

685   That youre groundis are no thing trewe   *premises*

Of youre beleve, neythir the elde ne the newe.

"Ye take the barke, whech is open to the yye,   *rind; can be plainly seen*

Then ye fede you ryght in youre dotage.   *in your stupidity you eat it*

The swete frute whech withinne doth lye,

690   Ye desyre it nought. Lo, swech is the wod rage   *madness*

Of youre customes in all youre age:

The leves ye take, the frute leve ye stille.
More opynly my sentens declare I wille:

"Who sekith roses there no rose growe?
695   Who sekith grapes oute of the brere?   *briar*
The hye very God, this may ye wel knowe,
Is not nowe visible among us here;
He is fer above, without any dwere,
Dwellyng in blysse with His servauntis alle.
700   Therfor, I sey yow, thow ye cry and calle

"Upon these stokkes to send yow good grace,   *chunks of wood*
To send you of myschef relef and socour,
Levyth this wele, ye shal it nevyr purchase   *obtain*
Because ye forsake youre creatour,
705   Worchip creatures and geve hem honour
To whom ye shulde no swech honour geve.
Be this example I may than wele preve

"The rotyn barke of thingis visible here,
Whech ye se outwarde, this byte ye and knawe;
710   The swete frute, the solace eke so dere,
Whech schuld be the parfytnes of youre lawe,   *ultimate achievement*
Fro that swetnes ye youreselve withdrawe
With ful grete hert of cursyd obstinacy
Whech hath you brought in ful grete heresy.

715   "And as long as ye thus dullyd be
In this same rudnes of opynyon,
Shul ye nevyr, sekyrly, leve now me,
Of very treuth have the possession.
Therfor repent you of youre transgressioun,
720   Than are ye able to receyve the feyth.
This is the treuth, what evyr ony man seyth."

Chapter 11

Thou myth a seyn at this tales ende
Many man there al othir wyse i-cheryde

	Than thei were here¹; summe her browes gune bende	*began to frown*
725	Rigth on thoo ydolis whech he had reryd.	*he (Maxentius); elevated*
	For peyne and deth had hem so i-feryd	*frightened*
	Befor this tyme, that in all her observauns	
	Onto the goddes thei made but feyned plesauns.	*feigned propitiation*

	But now this lady with hir wordis swete	
730	A newe lyth of grace onto her hertis all,	
	Whech befor her feyth thus had lete,	*abandoned*
	Hath brought in, for now thei gun to calle,	
	"Mercy Jesu, graunt us nomore to falle	
	Into swech errour, to swech apostasye."	
735	This was her noyse and thus gune thei crye.	*their*

	This sey the emperour and with ful hevy chere.	*saw*
	He gan to chaunge his coloure and his face.	
	"In evyl tyme," he thought, "I graunted here	
	Onto this mayde, whan sche cam to this place,	
740	To sey this sermone with a sory grace.²	
	Myn owne men, me thinkith, thei gyne despyse	
	Alle my goddes and all my sacryfyse.	

	"The othir seyde, whech thei Crysten calle,	*side*
	Thei have caute boldnes, and that mervelously,	*are marvelously infected with*
745	For in my presens thei have late down falle	*dropped*
	Alle her offeryngis, and that sodenly."	
	Thus thought this man and eke ful besyly.	
	He than beheld the beuté of this mayde,	
	And than ryght thus onto hir he seyd:	

750	"Mayde," he seyth, "here have we newly gunne	
	A blissyd sacryfyce onto oure goddys to make,	
	And ye ful onreverently ageyn oure god the sunne —	
	Whech every man for a god hath take —	

¹ Lines 722–24: *You might have seen by the end of her speech, / Many people disposed otherwise / Than they were before*

² Lines 738–40: *It was an evil hour when I made the mistake of allowing her to speak*

Spend youre spech. But now I rede ye slake   *I advise you to desist*

755   Till that oure servyse endyd be this tide,   *are over for the day*

That tyme we will ye drawe you asyde.

"Apollo graunt that ye no venjauns have   *are not punished*

For youre blaspheme newly here i-sowe!   *newly sown blasphemy*

He may you dampne and eke he may yow save —

760   Ye youreselve, I wote wele, this ye knowe.

Right for youre bewté aute ye stoupe ful lowe

To thanke him therof, thow there were not ellis;[1]

Now are ye most, I trowe, of his rebellys."   *the greatest*

Chapter 12

"Whi shuld Apollo bere any deité,"

765   Seyd the mayd, that all men myth here,

"And is but servaunt to Goddis magesté,   *Since he is only a servant*

With his bemes schynyng fayre and clere?

He walkith no cors, neythir farre ne nere,   *course*

But at the byddyng of his makere above,

770   Whom we are bownd only to drede and love.

"But traytouris are we the most part, dare I seyn,

And yete He suspendyth His grete venjauns.

A opyn example before yow will I leyn: *clear; offer*

Ye be a lord of ful grete pusauns;   *might*

775   Ther is no swech betwix this and Fraunce,   *this (i.e., Alexandria)*

For as I have lernyd of all the oryente,   *East*

Youre meny calle you kyng omnypotent.   *followers*

"I sett caase nowe that ageyn youre regalye   *Suppose that; sovereignty*

Certeyn of youre men wyth treson wold ryse,

780   Despite youre degré, youre persone defye.

Shuld ye not than as a trewe justyce

Youre grete powere fully exercyse

---

[1] Lines 760–62: *you know / That you should bow down and for your beauty / Thank him if for nothing else*

176

To kyll thoo traytouris that thei leve nomore?
But ye dede thus ye shuld repent it sore!   *Unless*

785   "Right thus it semeth be oure creatour,   *So it is with our creator*
God of hevene that all made of nought.
Ye take awey fro Him that dew honour
That He shuld have, whech He ful dere bought
Whan that in erde bysyly oure helth He soughte.   *welfare*
790   This same honour geve ye to develes ymages,
Whech ye have sett here solemply on stages.

"Loke nowe youreselve in what ye are falle —
Traytouris are ye and as traytouris shuld ye brenne,
For other name will I you non calle
795   Onto that tyme that ye youre Lord kenne!   *Until; recognize*
Lete all these vanytes fro youre brest renne,
Goode sere emperour, and turne to youre Lorde —
Than shul ye and I ful sone acorde."

Chapter 13

Now is the emperour steyned more and more.   *stunned*
800   All her servyse as for that day is done;
This tormentith him in his hert ful sore,
For neythir to sonne, to Venus, ne to mone   *sun*
Will no man lowte now and passed is the none.   *bow; it is past noon*
Wherfor he thinkyth ryth thus in his herte:
805   "Thow that I ponysh this lady with peynes smert,   *sore*

"Thow that I sle hir, strangill, or ellis brenne,
Yete shal hir doctrine no thing herby sees;   *cease*
Wherfor I thinke a slyer wey to renne,   *devise a slier plan*
That hir purpos schal not thus encrese.   *will not advance her cause*
810   Ageyn oure goddes is she and ageyn oure pees.
Therfor with resones will we hir oppresse —
This hold I best ageyn hir sotylnes."

Therfor hath he nowe — and that in grete hast —
Clepid his counsell into a pryvy place.   *summoned*

815 With ful grete sadnes thoo gan he cast   *deliberate*
   How that he may fro this lady race   *eradicate*
   Hir newe oppynyon — wheythir with solace *pleasure*
   Or ellis with peyne be best to procede.
   His counsell seyd rith thus in that stede,

820 That he shall send aftir grete clerkis,
   Lerned in gramer, rethoricke, and philosophie,
   Whech have in sciens so sekir merkis *learning; such expertise*
   That no man ageyn hem may replye.
   Thei shall sonest destroy this heresye *most expeditiously*
825 Of this same lady, thus seyd thei all.
   Anon the emperour dede forth i-calle

   Many messangeres, for letteris wille he sende
   Thoroweout the lond of Cipre and Surré.
   Alle thoo clerkys that will her lyvelode amende, *increase their income*
830 Thei must com nowe to this palustré,   *arena*
   Onto this place where this conflicte shal be. *debate*
   The letteres are wryte nowe and sealed ech on;
   The messageres in hast for these men are goon.

   The emperour himselve, as of a specialté, *to mark the occasion*
835 Sealed these letteres with a precious ryng,
   Whech was i-grave with ful grete sotilté.
   The sentens of the letteres whech that this kyng
   Wrote at that tyme, if youre desyryng
   Be forto lyst it, ye may here it sone:
840 "Maxence, the lorde, save sune and mone

   "Most grettest in erde whech hath i-be,
   Thre tymes consul in Rome, that cité hye,
   Fader of the puple and to the deité
   Of Jupiter the kyng of kynrod ful nye, *close in kinship*
845 Sendith love and helth to all the clergye *scholars*
   Of Surré and Cipre and othir provincis all
   Whech to his lordchip newly are falle. *recently have fallen under his rule*

"We will ye wyte, we send at this tyme
Onto youre Providens counsell to have.   *your Wisdoms (polite form of address)*
850 We ax not of you nethir taske ne dyme,   *toil; tithes*
But only oure feyth and oure sect to save,
For these Crysten folke make oure puple to rave
With sotill suasiones whech that thei use,   *arguments*
On whech sotiltees we oureselve muse.   *marvel*

855 "But most specialy a lady have we new i-caut,
Enforsed with eloquens mervelosly.   *Bolstered*
Mech of oure puple so hath sche taught
That fro oure feyth fle thei sodenly.
Thus party with witte, party nygromancy,   *partly by cleverness, partly by magic*
860 Sche pervertith oure lond in wondir wyse.
Therfor, we byd ye that are wyse,

"Ye hast now to Alisaundre for this same cause,
To loke if ye may this woman oppresse,   *suppress*
For this I telle you schortly in clause,
865 But she be ovyrcome with youre besynes,   *diligence*
All shul be Crysten, the more and the lesse,
And if ye convicte hir avaunsed schul ye be   *overcome; rewarded*
With plenté of ryches, if ye trost me."

Thus are the letteres wretyn and i-goo.
870 The emperour is walkid forth with the mayd
Onto the pales with lordes many moo,   *palace*
Whech was at that tyme ful wel arayd.
Many plesaunt wordis to hir he seyde,
And many grete behestis thoo he behyte,   *he made many great promises*
875 To turne hir opinion yf that he myth.

He hite hir, if she wold to him consent,   *promised*
To have ful powere of all maner thing,
More than any lord of his parlement,
For all men shuld bowe onto hir byddyng.
880 She shulde be qwene as he was kyng;
Hir ymage wold he sett in the merket place,
Whech shuld be like hir in bodye and in face,

179

And alle maner of men shull worchip geve
Onto that ymage as onto a goddesse.
885 Thei shal not chese, if that thei will leve,   *They shall have no choice*
Worchip shull thei hir both more and lesse.
That was his promysse, that with swech worthines
He will hir avaunce only if sche will forsake
Hir Cristen feyth and his feyth now take.

890 But all these promissis sett sche at nought,
This blessyd lady, ryth for Crystes sake.
This same vers was thoo in hir thought
Whech oure Lady hirselve gan make:
"Thei that are proud, God will hem forsake,
895 Meke He will lift for her mekenes."   *he will elevate the meek*
Than seyd she to the emperour with sadnes,

"All this world have I, for my Lordys love,
Jhesu I mene, forsake forevyre more.
There shall no mene of drede ne of love   *no strategy involving fear or love*
900 Put myn hert fro that grete tresore;
It shall ly full stille there as a good store
Till that I dey and yelde up my goost
Onto that Lord whom I love most.

"But sith that thi goddis of swech myth be
905 As thu hast pronounced here in this place,
Late hem take venjaunce nowe upon me —
If that thei may — late hem my body race.   *destroy*
Her myght is nought, ne nought is her grace;   *Their*
Therfor I despice hem as thei stand a rowe,   *in a row*
910 For fendis are thei — ful well that I knowe!   *fiends*

"And, sere, to you I will touch anothir thing:
I wole ye shull encline all youre entente   *devote all your attention*
To herkyne my wordis and my talkyng.
It is not unknowen to all the Orient
915 That both be descens and be testament   *by right of descent and of charter*
This cité is myn as for heritage
To whech ye have made nowe this pilgrimage.

180

"Sith ye are kyng and rythwisnes shuld kepe,   *should uphold the law*
Whi make ye swech mastries in otheris mennes londe,   *do you commit such outrages*
920 Compell my tenauntis, thow thei sore wepe,
To go with her offeryngis rith in her hondis,
With trumpes and taburs befor you to stonde,   *drums*
Withoute my leve, withoute my licence?
This is wronge to me and to God offence!

925 "If yowre goddis teche you for to do thys synne,
Than are they unryghtfull in her comaundment.
If ye ageyn her byddyng thus wil begynne,
Than do ye wronge ageyn her intent.
On what maner wise ye make youre went,   *No matter why you do this*
930 I wyl not tary you with no tales long,   *delay; speeches*
But thus I conclude — that ye do me wrong!"

Than was the emperour ful of malencolye.
He myght no lenger suffyr hir in his presens.
To a knyght he commawnded that stod fast by
935 He shal take thys lady and lede hir thens,
Put hir in prison for hir offence,
Loke he kepe hir so she go not awey —
For if that she doo full horrybyly shall he dey.

Gladly and jocundly with the knyght she goo,
940 As a spowse to chambre for hir Lordis love,   *a bride to her wedding chamber*
Nothyng dismayd, nothyng is she wroth:
Thus can oure Lord the paciens prove
Of hem that are chosyn to dwelle all above
In hevyn in His presens. But thus I lett hir lye,   *leave her for now*
945 And forth I shall telle of thys story.   *tell more*

Chapter 14

Whyll Kateryne is in prison thus i-closyd
The emperowr is rydyn into the lond
For certeyn causes; as it is supposed,
It was for brekyng of a certen bond   *breach of a certain agreement*
950 Betwyx too cites. As I undyrstond,

181

He rode to sesse the sisme that was new begun;   *mend the rift*
Iche of hem of othyr had spent many a gonne.   *made war on the other*

But he hath made pece and his jornay is sped.   *accomplished*
He is cum home now to Alisaundyr ageyn.
955 The messangeres that he sent eke thei hafe led
All theys clerkis to Alisaundre eke certeyn.
Thus be they cum both, shortly to seyn,
The emperour and the clerkis thus mete in fere;   *together*
A cowncell is sett now of lordis that were there.

960 The philosopheres are enterd into the same cowncell
To wete why the emperour for hem hath sent.
There was a fayre syght, withowtyn ony fayll,
For owt of the costes of all the Orient   *from all parts of the East*
Are theys maystires chose ryght for thys entent:
965 To conquer thys lady be philosofie.
The nombre of hem, if I shuld not lye,

Myn auctour seyth was fyfty evyn,
Lernyd men in arte and in arsmetrike,   *arithmetic*
In rethorike, gramer, and all the Sciens Sevyn.   *Seven Liberal Arts*
970 In all the world were non hem lyke:
They had stodyed the grownd of all musike.   *foundation*
The emperour is ful glad now of her cunnyng.   *their*
Thus seyd he to hem at her enteryng:

"Maysteres, we sent for yow for thys matere:
975 We hafe here a mayde whyche with obstinacye
Reneyhithe owre lawes whyche we use here,   *Repudiates*
For she is falle into that cursyd heresye
Whyche the Crysten clepeth, full of ypocrisye.   *Christian*
Sche eke so depe is into thys errowr falle
980 That all owre goddis devylles dothe she calle.

"And I suppose veryly ye teche but trewth,
Because that ye be so grete lernyd men.
To sle so yong a lady me thynketh rewthe;   *To kill; a shame*
Therfor, the ryght wey I wyll ye hir kene,   *teach*

182

985 To converte hir to owre lawe, ellys I must hir brenne.
   Thys is the cause why I sent for yowe.
   Go cast yowre wyttes in the best maner now

   "How ye wyll procede, for she shall cum anon.
   Hir answeres are sly; grete is hir lernyng.
990 I make yow sekyr, ye shall not hens gon   *I assure you*
   Onto that tyme that ye hir bryng   *Until*
   Into the same feyth whych hir fadyr the kyng
   Lyved all his lyf and hir modyr also:
   Thys is the matere whyche I wyll hafe do."

995 On answerd for all, and thus spake he:
   "We wene here is gadered swyche a cumpanye
   In all thys world shuld not a man fynd three
   So wyse, so studyous in philosofye.
   But ovyr all theys maystires Ariott is most worthy.
1000 He nedith not his labowr on a woman spend! *waste his energies on a woman*
   He shall unto hir but his disciples send,

   "And if she conclude hem be auctorité, *out-argues them by citing authorities*
   Or ellys be reson, leve me full wele,
   I wyll sey than that a goddes is she
1005 And most worthy to be sett on the whele
   Of naturall sciens. But I cannot fele
   In no maner that a woman shuld cum therto.
   I hafe not hard speke that ony woman dyde so."

   Aftyr thys sermonyng untyl the next day,   *discourse*
1010 The emperour comawnded knytes hem to chere, *knights to make them comfortable*
   To lede hem to her innes with full good aray —   *furnishings*
   In specyall of bokes and swyche othyr gere   *equipment*
   As longith onto men that swyche sciens lere.   *study*
   Thus leve I hem stylle in thowghtfull besynes,
1015 And Kateryne, oure maydyn, in prison and distres.

Chapter 15

The othyr day is cum, but the emperour thowght   *next*
To assay himselfe with his pryvy councele
For to conquer hir — but it avayleth nowght,
For whan most nede is, his resonys wyll whayle,   *arguments falter*
1020   So wele can owre mayd hir proporcyons rayle.   *set forth her argument*
Lordes were there many thoo in presence,
Statly, manfull, and of grete exspence.   *Dignified, manly, and generous*

The Kyng of Ermenye was tho in that place   *Armenia*
Where she was opposed of hir beleve;   *her faith was challenged*
1025   So was the Kyng of Mede, a fayre man of face;   *Media*
The Kyng eke of Macedon, whyche made many a preve   *Macedonia; effort*
Ageyn thys lady but he cowde hir not mend;
The Provoste of Perse was there also,   *Persia*
With bischoppis and lordys many moo.

1030   They made her resones but thei avayled nowght.   *made their points*
Fyrst seyd the emperowr ryght thus to thys may: *maiden*
"Myn owyn systir, hedyr I hafe yow browte
Befor my specyall frendis thys day
To se whedyr ye wyll stylle in your old lay   *law (Christianity)*
1035   Held your perseveraunce or ellys consent to us
And reney for evyr that traytour Jesus,   *renounce*

"To turn to Apollo, Venus, and Minerve,   *Minerva*
For your prison shuld cause yow, I suppose,   *imprisonment*
To chaunge your lyfe, leste that ye sterve,
1040   For of all maydenes, ye be the rose,
And to maydens it longeth to be led with glose. *for maidens it is fitting to follow advice*
Lat se now telle how ye avised be."   *Let it be seen*
Onto theys wordis thus answerd she:

"A love hafe I, syr, whyche lykyth me so   *pleases me so much*
1045   That all worldly delyte to me is but peyn
And all worldly joye to me is but wo,
If I very trewthe to yow shuld seyn.
Therfor know thys: for a certen

184

I wyll nevyr chaunge whyll I hafe lyfe;

1050   I shal be evyr to Him trewe spowse and wyfe."

Thoo seyd the emperour, "Than is all nowt   *for nothing*
That we with oure wyttes hafe laboured yow to safe.   *racked our brains*
Turn yowre wordis, turn eke yowre thowght,
Or ellys swyche ende must ye now hafe

1055   As longeth to traytours that thus wyll raffe.   *rave*
Avise yow of two thyngis whyche ye wyll take: *Pick one of these two things*
Ethyr shall ye dye or yowre lawe forsake."

And eke the grete Kyng of Armenye,   *Armenia*
Eem to Kateryne he was, as I wene,   *Uncle*

1060   "Cosyn," he seyd, "leve thys heresye.   *kinswoman*
Thynk of your kynrode, both kyng and qwene:
Was nevyr non of them swych thyng wold susteyn.   *hold such beliefs*
Alas! Why, woman, why, dyspyse ye Saturne?
He may and he wyll into a ston yow turn!"

1065   The Kyng of Mede, whyche sat thoo besyd,
In owre Lord Jhesu he put swyche blame:
"Your God Cryst," he seyd, "is know full wyd
That He was a wyche and so was His dame,   *sorcerer*
And the grettest in wycchecrafte as is the fame.

1070   Fye on swyche wysdam! Fye on swyche feyth!
Thys same recorde all the world seyth."   *Everyone says so*

Anothir thyng was there, and he hir thus reprevyd:
She stode in thys mater, he seyd, but alone.
There is non but she that in Cryst levyd.   *believed*

1075   "Loke now," he seyd, "whedir o persone
Is more worthy to be levyd than we ichone:
Reson wyll conclude that where multitude is
There is the trewthe — a man may not mys."   *fail [to find truth]*

The Kyng of Macedoyne, Syr Caspanus,

1080   Onto the lady full sobyrly thus sayd:
"Yowre God, yowre Lord, whyche ye calle Jesus,
As ye sayd He was bore of a mayde,

185

	But why sufferd He to be arayed	*treated*
	Of His owyn servauntis so as He was?	
1085	And a wyse lord had stond in that case,	*If a wise lord had been in his place*

"He wold have hanged hem of very justyce!"
Thus seyd the byschoppis, thus seyd they all,
Onto thys lady in her best wyse,   *as persuasively as they could*
And with besynes sore on hir they calle   *diligence; exhorted her*
1090 And she fro thys vanité nedis muste falle   *turn from*
And make of hir enmyes hir frendis dere.
Than spake thys lady, ryght as ye shall here:

Chapter 16

"Syr Emperour," seyd she, "I hafe or thys   *previously*
Onto yowre reverens declared ful wele
1095 Why my Lord Jhesu of servauntis His
Wold suffyr all thys peyn every dele,
But of my feyth nothyng ye fele,
So are ye hardyd with obstinacye.
Therfor hold I nowe but a grete folye   *I consider it*

1100 "Youre demonstraciounes for to declare.   *to argue with you*
But thus myche I say to yow everychon:
Yowre mahowude of whyche ye make swyche fare   *false god; display (commotion)*
Shall not save yow whan ye shall gon
Down into peynes, hevy as stone.   *i.e., hell*
1105 He may not deliver himsefe from that peyne
Where he is bownd with many a cheyn.

"But wycche was he nevyr, my Lord,   *sorcerer*
Ne His blyssed modyr Mary, that may,
He was God and man as bokes record,
1110 And all tho myrakyls were put in asay   *tested*
Be His mortayll enmes with full gret afray   *assault*
And evyr were thei fownde trew and stedfast.
Therfor, ley down that orible blaste

186

"Of your cursyd tungis, ye lordis, I yow praye.

1115 Berke now namore ageyn that holy name,   *Bark*

For ye shall sumtyme se that day

Ye shall for thys berkyng be put onto blame.   *be called to account*

Alas that ony wrechys shuld defame

So hyghe a Lord, so grete a dignité,

1120 To Whome mote nede bowe every kne!"   *must*

Than spake the Provost of Perse full sone: *forthwith*

"Sende aftir theys clerkis, syr, and let hem sey;

They can owre feythe, they wote what is to done. *know our doctrine*

Lat hir beleve hem or ellys shall she deye!

1125 She shall chese on, there is non othyr weye.

With thys long clateryng, tyme lese we here.

They wyll oppose hir in othyr manere."

Chapter 17

The phylosophers are enterd to the councell.

The emperowr seyd thus: "Thys is the howr

1130 In whyche we shall se if conyng wyll avaylle. *knowledge*

Therfor, maysters, do now yowre labowre,

For ye muste defende us from thys scharp schowre *assault*

With whyche we are haylyd now on every syde; *attacked*

But ife ye spede owre feyth wyll sone slyde." *Unless you succeed; fall*

1135 They answerd ageyn: thei seyd they had skorne *replied*

That so many men ageyn a mayden yinge   *young*

Shuld now dispute, for he is not borne

In erde as yete that durst stere ony thyng   *utter*

Ageyn her conclusyones, neythir duke ne kyng.

1140 Swyche grete rowse was made tho in that place: *commotion*

"Lete hir cum," they seyd, "lete us se hir face."

But whyll they were karpyng in thys matere,

A knyght is gun to hir in prison in haste,

Warnyng hir as a gentyll officere,

1145 In what manere the emperour will hir ataste.   *test*

What nedyth now moo wordys for to waste?

187

The lady seyd that it was glad tydyng;
There cowde no man gladdere to hir bryng.

Thoo fell sche down plat, all in a traunce,
1150   Commendyng hir cause ryght onto Godd alone:
"Graunt me," sche sayde, "Lord, perseveraunce,
To serve Thi Godhed whech syttyth in trone,
Of whech Godhed Thi Sone, the secunde persone,
Deyd in erde for synne of all mankynde,
1155   Whech onto Him ful ofte He fynt onkynde.   *untrue*

"Thou graunt me, Lord, this day eloquens
To safe Thi feyth ryght as Thu best can.
Suffyr not these clerkys to make resistens
Ageyn that doctrine whech Thu, God and man,
1160   Here in this worlde with woundis blew and wan   *black and blue*
Confermed thus. Geve me, Lord, that Gost   *i.e., the Holy Spirit*
Whech can put down soone all worldly booste,

"And as Thu grauntyd to Thin apostles here —
Whan thei schuld stande befor prynce or kyng,
1165   Thu sayd to hem thei schuld not be in dwere   *doubt*
What thei schuld speke, neyther to elde ne yyng,   *young*
For Thu shuld graunte hem wytt in answeryng
Ageyn whech there schuld no man replye,
Neyther of the secte of hethen ne of heresye —   *Neither heathens nor heretics*

1170   "Ryght so graunt now to me, Thi servaunt here,
That I hafe strength Thi cause for to defende,
That I may preve be resons scharpe and clere
Thi chyrches feyth, for whech Thu kan descende
Evene fro hevyn, oure maners to amende.   *our ways*
1175   This pray I Thee, put this in my breest,
As Thu art God and man, bothe kyng and preest.

"Thu art my conyng, Thu art my hardynesse,   *knowledge*
Thu art all in Whom oonly I trost.

188

There comth no vertew but of Thi worthinesse.[1]

1180   Let not Thi powere as this day be lost.
      Thu makyst all thing, bothe the hete and the frost,
      Wherfore, I pray, Lord, thow I a woman be,
      Yet for Thi worchepe yette so enforce me   *for your honor; strengthen*

      "That I may speke wordys to Thi plesaunce,

1185   As Thu graunted Ester to plese hir Assuere,   *Ahasuerus*
      To leve his stately solemne contenaunce   *set aside his somber formality*
      And spek to hir wordys of goodely chere,
      So graunt me now, Lord, Thi servaunt here,
      That I may plese and plete in Thi cause: *plead*

1190   This is the sentens that I pray, in clause."   *in brief*

Chapter 18

      Whan that this lady had made hir oryson,   *prayer*
      There cam an aungell glydyng down fro hevene,
      With mervelous noys cam he that tyme down,
      As bryth he semyd, as it were the levene.   *lightning*

1195   Alle the prison, whech had voutes sevene,   *vaults*
      Was lyght that tyme ryght of his presence.   *illuminated by his presence*
      The derke corneres coude make noo resistens,

      And sche myght not susteyn that vysyoun,
      So was sche ravyschyd with that new lyght;

1200   Ryght with his comyng sche fell sone down.
      The aungell comforted hir and bad hir be lyght: *to be cheerful*
      "Drede noght," he seyth, "thow that I be bryght.   *though*
      I am a servaunt bothe onto Godd and to yow,
      And for your comforte fro hevyn cam I now.

1205   "My Lord, your spouse, be me greteth yow wele.
      For very lofe this message now He sent:
      He comaunded yow to drede nevyre a dele   *fear nothing*
      Of theyse clerkys; ye schal not be circumvent.

---

[1] *All virtue proceeds from Your worthiness*

Ye schall conceyve full clerly her entent
1210 And yet moreovyre thei schul hafe no powere
For to conclude yow now, in noo manere.   *overcome*

"But your powere schal be ovyre hem more large,
For ye schall convycte hem with grete auctorite.   *convince*
Ye schall lede hem onto the Peteres barge,   *i.e., the Church of Rome*
1215 Whych fygureth oure feyth, as seyth dyvynyté,   *symbolizes*
And not only thus, but so devoute schul thei be,
That as martyres for Cryst thei schul deye.
This same prophecye whech I to yow seye

"Is determynde above be Goddis provydens.
1220 These clerkys schul now despyce her bokys alle,
In whech thei hafe had a full grete confidens;
Alle her grete trost now schall fro hem falle
With whech thei hauntyd her goddys for to calle.[1]
This schall oure Lorde do, lady, be youre laboure.   *through*
1225 Ryse up now and thank youre Savyoure.

"And ye youreself, aftyr that thei be dede,
Schul suffyr for Him mech more thinge
Than I hafe leysere to tell now in this stede.   *leisure*
But of thus mych I geve full warnyng:
1230 Ye schall make the qween for to forsake hir kyng
For Crystys love and dey soo in hir blode;
Ye schul be cause, lady, of all these werkys goode.

"Geve credens to me as to a trew messagere
And as no feyned spyryte with dobylnesse;   *duplicity*
1235 My name is Mychael, if ye wyll it here,   *hear*
Archaungell of hevyn, whech hath that besynesse   *occupation*
That all sowles, the more and eke the lesse,
That schall to blysse, I peyse all be wyght,   *weigh them all by weight*
Wheythyr in goodeness thei be hevy or lyght.   *[To determine] whether*

---

[1] Lines 1222–23: *They will lose the confidence / With which they used to call upon their gods*

1240   "This is myn offyce, leve me, lady, wele.

There is a sete ordeyned in hevyn above   *seat*

For yow, lady, aftyr your scharpe whele   *i.e., after you are tortured*

Whech ye schall suffyr for your spouses love.

Was nevyr no mayde to swech sete myght prove,   *attain*

1245   Safe Mary alone, Crystes modyr dere.

Farewell now, lady, and beth of ryght goode chere."

Thus was sche comforted and left all that nyght   *remained*

In prison stylle, in swete oryson alone.

The savour abode and sumwhat of the lyght

1250   Aftyr the tyme that the aungell was gone.

He hath made hir hardy and stable as the stone;

There schall noo peyn hir hert now remeve

Fro the feyth ne fro hir beleve.

Chapter 19

Now is the cité for to se this mayde

1255   Gadered in fere with noyse and rumour.

Every man there aftyr his cunnyng sayde,   *according to his understanding*

"Now is come the day and eke the houre

In whech there shall fall full grete honoure

On summe party, or ellys full grete schame."

1260   And because this lady was of so grete fame

Every man is bysy to stand that tyme ny,   *strains to get close*

That he myght here and se all that was doo.

The emperour is sette, the lordes sytt fast by;

The clerkys eke were sette be too and too.   *sitting in pairs*

1265   The may is sette in a sete also,   *maiden*

Ryght be hirself, for sche is left alone.

The emperour sittyng all hye in his trone,

Thus exorted he these noble clerkys alle:

"Maysters," he seyth, "here is this concionatrix,   *female conjurer*

1270   Here is the mayde on whom we dyd so calle,

Here is the new dyvynoure, here is the new Ulix,   *i.e., soothsayer; Ulysses*

Here is sche whos errour is so fix

And so sore glewyd sche wyl not fro it remeve!   *firmly glued*
Therfore, youre schaftys on hir now must ye preve."   *arrows (intellectual ammunition)*

1275 Than made the mayde onto the emperour
         A full straunge chalenge, seying on this wyse:
         "Onto these clerkys whych are here this hour
         Gadered togedyr befor yow as justise
         Ye hafe graunted a guerdon of grete apryse   *precious reward*
1280 If that thei convicte me; to me graunte ye noon.   *overcome*
         Wherfore, me thinkyth all wrong hafe ye goon.

         "But wold ye graunt now to my guerdon   *as my reward*
         That if I spede and convicte hem all o rowe,   *succeed; altogether*
         That ye schall leve your maumentrye ful sone,
1285 And my Lord Jhesu as for your Godd to know,   *acknowledge*
         Than wold I sey with wordys meke and lowe
         That ye were juge, juste man and trewe."
         With these wordes the emperour chaunged hewe.   *color*

         He seyd unto hir with ful stout cuntenaunce: *arrogance*
1290 "What hast thu to do of oure reward now?[1]
         Defende thi feyth with all the circumstauns
         That thu can; think it schall be lytyll enow.
         Lett be, damysell, make it not so towe.   *do not complicate matters*
         Entermet thee where thu hast to done;   *Mind your own business*
1295 If thu hafe wytte it wylle be sene ful sone."   *soon be evident*

         Thoo spake the mayde onto the clerkys alle:
         "Syth ye be gadered now into this place,
         Upon me only for to crye and calle,
         With youre argumentis to loke if ye may chase
1300 My wytt, my mynde, fro that new purchase
         Whech I hafe wunne, I mene fro Crysten feyth,
         Lette se what ony of yow to me seyth."

---

[1] *Just what has our reward got to do with you?*

192

Thoo spake a phylosophre of full grete age,
An honourable man, Amphos of Athene:
1305 "We are come," he seyth, "at the emperoures wage,   *expense*
For a mayde, he wrote, of yerys eytene —   *eighteen*
That same is ye, pleynly, as I wene.
But wherfore we come as yet know we not now —   *why*
Of that matere the answere lythe in yow.

1310 "Syth ye be causere than of this afray,   *cause; proceedings*
Sey ye your growndis and we schull purveye   *beliefs; give*
Answeres therto or we goo hens this day.
We cast us sekyre newly yow to conveye   *We are resolved to return you*
Onto that feyth whech ye dyd reneye   *renounce*
1315 Be wykkyd counsayle. Therfore, fyrst schall ye   *By*
Speke in this matere and than answere we."

Chapter 20

The mayde stode up and with full goode chere
Sche crossed hir heed, hir mouth, and hir breeste,
Than spake sche to hem ryght as ye schall here:
1320 "In me it lyghte at the begynnyng of this feest   *It falls to me*
To pronounce fyrst, thow that I be leest
And most unworthy. But oure Lorde Jhesu,
Blessyd be He, syth tyme that I Him knew,

"I hafe left all my auctoures olde,
1325 I fonde noo frute in hem but eloquens.   *no substance; only literary skill*
My bokes be go, goven or elles solde.   *given away*
Farwell Arystotyll, for full grete expens
Made my fadyr and had full grete diligens
To lerne me thi sotill bokes alle,   *teach*
1330 Of dyverse names as thu ded hem calle.

"Of Omere eke hafe I take my leve,   *Homer*
With his fayre termes in vers and eke in prose
Ful erly sat I and eke full late at eve
To lerne the texte and to lern the glose —   *commentary on the text*
1335 I hafe chose bettyr, treuly, I not suppose   *I do not think*

But wote full well. Farwell eke Ovyde;   *But know for certain*
Thou loved full wele blynd Venus and Cupyde.

"I hafe take leve of Esculape and Galyene   *Aesculapius; Galen*
And of all her pryvy sergyng of nature.   *searching into nature's secrets*
1340   I hafe a lessoun mech trewere to susteyne
And more directe to know creature.[1]
Ye, Plato bokes eke I yow ensure   *Plato's*
We hafe do now, we schall nevyr more mete,   *finished with; encounter*
Ne him Phylystyoun, bothe phylosophyre and poete.

1345   "Behelde, ye maystrys, alle these mennys werkys
Have I stodyed and lerned full besyly.
Thei were red me of full sotell clerkys;   *clever*
There lyve noo bettyr at this day hardyly.
And in these bokes no othyr thing fond I
1350   But vanyté or thing that schall not lest.   *endure*
And evyr me thowte that swech lernyng was best

"That tretyth of thing whech evyr schall endure.
Swech thing lerne I now, turned to Criste Jhesu:
I lerne how Godd is Lord of creature;   *creation*
1355   I lerne how He the hevyn whyght and blew,   *blue and white sky*
The watyr, the fyyre, the erde or that it grew,   *i.e., before it became fertile*
Made all of noght—this is now my lernyng.
I lerne also that He, a chyld full yyng,

"Was bore in erde of Mary, and sche a mayde,
1360   Grew onto manhode to thirti wyntyr and thre,
And than wylfully, as the prophetys sayde,   *by his own choice*
For synne of man hyng upon a tre.
Many miracles in erde thoo dyd He
Whyll He went here, this I yow ensure;   *walked*
1365   By dyvers werkys know was sundry nature: *his dual nature was known*

---

[1] Lines 1340–41: *I have a teaching (Christianity) to uphold that is truer [than paganism] / And that leads more directly to an understanding of creation*

194

"That He was Godd He schewyd be werkis grete,
For all the elementys obeyd his comaundment.
That He was man ful esy is to trete: *is easily established*
Thei sey and felt Him that with Him were present.

1370 I tell yow pleynly now all myn entent.
This is my scole, this is my philosophye;
Thys is the sciens I hope schall nevyr lye;   *knowledge; trust*

"Thys is my feyth; this is my victorye.
What evyr men sey, a Godd must we hafe,

1375 Above all men that evyr reygned erdely,   *on earth*
Most sofren Lord whos powere may all safe.   *sovereign*
Loke on your goddys, how thei tumbyll and wafe   *tumble; waver*
Ryght whan men swepe hem, so lytyll is her myght.   *brush*
Wype ye that blyndenesse whech hath hyllyd your syght, *obstructed*

1380 "For Cryst seyd so whan He the Gospell sew: *sowed*
'Thei that se,' He seyth, 'schall be blynde,
And thei that nevyr of My vertew knew,
Ful truly wyll thei hafe Me in her mynde.'
But pull we the frute owte of the rynde

1385 To tell yow platly what this sentens is:
The seeyng men betokne yow, iwys,

"For ye can se all thing that to nature
Perteyneth, be crafte whech ye of bokes hafe.
But your savacyon, that I yow ensure,

1390 Consyder ye nowte, ne how ye may be safe.   *nor how you may be saved*
Youre blasyng scyens make yow so to rafe   *brilliant learning*
That endles treuthe can ye nevyre more fynde.
This same errour is that makyth yow blynde.

"But in His name whom I now rehers,   *declare*

1395 I schal be strong all materes to conclude.   *settle*
There schall no man have myght me to reverse,   *confound*
Thow ye bryng a grettere multitude.
He can make wyttys that be ful dull and rude
To schyne with sciens on the freschest wyse,

1400 My Lord Jhesu, and foles ofte He make wyse."

Chapter 21

> Whan this mayde of this fayre processe
> Had made a hende, there stode up thoo a man — *an end*
> Of fers corage, thow it were wodeness, — *haughty disposition; madness*
> Maystir Astenes so thei called him than;
1405 For very angyr of coloure was he wan.
> With cryyng voyse, he fyllyd thoo the place.
> Thus spak he than: "Alas what is oure grace? — *special virtue*
>
> "Ye of Rome, lordes and citeceyns alle,
> Ye bloode ryall, ye men of nobylnesse,
1410 What cause schul men hafe yow to calle — *Why should people call you*
> Wyse men endewyd with sobyrnesse?
> If wysdam were with yow, than wold I gesse
> Ye schuld not suffyr these Crysten folke here
> Reprove oure goddys with swech veniable manere. — *vindictive*
>
1415 "For we were called be oure emperour,
> Fadyr and keper ful gracyous of this londe,
> To convicte, he seyd, here a new errour—
> Whech is not new ye may well undyrstonde.
> Many of hem hafe I brent with bronde — *fire*
1420 Of these Crysten, ryght for this entent:
> That thei call feyth, we calle delyrament. — *lunacy*
>
> "Oure goddys may sey that we be onkynde, — *unnatural*
> For all the benefetis that thei to us sende
> We to suffyr the yyngth of womankynde — *youth*
1425 Thus openly Cryst for to commende
> And all His tresoun with coloures to defende, — *rhetorical tricks*
> Oure goddys eke develes for to calle,
> This suffyr we, and that is werst of alle.
>
> "Wherfore, syre kyng, beware of here offens —
1430 Suffyr now this lady no lengere for to speke.
> These lewyd folk that lysten with gret sylence, — *ignorant*
> With apparent resons sche schall sone i-cheke — *entrap with spurious arguments*
> That fro her feyth sche schall sone hem breke.

196

| | Thei come nevyr home, thow we wold hem drawe. | *i.e., return to our faith* |
| 1435 | To suffyr swech prechouris, it is ageyn oure lawe. | |

	"We cam now hedyr to here summe novelté,	
	And sche begynnyth with Jhesu Nazareth,	
	Cryst thei call Him and prophete of Galilé,	*Galilee*
	Sche callyth him Lorde of wynde and of breth,	
1440	Of erde, of watyr, of londe, and of heth.	*heath*
	This elde errour know we well enow:	
	I hafe myselfe convicte many of yow —	

	"Of your secte, I mene. How may ye for schame	
	Reherse of Jhesu that grete dobylnesse?	*duplicity*
1445	Summe men seyn that He had a dame	*mother*
	Whech was a mayde in very sothfastenesse	
	Aftyr the tyme that sche had suffred dystresse	
	Of chyldbyrth: this know all men a lye —	
	This lewyd doctrine is not worth a flye!	*i.e., silly*

	"Ye magnyfye Him for this cause alsoo:	
1450	Ye sey He roos fro deth to lyffe ageyn,	*rose*
	But of His disciples in sekyrnesse were there too	
	Whech went to the grave, as I herde Jewys seyn.	
	Thei stole the body ful pryvyly in a reyn,	*secretly during a storm*
1455	And than seyd thei her mayster was i-goo	
	Be very myracle, and thus seyd many moo."	

Chapter 22

	Onto these wordes, onto this blaspheme,	
	Answerd the mayde, with most goodely chere.	
	Sche seyd thus: "At my Lord of hevene	
1460	Toke I begynnyng of my conflycte here.[1]	
	A makere is there withouten any dwere	*creator; doubt*
	Ovyr all this worlde whech was or it began.	*before the world's creation*
	For, as I hafe provyd, Jubiter was but a man;	

---

[1] Lines 1459–60: *I began my disputation here by speaking of my Lord of heaven*

    "No more was Saturn, whech his fadyr is.

1465   Than syth thei were men and toke here begynnyng,   *had a beginning*

    Than must we ferther procede now, iwys,

    To seke Him whech befor this thing

    Was evyr in heven eterne regnyng.

    This same is Godd of whom now I preche,

1470   Ageyn all synnys most sovereyn noted leche,   *physician*

    "Spryng of all thing that evyr begynnyng hadde,   *Source*

    So is He called, in whom all thing is eke,   *the same*

    Of whom all good thing and no thing badde

    Procedyth newly bothe be day and be weke,   *every day and week*

1475   Be whom all creatures be thei wylde or meke   *tame*

    Are conserved, at Him thus I began —   *preserved*

    But if I dede, I were no wyse woman.   *Unless I did so*

    "Make no comparison betwyx your godd and myn,

    For my Godd hath made all thing of nowte,

1480   Eke youre goddis are not so goode as swyn —   *swine*

    Thei can not gruntyn whan hem ayleth owte!   *grunt; something ails them*

    As sore as ye in this matere hafe I sowte;   *diligently; sought*

    I fonde no trewth, therfore fro yow I flede.

    In trewer weyes ful sykir am I lede."   *securely*

1485   Thys man was thoo of these resones grete

    So troubled, he qwok betwyx ire and drede.   *quaked*

    Lett othir men now in this matere trete,

    For he hath done, he hath sowe his sede,   *sown; seed*

    A sikyr helpe whan there cometh grete nede.

1490   But God wold hafe him turned in this manere —

    His mervelous menes schul we nevyre lere.   *ways; fathom*

Chapter 23

    Anothyr clerk stode up thoo in hast.

    Onto the mayde he made swech evydens: *presented this argument*

    "All your wordes hafe ye not spent in waste.   *said in vain*

1495   I undyrstand full wele your grete eloquens.

    Ageyn oure goddis ye make this defens: *argument*

Ye sey her ymages whech we worchep here   *their*
May not fele, ne hafe no powere.

"Thys wote I wele — thei be but figures
1500   Representyng othir manere thing.
Lych to these fayre rych sepulcures
Whech betokyn in her representyng
That there is byryed duke or ellys kyng,   *is buried there*
So are these ymages toknes of goddis oure
1505   To whom we geve with hert gret honoure

"Not for her cause but for significacyoun   *not in themselves*
Of the worthy whom thei represent.
Therfor I answere to your replicacyoun,   *reply*
Servyng sumwhat now youre entent: *Agreeing with you somewhat*
1510   Thei that made hem nevyr othir wyse ment
To sett hem up but for this cause only —
That to hyere devocyoun men schuld go therby."[1]

Than seyde the mayde, "I wold ye schuld now schew
Of all these goddys whech that worthyest be.   *Which of these gods is worthiest*
1515   For as thei stande in your temple o rewe   *in a row*
I can perceyve in hem no dyvynyté
More in on than othyr, for your Saturn, pardé,
Whyl that he lyved was a fals traytoure —
Homycyde cruell, debatere and robboure.   *brawler*

1520   "His wyffe was a woman nye of that same vyce: *equally vicious*
Veniable, dispytous, chydere every tyde,   *Vengeful, mean, always complaining*
Of hir condycyon unstable and ful nyce.   *character; foolish*
There myght no man with hir no whyle abyde —   *remain for long*
Hir owyn chyldren kyllyd sche be hir syde.
1525   Jubiter was gelt of his fadyr Saturn, eke,   *was castrator of*
Banyched his lond, his herborow gan he seke.   *dwelling*

---

[1] *So that people should proceed through them to a higher devotion*

"His owyn syster Jubiter defouled thoo.

His fadyr aftyr banychid he owte of londe.　　　*he then banished*

These are the dedys of your goddys, loo!

1530　How may your lawe eternaly thus stonde

Whan it is bylyd on so brytyll bonde?　　　*built from such weak bonds*

Pluto was ravyscere of maydenes ful violentt;　　　*ravisher*

Venus was lecherows and also violent.

"Vulcane was cruell and yet was he cokholde;

1535　How schuld swech persones to ony Godhed prove!　　　*attain the status of gods*

Summe are yong, summe of hem are olde.

Cupyde encresyth in men that unclene love.

These grete vylonyes can ye nevyr fro hem schove.　　　*misdeeds; dissociate*

Of wychcraft nooted was your godd Mercurye,

1540　Maystir of charmes and of swech sorcerye.

"Youre godd Apollo, whan he was drunk of wyne

Than wold he jangyll in manere of prophecye,　　　*chatter as if he were prophesizing*

Ful sotyll lesyngys wold he thoo dyvyne　　　*subtle lies*

To hem that knew not his trescerye.　　　*treachery*

1545　Sumetyme soth sawed, sumetyme dyd he lye.　　　*he spoke truly*

These are your goddys whech that ye honoure —

Alle to vyces sett was her laboure.　　　*their energies were given to vice*

"Youre offeryngis, eke, thei be abhominable:

To summe goddys offyr ye swynys dunge;　　　*swine's dung*

1550　There comth noo mete befor yow at the table

Tyll youre godd hath awey the tunge.[1]

If all youre harlotrye thus openly were i-runge　　　*recited*

It wolde schame yow. Therfor, ye that be wyse

Fle this folye, drede the hye justyse."

1555　Thoo stode the man, afrayd as owte of mynde.

He cowde not speke to hir o word moo.

Oure blessed Lord his hert gan thoo bynde

Onto His servyce; therfor, let him goo

---

[1] Lines 1550–51: *No meat is served at your table / Until your god has been given the tongue*

Sitt and rest, as for that tyme with woo.   *unhappily for the time being*
1560 Thus schull thei stynt whan God wyl sey "pees";   *stop*
Of all wysdam He can sone make relees.   *an end*

Chapter 24

Anothyr clerke thouth deppere to procede.
He stode up thoo and this was his sentens:
"Of oure goddys ye schew the schamful dede;   *expose; deeds*
1565 Nothyng speke ye of her good provydens.   *wisdom*
We hafe in this matere ful mysty intellygens   *a very dim understanding*
Whech may not be comyn to every man,   *be conveyed*
But to yow, lady, so now as I can,

"Wyl I that comown, ryght for this entent: *impart*
1570 Because yourselve of wytt sotyll be
And for these lordes eke that be present,
These same motyves at this tyme meve me,   *considerations*
For I wyll tell now the most pryvy secré
Whech that we have in oure philosophye
1575 Towchyng the goddys and her progenye.

"Saturne the fyrst, whom ye so dyspreve,   *refute*
Him take we for tyme because he is olde,   *He represents time*
And tyme, pardé, aftyr oure beleve,   *according to our faith*
As for a godd amongis us now is holde.   *is considered a god*
1580 Jubiter the kyng, as the treuth is tolde,
He is take for fyre, and Juno eke his wyffe,
Sche is take for eyre that us gevyth lyffe.   *air*

"Thus are oure goddys in manere of allegorye
Resemble to natures whech that be eterne.   *Equated with natural elements*
1585 Than is oure feyth groundyd on no lye
But on swech thing whech is sempyterne.   *eternal*
Myn owne lady, ye sowt not well this herne   *examined; [intellectual] nook*
Whan ye blasphemyd oure goddys all o rowe.
I tell yow this; I wold all men it knowe."

1590 The lady answerd with sad avysement.
Sche seyd sche know his circumlocucyoun;   *what he paraphrased*
The Kyng of Thebes a book had hir sent
In whech sche fonde swech exposicyoun,
But sche halt it now but for abusyoun.   *considers; deceit*
1595 Yet these resones whech the man had schewyd
Be very resoun sche wyll prove hem lewyd.   *foolish*

For at the tale whech this man had tolde   *as this man spoke*
Gladed the emperour, tremelyng evyn for joye.   *trembling*
To speke than was he wax ful bolde:
1600 "Clerke," he seyd, "Saturne kepe thee fro noye!   *harm*
I trost this ladye wyll bere hir now more koye.   *demurely*
What sey ye mayde — where is youre answere?
If ye can owte, lete us now it lere."

The mayde seyd onto the mayster sone,   *replied; promptly*
1605 "Your schamful doctrine wold ye ful fayn hyde
With fygure and coloure, as ye are wone to done,[1]
But ye must ley these exposicyouns asyde.
Are not these planetys knowyn wondyr wyde?
May we not se hem whan thei schyne so clere —
1610 The sune, the mone, whych schyne onto us here?

"Thys wote we wele that thei be no men —   *know*
Why are thei grave thus of ston and of tre?
This errour is ful esy for to ken: *explain*
That men are thei not ne nevyr more schal be.
1615 In these figures than full fowle erre ye;   *images*
Ye worchep the schadow and leve the substauns.
Here is in yow a full grete varyauns.   *fickleness*

"Eke the planetys whech schyne thus above,
Thow thei schuld stand evyr and be eterne
1620 Yet can ye not with youre bokes prove
That thei hafe evyr before be sempiterne.   *always existed*

---

[1] *With rhetorical flourishes and ornaments, as you are accustomed to do*

If phylosophye were loked in his pryvy herne,
Ye schuld fynde there that planetys all be made.[1]
What wyl ye ferther in this matere wade?

1625   "If thei be made, than are thei creatures,
        And he that made hem, he is Godd alone,
        Ley hem in watyr all your mysty figures,   *Give up*
        For nowt are thei, neyther the stok ne stone.   *they are nothing*
        Onto that hye God loke ye make youre mone;
1630   Prey Him to send you of errour repentauns,
        Than have ye of treuth the very assurauns."

Chapter 25

        The phylosophres merveylyd of this answere,
        Of hir wytt and of hir eloquens.
        Thei that now in presens are there
1635   Herd nevyr before swech manere sentens —
        Sche can al thing of very experiens.
        A mastere stode up and spake thoo to hem alle:
        "I wold a supposyd," he seyd, "that the hevyn schuld falle

        "Rathere than woman swech sciens schuld atame.   *learning; master*
1640   Lete us leve, felawes, now oure elde scole,
        Geve entendauns at this tyme to this dame,   *Pay attention*
        For in this worlde in cunnyng stand sche sole.   *her knowledge is peerless*
        All oure lernyng wyll turne us to dole   *cause us grief*
        But if we folow as mech as we may
1645   To lerne the treuth whech schall lestyn ay.   *last forever*

        "Wherfore lete us lerne now of this mayde
        What that God is whech made thus all thing.
        With this matere hafe I be oft dysmayde,   *On this subject; frustrated*
        For I cowde nevyr with naturall arguyng
1650   Dyvyne so fere, and evyr oure stodyyng

---

[1] Lines 1622–23: *If you explored philosophy's secret recesses, / You would find that all the planets were created*

203

Hath be therto ful directe, as me semeth.   *directed*
I wyl beleve now as this lady demeth."   *says*

Thus is consentyd now all the cumpanye.
Thei wyll lere of hir, thei sey plat and pleyn,
1655   For it is above alle her phylosophye   *i.e., their philosophy cannot reveal*
What Lorde He is that made the wynde and reyne.
That there is swech on can thei wele i-seyne,   *a one*
But what He is or what is His name
This desyre thei to lerne now of this dame.

1660   The mayde eke was as glad as thei
To enforme hem in this same matere.   *inform*
Onto these men ful sadly gan sche sey,
"Syth that ye take the forme now of scolere,   *Since you take the attitude of pupils*
Ye are the redyere these mysteries for to lere.   *better prepared*
1665   But we wyll leve this Godhed for a tyme
And of the manhode a whyle wyll we ryme.

"Ye schall know fyrst that oo God is in heven,
Distinct in persones, as we beleve, thre:
Fadyr and Sune and Holy Gost ful evene.
1670   These same persones oonly oo God be.
Oure auctoures sey that if Godd had be
Oonly o persone than schuld not His holy blys
Be comounde to other so parfytly as it is,   *conveyed*

"For creature non myght receyve no swech: *comprehend*
1675   Therfore He ordeyned be His eterne counsayle
That thre persones in myght and nature lych   *alike*
In oo Godhed, to us ful gret mervayle,
Schuld be consederyd to mannys grete avayle;   *be seen; benefit*
And ech of other His substauns schuld thus take,
1680   Non lesse, non more; thus oure feyth we make.

"Of the thre persones, the secunde, whech is the Sune,
Cam down to erde here; He tok mankynde,   *assumed manhood*
For man had lost all that evyr was done   *lost all he had*
Whan he to God was fall so unkynde —   *behaved so unnaturally*

1685	He brake the precept with whech he gan him bynde	*God's commandment*
	Amongis the trees in the place of delyce	*delight*
	Whech that we clepe in bokes paradyce.	

	"And for there was no man able in erde therto	
	To make unyté betwyx God and man,	*reconcile*
1690	This was the cause that that Lorde dede soo.	
	He lyght to herde and in a yong woman,	*descended to earth*
	A clene maydyn, of flesch and bloode He nam.	*chose (took)*
	Therin He deyd to sle oure synnes alle.	*kill*
	This is the God on whom we Crysten calle."	

Chapter 26

1695	The mayster principale whech the wordis hadde	
	For hem alle at that same day and tyme	
	Of hir doctryne was ful joyful and gladde,	
	For God hath poyntyd in him a newe pryme.	*ordained; new beginning*
	Oure Lord Jhesu had purged him of his cryme,	*sin*
1700	Made him dysposed to his conversyoun.	
	But he mervelyth sore of this informacyoun.	*wonders greatly at*

	He seyd to the lady in ful fayre manere,	
	"O thing there is here in youre techyng	
	Whech I cannot conceyve it yet ful clere:	
1705	For God and man in her coupelyng	
	Be ful diverse, and yet sey ye this thing:	
	That bothe natures be joyned in oo persone	
	There was nevyr swych but if it be He alone,	

	"For if He be God, than must He be eterne,	
1710	If He be man, than is He coruptible;	
	A nature or persone whech is sempiterne	
	To sey of it that it is passible	*transitory*
	Semeth to me a ful grete insolible.	*contradiction*
	This is the mocyoun, lady, ye must declare,	*proposition; explain*
1715	For in this matere oure wyttys be but bare."	

Thus to this mocyoun answerd thoo the mayde,
"Ye must conceyve," sche seyde, "in your mynde
That these too natures in oure Lord Jhesu were layde
And coupled togedyr ageyn used kynde: *ordinary nature*
1720   Thus we of Him in solempne bokys fynde.
But the very prove of His werkys grete
Is ryght enow this matere for to trete,   *sufficient to settle this matter*

"For He that reysyde Lazare fro the grave
Where he had loy four dayes evene,   *lain*
1725   He that Petyr in the see dyd save   *sea*
And walkyd there as men do on a grene,   *lawn*
He that comaunded the wynd that was so kene   *sharp*
That he schuld cese and blow no more that tyde,   *it; time*
He that so mervelously onto heven gan glyde

1730   "Body and all, He was more than a man,
For be His Godhede wrowt He these mervayles.   *brought about*
Mech more thing now reherse I kan,
But I pase ovyr, gevyng to your assayles   *attacks*
Tyme and space. I pray God that youre entrayles   *hearts*
1735   He endew with grace that ye may know the treuth;
Of your dampnacyoun have I ful grete reuth.   *I would hate to see you damned*

"But all these werkys whech were so grete
Schew be reson that more than man was He.
Whan He the Jewys met ryght in the strete
1740   There schewyd He than His dyvynyté;
Thei durst not loke but fel down at his kne.
There myght no creature be resone do these werkys
But He were God, thus prove oure clerkys.

"And that He ete His mete, slepe, and went,
1745   Spak and drank, restyd and wery was eke —
This servyth ful pleynly to your argument   *answers fully*
In whech ye gan ful sotylly for to seke.
Youre answere hafe ye, if it may yow leke,   *if you please*
That these too natures whech in Him were
1750   Dyverse werkynges had whyll He was here.   *manifested themselves differently*

"Yet of your auctouris may we take wyttnesse.
Sybylle seyd mervelously in this matere: *Sybil*
'That holy God,' sche seyd, 'evyr be in blesse,
Whech schall be hankyd lech a thefe here   *hanged like a thief*
1755   Ryght on a tre and aftyr leyd on bere.'   *bier*
What wyll ye more what schuld I to yow say?
Onto this auctrix ye may nevyr sey nay,   *female authority*

"For as an auctoure admittede in your lawe   *as an acknowledged authority*
Is sche receyvyd, and pleynly to oure feyth
1760   Beryth sche wyttness in hir mysty sawe,   *vision (prophesy)*
For these too natures in oure Lord sche leyth: *attributes*
God He is full byssyd, as sche seyth,
And manhod it is that hyng upon the tre —
Oute of youre lawe cometh this auctoryté."

Chapter 27

1765   Anothyr mayster evene ful of eloquens,
Of curtesye eke, and a ful semely man,
Spak to this lady with full grete reverens.
He seyd hir wytt before her wyttes ran
So grete apace it cannot be ovyrtan,   *So far ahead; overtaken*
1770   But yet he prayed hir that he myght seye.
In his arguyng ful naturaly he toke the weye,

For nature, he seyd, be swech influens   *the flowing of such a medium*
Was so confermed that it myght not fayle.   *strengthened*
Every thing, therfore, that makyth resystens
1775   Ageyn nature ful sone wyll it qwayle.   *give way*
Withoutyn nature may nothing avayle,
Wherfor he wolde swech thing as sche shall preche
Be naturall resones hir thingis shuld she teche,

For harde it is to constreyn a mannes wil   *persuade someone*
1780   To trow a thing whech he cannot prove.   *believe*
Who shal beleve good thing or ellis il,
That same beleve must com of very love
And very trost whech is onto his hond.

Therfor this man desyrith that naturaly
1785 Hir conclusiones she prove now openly.

She seyd she wold with good entent,
So as hir wit wold serve hir for this tyme   *Insofar as*
And so as God of His grace hath sent
Onto hir knowlech at that day to dyvyne,   *impart*
1790 Ful fayn wold she now this maystir enclyne,   *persuade*
For she to Cryst cast hir him to drawe;
He shall no more trost now on his lawe.   *religion*

This same example put she to him tho,
Of body and sowle whech we bere abouth,
1795 How thei are joyned in on thus these too,
And on his hyd, the othir is sene withouth.   *one is hidden*
She seyd, "To all men it is ful grete douth
How that the sowle, whech that mevere is,   *mover*
Cam to the body whan he cam fro blys,   *when it (the soul) came from heaven*

1800 "What wey he cam or ellis in what hour
Whan to the body he cam it for to qweke   *infuse with life*
It is but foly to spend oure labour
Swech prevy thingis for to serge and seke.   *search*
Ye may leve this thing if ye like:
1805 That soule and body are joynyd now in fere   *together*
In what persone that ye se walke here.   *every living person*

"And if ye list not to beleve this thing,
Ye may leve but ye shall it nevyr i-knowe
The maner or tyme of this pryvy werkyng.
1810 Youre scole therto is yete ovyr lowe;[1]
Ye may wele bost of youre conyng and blowe,   *knowledge; brag*
But ye shal fayle whan ye com to the poynt —   *in the final analysis*
Oure Lord God hath hyd fro you that joynt.   *hidden; position*

---

[1] Lines 1807–10: *And if you do not want to believe this thing, / You may believe only [that] you shall never know it, / [Namely] the time and manner of this mysterious occurrence. / Your learning is too inferior to reveal it*

"Than sith ye may be no naturall weye
1815 Have the knowlech of these creatures here,
How shuld we of you now than sey
That ye shuld know thing above clere? *understand heavenly matters*
How schuld ye knowe that Lord that hath powere
Ovyr all thing? How schuld ye to Him gesse *speculate about him*
1820 Whan that ye may not know mech thing lesse?" *much lesser matters*

Chapter 28

Whan that this answere was gove thus to this man,
Ech man besyde that stod thoo aboute *bystanders*
Ful mervelosly chaunge thei began,
For thei that Cristen were, withouten doute,
1825 Whech to the maumentis befor tyme dede loute,
Now wayle thei sore with grete repentauns,
Demyng hemselve ful worthy grete penauns.[1]

Thei have remembred her God most of myth, *most powerful God*
And wher that a woman prechith constantly, *whereas*
1830 There thei forsake Him. "This thing goth no ryth, *is inappropriate*
That the freler kynd shall so stabyly *frailer sex*
Confesse oure feith, wher that more myty *stronger ones (i.e., men)*
Held her pees and dare speke rith nought":
Of the Cristen this was both cry and thought.

1835 The othir syde, thoo, that paynemes were, *pagans*
Thei sey hir resones and hir grete evydens
Whech stoyned the clerkis all that be there.
This put the puple in conceytis ful suspens, *confused the people*
For all her labour and all her grete expens,
1840 For this thing her reward shal be woo.
Grete murmur was there and summe begun to goo.

---

[1] Lines 1824–27: *For indeed those Christians / Who had just rendered service to the idols / Now wail out of deep repentance, / Judging that they deserve a severe penance*

Ovyr all this the emperour he is now woode.   *mad*
Onto the clerkis with full angry face
He cryed: "Be armes, bones, and be blode,   *By*
1845   It was a shame and a sory grace   *misfortune*
That fele clerkis gaderid in a place
Shulde be astoyned sodenly of a mayde!
Coward churles," rith thus to hem he seyde,

"Plucke up youre hertis; lete not oure lawe thus falle!
1850   Lete not oure goddis suffir thus this wronge —
But if ye do, the most part of you shall,   *otherwise*
Ere long tyme, by the necke shul be honge!
Speke, men, for shame; the tyme is not longe —
It passith fast and we do no note;   *accomplish nothing*
1855   Me thinkith ye stand evene as men that dote!"   *fools*

Chapter 29

Thoo stode up with a new motiffe   *argument*
A freshe clerke, maystir Apollimas.   *young*
So aferde was he nevyr in all his lyffe
Of no matere ne of no dyvers cas   *adverse circumstance*
1860   So as of this matere now he fesed was.   *disturbed*
But thus sayd he than softly to the mayde:
"In youre declaryng, lady, me thought ye sayde

"Too sundry thingis; if we considre weele,   *different*
Contradiccion ful sone in hem shal be founde:
1865   Youre Lord Jhesu, whech is know full weele,
As ye sey, He made this world so rounde.
Adam and Eve He formed fro the ground,
And all othir thing whech that have substauns —
It was made, ye sey, be His ordinauns.

1870   "Ageyn you now thus I will replye,
Provyng ontreuth in youre marred feyth,   *problematic*
I have made rekenyng whech may not lye,   *an infallible calculation*
Amongis oure stores what ony man seyth.   *histories*
The byrth of Jhesu full treuly oure booke leyth,   *sets forth*

210

1875	For He was born undir Octavyane,	*Since; Octavian*
	At litil Bethlem in a lewde lane;	*Bethlehem; lowly*

"It is not fully yete thre hundred yere
Sith that youre Jhesu was of His modir bore.
How dare ye than in swech presens here
1880 Afferme of thing that was so long before
That He this worlde shuld make or restore?
How myth He make thing whech thousandis fyve
Had here duracion er that He toke lyve?   *existed*

"This is my motiff — an answere I desyre   *proposition*
1885 In pleyn langage, without distinction.   *rhetorical tricks*
This sympil puple have ye set on fyre
With youre crafty circumlocucion!
Answere in schort to this conclusion;
Than schal I sey that ye be that mayde
1890 Swech anothir no man hath assayde."   *encountered*

Chapter 30

Thus spak the lady onto the clerk ageyn:
"Alle youre groundis, sere, in youre arguyng   *premises*
Have take oo partye and, schortly for to seyn,   *considered*
Lefte the othir; wherfore the concludyng
1895 Fayleth ful foule now in your rekkenyng:
His manhod counte ye and His birth temporal
And not that birth whech is eternal,

"For this temporal birth, as ye seyde late,   *as you just said*
Was now before us not many yeeres goo,   *past*
1900 As to comparison of the largere date   *i.e., His existence as God*
It may be counted but for a yeer or too.
But of this mater the mistery wil I ondoo,
For of this same have ye grete mervayle,
As me semeth rith be youre assayle.   *to judge from your attack (lines 1862-90)*

1905 "At the gynnynge first schul ye undirstande   *To begin with*
That God eternally hath evyre oure Jesu be,   *Jesus has always been God*

211

Makere and schapere of all thing that is levande,
Thus is He called and thus beleve we.
But now of late dayes, of His charité,   *Recently, out of charity,*
1910 He took oure kende to oure redempcion,   *assumed our nature to redeem us*
In whech kende He suffred passion.

"For the manhod was not able to doo this thing   *Because; i.e., redeem*
And the Godhed mith not suffre swech desese,   *i.e., death*
Wherfore of these too He made a coupeling,
1915 The Faderes offens thus for to plese,   *atone for the offense to His Father*
The develes power thus for to fese.   *rout*
In Godhed and manhed He took this batayle,   *engaged*
For manhed alone mith not avayle.

"Thus, for His Godhed hath be eternally,
1920 Therfore sey we that He made al thing
Thurgh power of the same, and eke that body
Whech was conceyved of a mayde yinge,   *young*
That same body on the crosse hyng,
That same body at Bethlem was bore,
1925 For the Godhed hath be eternally before."

Whan sche had sayde this glorious vers,
The man stood stoyned and marred in mende.   *thunderstruck*
Noon of hir wordes coude he revers;   *refute*
Thei passed of his lernyng al the kende.   *capacity*
1930 Resons ageyn hir coude he noon fynde,
But thus seyde he tho openly with cry:
"As ye beleve, lady, soo beleve I."

Chapter 31

Anothir maystir made hir this motif:
"Ye preche of Crist," he seith, "and of His dede,   *death*
1935 How He for man thus frely lost His lif
For to brynge him to that hevenly mede.   *reward*
His deth, ye sey, awey tho gan lede   *took away*
Alle maner synne, the power eke of helle
With His deth that Lord gan than felle.   *defeated*

1940   "Mith not that Lord with His real power
        A maistred the devel and putte him soo to flith?   *Have overcome*
        Mith He not a sente an aungell or a messager?   *have*
        What was the cause that He Himself wolde fith,   *fight*
        Suffre swech passion and lese soo His rith?
1945   If He was myty, why suffred He that wrong?
        Answere my tale for it is nowt long!

        "If He Himselve mith not redresse this thing,
        Than was it foly to take it on hande,
        And if He were, as ye seye, soo myty a king,
1950   There mith no powere than ageyn Him stande.
        Youre prophete seyde that He with yrn wande   *iron rod*
        Alle His enemyes schulde bothe bete and bynde.
        In swiche sufferaunce me thinkith He was blynde."   *He was foolish to suffer so*

        "Youre motif, sir," seyde the noble qween,   *proposition*
1955   "Hath grete colour, but yet I voyde it thus: *seems plausible; refute*
        As I have lerned in bookes that I have seen,
        Oure Lord Crist, oure Savyour Jesus,
        List for to feyten with the devel for us   *Desired to fight*
        And ovyrcome him in swech kende as he toke.   *nature*
1960   For the synne of Adam, if we wil loke,

        "Must been redressed oonly be mankynde,
        And because there were amongis men non able —
        For in all erde myth He than non fynde
        Man so clene, so parfyth, so profithable   *valuable*
1965   As Adam was whil that He was stable
        In blessed paradyse or he dede offens —   *before*
        Therfor oure Lord with His fleshly presens

        "Toke this jornay and deyed on a tre,   *expedition*
        That evene as synne in the tre was doo,
1970   Rith so on the tre deth suffered He.
        It was convenient He shuld fyte so: *appropriate*
        In the tre was joy bore and in the tre woo;
        Woo be Sathan, joy be oure Lorde Jhesu —
        Out of that tre a blyssyd frute grewe!"

1975 Ther stood up than with ful bold face
A grete clerke thei callyd Alfragan —
He thought to have worchip in that place.   *gain honor*
His apposayle rith thus he began: *examination*
"Youre Jhesu Crist, He is both God and man,
1980 As ye sey, lady, but ley that osyde
As for a space — lete that matere abyde.

"Ye Cristen put evyr in youre posicioun   *hold*
That there be namoo goddes but on.   *no more than one god*
But if youre owne booke come to revolucion,   *is examined*
1985 I trow oo God shal not be found there alone.
I red in a Crysten prophete not long agone —
I wot not veryly yet what ye him calle —
Thus spekth he that ye be goddes alle.   *you are all gods*

"Whom mente he here in this pluralité
1990 But God whech ye singulere confesse?
Betwix these too is no neutralité,   *These two views cannot be reconciled*
But be thei more goddis or be thei lesse,
Youre owne bokes of hem bere witnesse
That many be there and moo than on —
1995 Lete se what wey that ye will now gon.   *which position you will adopt*

"Ye put to us here a grete God of hevene
Whech hath a Son ye sey hith Jhesu,
And in youre bokes fynd we full evene
Of anothir god both juste and trewe —
2000 Thei calle him Baal; I trow ye him knewe.
Thre hundred prophetis onto his servyse
Were endewid there, full sad men and wyse.   *committed*

"How may ye sey thanne that God is but on?   *there is only one God*
How may ye forbarre oure opynyon?   *reject*
2005 If that youre God be regnand thus alone,   *ruling*
Why speke youre bokes of swech divysion?
Whi may not Jupiter make his conjunction

With Juno, his wiff, sith there be goddis fele?[1]
Youre resones, lady, avayle not a rake stele." *are not worth a rake-handle*

2010 "Ye must conceyve, sere," seyd the mayde, *understand*
"That oure Scripture in his mysty speche *its veiled*
Hath many figures, if thei be assayde. *examined*
Oure Lord God is sumtyme callyd a leche, *doctor*
Sumtyme a justise and full of wreche, *wrath*
2015 Sumtyme a fader all ful of love.
Swech sundry predicates in him wil prove *designations*

"The sundry effectis that in Him be. *capacities*
Wherfor I telle you, ser, if ye wil here,
Of oure feyth a ful grete verité.
2020 Ye may considre now and ye wil lere,
Goddes are there non ne nevyr more were
But on alone, Whech made erde and hevene,
Hayle, reyne, wynd, thundir, and levene. *Hail, rain; lightning*

"And be nature is He God regnyng thus alone,
2025 But yet of His godnes He hath to him chose *generosity*
Certeyn personys to dwelle in His wone; *live with Him*
Thoo calleth He goddes, as I suppose.
This that I sey now is no fals glose *commentary*
But folowith of the texte, if ye take hede, *derives from the text (Scripture)*
2030 For there that ye now on this wise gan rede *in this manner*

"'I sey ye be goddis,' there folowith thus,
'And sones of Him that syttith hyest.'
This is a grete distinction, ser, amongis us
Of nature and adopcion, whech is the best: *Between*
2035 Adopcion we sey is but as a gest, *like being a guest*
For he is chose in rith be fre will;
But naturall regnyng hath a hier skyll, *greater entitlement*

---

[1] Lines 2007–08: *Since there are so many gods [referred to in Christian books], why cannot Jupiter and Juno, his wife, be counted among them?*

      "For who so regnyth naturaly in ony place,

      He may not be put oute but he have wrong,   *without being wronged*

2040   And he that chosyn is, he comth in be grace.   *invited*

      Myn answere wil I bregge and make not longe,   *curtail*

      For catch now this conceyt and in youre wit it fong: *examine*

      That naturaly God regneth al alone

      Whech of His goodnesse hath called to His trone

2045   "Certeyn folkis rith of His good grace,

      Whech goddis we calle because thei have blys: *are in heaven*

      Thus ar thei with Him evyr and se His face,

      Regne ther in joy whech may nevyr mysse —   *fail*

      There are thei tretyd rith as childirn His.

2050   This is the entent of that auctorité.

      Anothir thing eft alegge ye   *you further allege*

      "Of Baal, that god, and of his servauntis alle

      But no thing to purpos is that ye conclude.   *your conclusion has no merit*

      Oure Scripture rehersith thei dede him so calle

2055   Thoo same prophetis of his similitude.   *likeness*

      Rede bettir that booke of thoo dyvynouris rude,

      For there shal ye fynd that thei dampned were

      For her fals beleve all that were there."[1]

Chapter 32

      The maystir avisyd him and than cryed loude,

2060   "This mayde wil evyr lede us, seres, we are caut

      In oure artes, be we nevyr so proude.

      A newe maystresse, sekirly, have we laut;   *got*

      All oure lernyng as now avaylith naut.

      Therfor I sey, as for me, I geve it up —

2065   This lady hath drunke of a hier cupp

---

[1] Lines 2056–58: *Read that book (Scripture) more attentively and you will see that those ignorant prophets were damned for their false beliefs, every last one of them*

"Of prevyer secres than evyr we coud fynd: *more profound*
Sche passyth Plato, she passeth philosophie,
Sche spekith of Him that autour is of kynd.
That she seyth, I wote wele, is no lye;
2070   Wherfor of hert enterly thus I crye,   *wholeheartedly*
I can nomore — I wil turne to hir feyth
And leve myn elde, what any man seyth.   *no matter what*

"Ye shul do so eke, be my consent,   *in my opinion*
For o God I knowlech and non but Him alone,   *acknowledge*
2075   Thow I seyd nought, evyr have I so ment.   *I always believed this*
Lete us submytt us therfore to His trone:
I am converted; I sey for my persone   *resolve*
I schall nevyr berke ageyn that deyté.   *bark*
In this matere, seres, what sey ye?"

2080   Thei cryed alle comoursly with oo voys   *(see note)*
That thei consent to his conclusyoun.
O God confess thei, whech thei calle Noys;   *Greek:* nous/noos *mind*
What he comandeth, of nede it must be don.   *necessarily*
But yett her conceytes wyll thei uttyr soon
2085   Of othir thinges longyng to this crede.
To telle the rumore, I trow it is no nede,   *report the talk*

Whech in the puple is encresyd this tyde.   *among; resonates at this time*
"Alas!" thei sey, "What lyffe hafe thei ledde,
Oure grete clerkis whech are know so wyde.
2090   It were as good thei had loy in bedde,   *lain*
Whan thei teche thing whech must be fledde,   *abandoned*
Whych thing is holde but for a vanyté!"
The lordes eke there aftyr her degré

Dysputed this mater and beet it up and down: *beat*
2095   "No Godd but on?" thei seyd, "What is than Saturn?"
Eche to othir ful pryvyly thus dede rowan: *whisper*
"Fro these maumentys goode is that we turn,
Lete us despyce hem and with oure fete hem spurn,   *feet*
For this falshede have we folowyd to longe."
2100   This was the noyse than there hem amonge.

217

The emperour lokyth, but I trow he is wrothe:
"Fy on feynt harlotys that thus rendyth oure lawe!"   *weak knaves; destroy*
Thus seyd he than, he thowt his lyffe full lothe   *hateful*
That any mayden clerkys schul thus drawe,   *convince*
2105   That sche schuld be wyser in hir sawe;   *speech*
This grevyth him sore, but yet in his grevauns
Stod up a clerke whych with his dalyauns   *talk*

Seyd he wold prove be reson naturale
That mech thing towchyd was full ontrewe: *matter touched upon*
2110   "O persone eterne and eke mortale:
This doctrine," he seyd, "was come on thee newe."   *recently*
But the same resones that othir dyd sewe   *arguments that others put forth*
Rehersyth myn auctour, as he doth ful ofte.
I suffyr thoo levys to lye styll ful softe.   *I will skip over those pages*

2115   Lete othir men here hem that love nugacyoun,   *trifling*
For othir many materes mote com on hande.   *be treated*
I wyll rehers fyrst the grete disputacyoun   *debate*
In whych that this lady feythfully gan stande
With mayster Aryot, thorowoute that lande
2120   Most famose man noysed in that tyme.   *by reputation*
Of this matere wyll we now ryme.

Chapter 33

Thys Ariot was chose be comoun asent
To dyspute with hir, to loke, if that he may,
Dystroy hir feyth and all hir fundament.   *the foundation [of her faith]*
2125   On him hafe thei put now all this affray.   *contest*
Now schal be sene who schal have the day:
If he be convycte, thei wyll yelde hem alle;
If he be victoure, than wyll the revers falle,

For victores be thei than be his conquest.
2130   He stod up full solemply, with sobyr chere,
Commendyng the lady as him thowt best.
Than seyd he to hir in this manere:
"Many thingys hafe be rehersyd here.

218

I herd all and yet I held my pees.
2135 But now is this matere thus sett douteles.

"It is put in us too all this thing to trete,   *It is now up to us to settle everything*
Oure Lord Godd send us good spede: *luck*
If so befall that I, with argumentis grete
Or ellys with auctoryté, that I may yow leede
2140 From all your feyth and fro your fekyll crede,   *false belief*
Than have we wun, and if that ye lede me,
Than have we do, for victoure thoo are ye."   *Then we are through*

His fyrst questyoun, as I undyrstande,
Was of too natures whech we in Cryst rede,   *understand to be*
2145 Whech matere before have be in hande,   *we have covered before*
And for that cause me thinkyth it no nede
With swech prolixité oure book ferther to lede.
Turne and rede, ye that wyll it renewe.   *review*
Anothyr matere this phylosophre gan pursewe:

2150 Of Crystys Incarnacyoun, how that it myght be,
And how He in Bethlem thus born was.
Eke all this matere, as thinkith me,
Aforn in his werk this man dede it tras.   *my author covered before*
Wherfore fro all these thus schortly I pas,
2155 Supposyng that this same prolixité
Wolde make men wery of redyng to be.   *make people tired of reading*

Yete anothir mater touchid he to the mayde:
Of oure Ladies clennes in hir concepcion.
He had ful grete merveyle, as he seyde,
2160 Sith the synne of Adam in his progression
Was gove to mannys flesshe as possession,
How myth she have clennes and maydenhed
Whan she cam of that corrupt seede?

The mayde answerd rith thus to his tale:
2165 "Thing that is foule oure Lord may make clene;
He is very medecyn ageyn all oure bale.
His wondirful werkis are hard forto sene,   *understand*

219

But be ensaumples we may prove, I wene,
That this conjunction of mayde and of man
2170   Withoute ony synne this Lord thus began.

"Fro the seed first of all mankynde,
It was so corrupt, He preservyd this mayd —
It had ellis ful mech be ageyn kynde
But if hir soule had be arayde
2175   With vertues grete and no thing afrayd
With no vyce of synne or velonye.
Thus dede this Lord that sittith thus hye.

"Ferthermore, whan He cam to that herbourgage,   *dwelling (Mary's body)*
His comyng was lich the sune schynyng bryth;
2180   Lich to the glas I lykne that maydenes cage: *womb*
The sune schynyth theron with bemes lyght
And thorow it goth, as we se in syght,
Yet is the glas persed in noo manere.   *pierced*
So ferde that Lord whan He cam down here.

2185   "Thus was she clene in hir concepcion,
Thus hath she receyvyd the Godhed of blys,
Yet was she clenner in His carnacion,   *conception*
Of whech clennes shall she not mys.   *lose*
This must ye beleve, sere, if ye wil be His.
2190   Than shul ye know that ye nevyr knewe;
In my behestis ye found me nevyr untrewe."   *promises*

Chapter 34

Anothir qwestion mevyd this man that tyme,   *raised*
Replying sore ageyn hir declaracion.
It is ful hard swech thingis forto ryme,
2195   To uttir pleynly in langage of oure nacion,
Swech straunge doutes that long to the Incarnacion.   *mysteries; pertain to*
But that myn auctour toke swech thing on hand,   *since; undertook*
And yete his langage unneth I undirstande,   *barely*

220

	Wherfor with othir auctouris I enforce him thus,	*fortify*
2200	Whech spoke more pregnantly as in this matere,	*clearly*
	For ageyn the byrth of oure Lorde Jesus	
	And His concepcion argued thoo this sere:	
	"Youre oppynyon sett ye all in mere,"	*you bungle hopelessly*
	Thus seyd this man onto this lady mylde,	
2205	"For ye rehers who that God and childe	

	"Both togedir, coupled in oo persone,	
	Was youre Jesu, and eke ye thus confesse	*acknowledge*
	That this myracle dede He not alone,	
	But it was do be all thre, I gesse.	
2210	This is youre feyth, to this ye you professe,	
	That be the Fader, the Goost, and eke the Sune	
	Wrought was thus this Incarnacion.	*the Incarnation was effected*

	"Whi shall we not than of youre wordis conclude	
	That Fader and Sun and Holy Gost in fere,	*together*
2215	Sith that Thei be all of o similitude,	*one likeness*
	That ech of Hem flesshe and blood tooke here.	
	Thre sundry men than are Thei, withouten dwere,	
	And eke o God — how acordith this tale?	*how can this make sense?*
	All a wrong me thinkith wryhith the male,	*things turn out (lit., the bag turns)*

2220	"For ye sey eke that but on was incarnat,	*incarnated*
	On and no mo, and that was Jhesu youre Lorde.	
	Therto the Fader put ye in that astate	*condition*
	That He did this.[1] How may this acorde?	
	Sith that He wrout this of youre owne record,	*did; by your own account*
2225	Than was He joyned on that same werke —	
	That it thus folowyth perceyveth every clerke."	

	This motif preysid the qween with the best.	*highly*
	Sche seyd onto him, "Sere, ye lacke nothing	
	That longith of vertu to youre soules rest	
2230	But feyth alone. I pray that hevyn kyng	

---

[1] Lines 2222–23: *Moreover, you say that He (the Father) did this (the Incarnation)*

That He may touch you with sum pryvy merkyng
That ye may knowe whech is the very truth,
But if He did it were ellis grete reuth.   *Unless He did; pity*

"As mech as Nature may, she hath you taught —
2235   She coude no farder in hir wey procede;
But the wisdam of God, that may naught
Because of Nature, lerne this as youre crede.   *Be derived from Nature*
Yete as I can I will you mekely lede
Onto oure scole and telle of this matere
2240   The exposicion, if ye will it lere.

"Thus seyn oure bokes: To the Faderes astate   *condition*
Longith powere, whech we belevyn alle,
And to the Sone longith thus a parte
Whech we callen wisdam. The worlde round as a balle
2245   And hevyn eke also whech may not falle
Were made in Him. To the Gost longith goodnes.
This is oure scole withouten more or lesse.

"Than folowith thus that the Fader all thing
Made in His wisdam; it was ful convenient   *appropriate*
2250   That be that same grete reformyng
Of all mankynde, whech with synne was shent,   *ruined*
Shuld be redressyd. Lo, this is Her entent.   *plan*
That provyth be feyth and be demostracion
That most to the Sone perteynyth the Incarnacion

2255   "As in praktyke, but the sond and the provydens
As the menes of mercy whech were there doo,
Tho longen to the Trynyté[1] — o God in existens,
Thre in persones, we discryve Hem soo.
Example, sire, may we put thertoo,

---

[1] Lines 2253–57: *It is shown by faith and logic / That the Son was responsible for implementing the Incarnation, / But the grace and providence that conveyed mercy through the Incarnation, / Those were attributable to the Trinity as a whole*

2260	As putten oure clerkys in her bokes wysse,	
	Whech were wretyn with ful good avysse.	
	"Davyd, he seyd, whan he thristid sore	
	He desyred sore to drynke of that well	
	Whech stood in Bethlem where he was bore.	
2265	He sent thre prynces, soth for to telle,	
	Thorow all the hoost of Philestis so felle.	*Philistines; cruel*
	Thei browth this water with parell to the kyng —	*at great risk*
	On of hem in a basnet bare this thing.	*vessel*
	"All had thei labour egal, as I wene,	
2270	And yet on bare the vessell and no moo.	
	This same figure oure clerks thus remene:	*interpret*
	That thowe the Fader and the Goost both too	
	Wrought this thing and ordeyn it shuld be soo,	
	Yete was the bordeyn in oure Lorde alone,	*burden on*
2275	Jhesu, I mene, the Sone the secund persone."	

Chapter 35

	Aftir this had thei ful grete comunicacion	*long discussion*
	Of the synne of Adam and of the serpente,	
	Enterfered with spechis, but dilatacion	*Full of speeches; amplification*
	As me thinkith, longith noth to lyffe presente —	*is not relevant to this life*
2280	It occupieth ny all the Newe Testament,	
	That myth it here if that hem list.	*Whoever wishes can hear about it*
	Wherfor myn entent I wold that ye wist:	
	I love no long tale, evyr hangyng in on,	*dragging on*
	Wherfor as of this boke I wil make an ende	*Therefore*
2285	Right in this chapter; me thinkith it long agone	
	Sithen I began this boke for to bende	*direct*
	Onto youre eres and onto youre mende.	*mind*
	Knowith weel first that this noble qwene	
	Hath concluded these maystires thus bedene,	*overcome*
2290	And in speciall Ariot, for that he coud replye	
	It avaylith as nouth — his witte is but bost.	*vanity*

223

	He standith amasid and nothing hardy	*no longer daring*
	To spekyn o worde; thus can the good Goost	*i.e., Holy Spirit*
	Gadir to Him all this wisse hoost	
2295	And maykyn hem to trowe as the mayden taught,	
	For all her philosophye thus are thei caught.	*their*

	For aftir thei had spokyn of the filiacion	
	Of Cryst oure Lord, wheyther there were too or on,	
	And eke the Holy Gost with His procession,	
2300	Wher that this fayled, answere was non.[1]	
	This same Ariott stod stille as a stone,	
	For the Holy Trinité she provyde him be kynde,	*nature*
	He coud fro the resones no wey fynde.	

	Onto his felaws thus full lowd he seyd,	
2305	"We have gon wrong evyr into this day.	*until*
	Blissid be God and this holy mayde	
	That to us have tauth a trew way.	
	Sey ye as ye leke, I can not sey nay,	
	For o God I beleve, whech is in blys.	*heaven*
2310	I leve on Jhesu eke, whech His Son is,	

	"And I leve on the Gost, knyte of Hem too.	*joined with*
	I leve that this Jhesu deyed for my sake;	
	Thus were oure synnes be Him clensid soo.	
	Onto His handis my soule I betake,	*commit*
2315	Prayng Him hertily that fro the fendes blake	
	He now defend me, that I not dampned be:	
	This is my crede, felawis, what sey ye?"	*creed*

	Thei answerd all that thei had now found	
	Thing thei had south all her lyve dayes.	*sought*
2320	This will thei kepyn as a trew ground,	*hold as truth*
	For thei had walkid many perlous weyes,	

---

[1] Lines 2297–2300: *There was nothing to do after they failed to perturb her when they spoke of the descent of Christ, whether there were two or one [persons in the flesh], and of the emanation of the Holy Spirit*

With veyne argumentis jangelyng evyr as jayyes.   *bickering like jays*
Now will thei levyn it and to Crist turne;
With Aristotill nen Ovide will thei nomore sojorn,   *nor*

2325 But put hem in the mercy of oure Lord Jhesu,
Prayng this mayde that sche be mene   *intercede*
To purchas pardon of her feyth untrewe   *their*
That thei so long shuld it susteyne.[1]
Thei fellen on knees, these clerkys all bedene,
2330 Crying long, with ful grete devocion,
"O Jhesu Crist, for Thi swete passion,

"Have mercy upon us, forgefe us oure trespas.
Deme us not, Lorde, aftir oure mysdede.   *Judge*
As Thu art petous, graunt us of Thi grace,   *merciful*
2335 Of Thi protection have we ful grete nede.
We wil don oure diligens for to lern Youre crede,   *apply ourselves*
To maynten it and susteyne with all oure myth —
There shall nevyr man bryngen us in othir plyght."   *condition (religion)*

Thus are thei convertid; this counsell is i-doo.
2340 Oure boke is at an ende, a new we will begynne.
It is ful convenient that we shuld do soo.
God and Seynt Kateryn, kepe us oute of synne
And send us the hey weyes hevyn blys to wynne,   *means to earn heaven*
Wher we may dwellyn and lokyn on that face   *i.e., Christ's face*
2345 Whech gladith all men that ben in that place.   *delights*

---

[1] Lines 2327–28: *For having supported so long their false religion*

Book 5

[The martyrdom of the philosophers and of Katherine]

Prologue

Now is come oure leyser and oure space
In whech we may — aftir oure grete labour
Of other materis, now we have grace —
Turne ageyn and tast the swete savour

5   Of this clene virgine, of this wele savoured flour,
Whech with fyve braunchis grewe thus here in erde: *branches*
The first, the secund, the thrid, and the ferde

Have ye perseyvyd if ye have red alle;
Now shall the fyft be schewid unto youre syght,
10   For now me lyst this lady a rose to calle,
Of fyve braunches full preciously i-dyth.   *richly composed*
The rede coloure that shon in hir so bryght,
That was hir martirdam. The fyve leves grene
Betokne hir lyffe, thus distincte, I wene,

15   In dyvers bokes, like as we have dyvysyd   *as we have set out*
Beforn this tyme; and now this is the last.
These fyve leves, rith thus are thei sysyd   *arranged*
That on the stalke thei cleven wondir fast;   *cling*
The reed floures kepe thei fro the blast   *protect; wind*
20   Or thei hemselfe thus lateth hem abrode,   *wide open*
And aftir that thei make here than abode

Even undir the same swete floures —
Betokynyng that hir liffe was sprede
With martirdam and with scharp schoures   *afflictions*
25   Whech for Crist both suffered and dede,
For in divers bokes, as I have oftyn rede,

Martirdam hath a suffereyn dignyté   *sovereign*
Above all vertues whech that gostly bee.

Thus grew this rose oute of the thorny brere   *briar*
30   Whan that this martir of hethen was bore.
I will declare yete, if ye will here,
Why that these leves clevyn so sore:
Thre of hem are berdyd and noo more,   *fuzzy*
And too stand nakyd withouten dagge or berde —   *points hanging down; fuzz*
35   Thus are thei wont to growen in oure yerde.

These fyve leves, as I seyd wolate,   *lately*
Betokenes these bokes whech we haven in hand:
Too of hem expresse the tyme and the date
In which this lady, as I undirstande,
40   Leved as hethen and so dede al hir land.
Therfor are thei naked in her kynde,
Expressyng thus this ladies levyng blynde.

Blynd I calle hir whill she was in that lyffe,
Knew not Criste baptem, ne had non take,
45   Of hevynly thinges litil inquisitiffe —   *curiosity*
Hir elde oppynyones had she noth forsake.
Fro this blyndnes Crist made hir awake
In oure third boke, rith as we seyd before —
It nedith not as now it rehers nomore.

50   The othir thre with berdis are so i-growe   *so fuzzy*
That leves of vertu men may hem calle.
To all the world opynly thus it is knowe
That she hath grace whech may not falle.
So are hir leves endewyd and evyr shall:
55   Evyr are thei grene and evyr more shall bee,
Regnyng with Cryst in very felicyté.

And in hir honour now I will procede
To myn fyfte boke, in whech I will speke
Of hir martirdam, so as the story will lede —
60   How God the quelys for His cause dede breke   *wheels*

And on the puple took full grete wreke.   *vengeance*
Thus shall it be translate now new fro Lateyn,   *newly*
To the worchip of God and of Seynt Kateryn.

Chapter 1

Whan these clerkys had made thus her compleynt   *lamentation*
65   Of all her errour and wrong credulyté,
The emperoures hert for sorow gan to feynt,
For now is none that dare speke but he —
In all these materis convicte is this mené.   *company*
Wherfor with angry chere and wordys full dispitous   *contemptuous*
70   Thus seyd he to hem as he stode in that hous:

"Fy on youre scole! We had ful grete trost
Ye schuld a made wele all that was amysse.   *have remedied*
All oure expens, all oure consayle is loste!   *purpose*
Ye have reved me of this worldly blys —   *robbed*
75   Noth worldly but gostly, for I seyd amysse —   *misspoke*
It is gostly joye and longith to oure feyth.
Here ye noth now what that the puple seyth?

"Thei seyn a maydyn hath convicte in this place
Fyfty clerkis in this world non lych.   *unmatched*
80   Thei sey thei wollyn the same feyth purchace —
Thus sey thei all, the pore and the rych.
Wold God ye had be byryed in a dych
Whan ye cam heder, for now all is lost:
Labour and connyng, rydyng and mechil coost.   *travel*

85   "Lete now youre prudens make yow a new corage,   *renew your spirits*
That ye lese noth youre cunnyng and youre fame —
Thinke what I hyth you, worchep and wage;   *promise you*
Lyft up youre hertis, men, for very shame!
Beth noth aferd, for than ye lesen youre name.   *reputation*
90   Speke to this woman, with reson bere hir down,
Than are ye worthy in scyens to bere the crowne.

228

"Ye stand all hertles. Wher is youre cunnyng goo
That been astoyned with nature femynyne?
Be holy Saturne, I wold a supposed soo   *have*
95   That on of you myth a ben for swech nyne.[1]
Ye faren as ye were bound with lyne: *rope*
What answere will ye gevyn of youre conyng,
Whech that at nede avaylith nothing?"   *in need*

Chapter 2

The grettest of hem and leder eke,   *leader also*
100   The same Ariot of whech I spake before,
Onto the emperour thus he gan to speke:
"Onto thi courte come we, lesse and more,
Thi goddes servyse to gefe and restore,
And, as I wene, of all the est syde
105   Of all this world to seke fer and wyde

"Shuldist noth fynd swech a pykyd cumpany   *distinguished*
In gramer, rethoricke, and thoo artes alle,
But speciall in naturall philosophie
Are we endewid. But to sciens whech thei calle
110   Theologie, to that coud we not falle   *come into the possession of*
Till that this lady bryngyth us to induction —
Evyr blyssyd be she for hir good instruction!

"What manere man that wolde or this tyme
Dispute with us be reson and auctorité,
115   His demonstracyouns cowde us neyther trappe ne lyme,   *ensnare*
But he was caute for all his sotelté.
He pased not fro us withoute a velonye —   *humiliation*
This was oure usage ryght than for victorye,
So loved we these wordes of veynglorye.

120   "Now it is turned, oure fortune and oure chaunce,
Oure appetyte eke — I wote nevyr how it is went.   *desire*

---

[1] Lines 94–95: *I would have thought / That one of you could handle nine of her*

This mayden makyth that we falle in traunce;
Oure conyng now, it semyth that it is spent.
Sche spekyth of Godd whech that was hangen and rent
125 And gostly spech hath sche browte to place;
Naturall scyens hath in this matere no space.

"Therfore can we as in this solemnyté
Speke ryght nowte, but resones make sche grete.
Hir prechyng paseth all oure carnalyté,   *lecture allegorically*
130 For whan I fyrst thus mystly herd hir trete
In my body my bowelles sore gune bete,
For very rebuke that I hir langage   *shame*
Cowde not conceyve. Wherfore, syre, alle your wage,

"Alle your rewardes whech ye profyrd us,
135 We refusen; youre goddes and youre lawe
We renunce for the love of oure Lorde Jhesus.
Schew ye summe resone pleynly that we may knawe
If that your goddes with her rowe pawe   *their rough hands*
Have othir evidens that ye can preve this tyde,   *demonstrate*
140 For in this errour we wyll no lengere abyde.

"Cryst, Goddes Sone, that with His blyssyd passyoun
Bowt all mankynde, here we now confesse.   *Redeemed; acknowledge*
Onto His mercy ryght with goode devocyoun
We now commend us, the more and eke the lesse.
145 Slee and flee, brenne and put in dystresse,
Other feyth schall thu nevyr plant
Into oure hert, for nothing now we want

"But of baptyme, this holy sacrament.
God, as He bowte us, on us have mercye."
150 Thus seyden his felawys all with oon entent,   *unanimously*
"There is no Godd but He that syttyth on hye;
On all these maumentys evyre sey we 'fye!'
We schuld dey rathere than we schuld forsake
The Crysten feyth whech we have now take."

Chapter 3

155	Now wax the emperour ny wode and oute of mynde:	*crazy*
	His eyne rolled as thei wold fall oute.	
	"Fy on yow," he seyd, "charles unkynde!"	*churls*
	Now is oure feyth for yow more in doute	*thanks to you*
	Than evyr it was to hem that stonden aboute!"	
160	He thoo comaundyd in ful hasty wyse:	*ordered [his henchmen]*
	"I wyll her deth that ye thus devyse.	*their*

"A fyre I wyll that ye hastely make,
Ryght in the myddes of the grete cetee — *middle*
Spare no wode for holy Saturn sake.
165 Spede yow fast these renegatys that ye see, *those renegades (the philosophers)*
Frye hem in her grece, for be that deyté *deity*
Of swete Apollo, I schall not ete ne drynk
Tyll that I se hem bothe brened and stynke. *stinking*

"Put in rosyn, pych, and othir gere; *rosin; pitch; material*
170 Spare no coste, for in this do ye servyse
Onto oure goddys, withouten any fere. *doubt*
Thus schul thei dey that oure goddis despyce.
I schall be there myself as justyse
And see these I wele don in dede.
175 Whan ye have don ye schall have ryght goode mede. *reward*

"I wyll ye bynde hem bothe fote and hande, *commend you*
Drawe hem forthe as dogges unto the place.
Youre ropes loke thei be myghty and youre bande — *shackles*
Spare neythir body, heedys, nyn her face. *nor*
180 God gefe hem all swech a sorye grace
That thus forsake oure goddys that be eterne!
Loke none of hem skape yow in non hyrn. *them escape; hiding place*

"Thei schal be brent dede, ryght as I have seyde,
Brent into askes — thei gete no remedye.
185 Lete hem crye now on this wylfull mayde *call upon*
Whech hath browte hem into that heresye!
I wyll noo wordes as now multyplye: *I will say no more*

Goo now forth in hast and do youre dede;
Whan it is done, treuly schall ye have your mede."

Chapter 4

190   Thus are thei draw with grete vylony
       Onto her dome — thei wrestyll not ageyn.   *their judgment; against [it]*
       Men myght se there many a wepyng eye,
       But for fere no man dare now seyn.   *speak*
       Glad are these meny alle of very peyn.
195   The mayster of hem thus he cryed that tyme:
       "To God be it that for no synne ne cryme

       "Be we appechyd but only for trew feyth.   *charged with*
       Therfor, felawys, in Cryst youreselfe comfort.
       Whatevyr this tyraunt doth or seyth,
200   Thank oure Lorde, for we are in His port   *haven*
       Whech that ledyth us to that blyssyd comfort,
       Where all seyntys are gadered togedyr be grace
       In an hevynly, joyful, blessed place.

       "Oure Lorde hath called us fro oure olde erroure
205   Onto this ende: thank we Him therfore
       Whech onto the beuté of His meroure   *image*
       Wold of His goodeness newly us restore.
       In this world, as for me, I wyll no more   *wish nothing else*
       But that we schuld ben baptized or we deye;   *before*
210   Than were we redy for to walke that goode weye.

       "For that same baptem is an holy werke:
       It causeth grace and feyth and eke endewyth;   *bestows [them]*
       Betwyx God and man it is a very merke
       That whosoevyr Crystes steppes sewyth   *follows*
215   All his levyng sothely he renewyth,   *living*
       Whan that he waschyth in this watyr his synne.
       Oure Lorde Himselfe was wasched therinne

       "Ryght for this cause: that no man shulde dysdeyne
       To use the same whech that this Lorde used.

220 Of my conceyte I wyll no more now feyne,   *dissemble*
    For in this matere ofte tyme hafe I musede.
    Many yere this sacrament I refusede;
    That I repent now, and evyr I schall it rewe,
    That I so long leved a lyffe untrewe.

225 "Werfore my care now is this onlye:
    That sythe we schall and nedys must deye,
    Of all oure synnes mercy for to crye,
    And all oure defautes undyr fote to ley,
    To treden hem down. Than savely may we sey
230 That we are purged and of all made clene —
    Thus must we beleven, felawys, all bedene."   *one and all*

Chapter 5

    And onto the mayden he turned him with his voys:
    "Lady," he seyd, "for God that syttyth above
    And for the passyoun that Cryst had on crosse,
235 Prey for us to Him that is thi love;
    Thu seyst full welle we may no lengere schove   *prolong*
    Oure lyvyng dayes, for thei are nye at ende;
    Prey that He wyll His mercy sende

    "Onto His servauntys and spare hem at this tyme.
240 Suffyr us eke that we may waschyd be
    With holy baptem, that we may the bettyr clyme
    To that place of grete felicité;
    And if this prayere plese not Him, but He
    Wyll allgatys that we schall wante this thinge,   *nevertheless*
245 We wolde desyre than of this blyssyd kinge

    "He wold with us make dispensacyoun,   *make an exception for us*
    For all this may He; He is omnipotent.
    He lovyth all men, He lovyth every nacyoun
    Egaly, ye sey, this is oure fundament.   *premise*
250 If He dyspence with us of this sacrament,   *exempts us from*
    Than for wantyng may we bere no blame,   *We cannot be blamed for lacking it*
    Than schall oure deth be tyl us but game."

Than seyd the mayd untyll hem all in fere:
"Fere ye ryght nowght, thow ye want this thing.
255 So as I can now wyll I yow lere.
Thoo men that for love of Cryst oure kinge,
Whech wante of baptem, that holy waschynge,
Thei schall to blys, for aungellys schall hem carye —
The fendes powere no thinge may hem tarye.   *hinder*

260 "In stede of baptem servyth His passyoun:
Not only blode whech that He for hem dyd blede
But all othir deth whech with devocyoun
Thus thei suffred unto hem grete mede.
Leve ye wel this doctrine trostly as your crede,
265 The grete peyne the whech is dempte to yow   *decreed for you*
In stede of baptem schal be as now.

"God may with fyre purgen mannys synne,
With watyr eke as Him lyst demene;   *as He chooses*
Summe men are baptyzed, heven for to wynne,
270 With that watyr whech in the fonte is sene.   *seen*
Summe are purgede with her blode, I wene —
Thei deyn as marteres, this is oure decré.
Summe are baptyzed, eke, as leve we —

"Thys calle oure clerkys baptem of the Goste —
275 In Goddys mercy, and deyen oute of synne
Ryght in her feyth that stedfastly troste.
Therfore ye knytes of Cryste new begune,
To cleym youre herytage that ye were therinne
Beth not aferde, but suffre the peyn mekely —
280 Than are ye baptized, trost me now trewly."

Chapter 6

Whan that thei weren of this holy mayde
Thus comforted, the offyceres comen anoon:
Thei bondyn her handys, ryght as I seyde;
Thei leden hem forth, fast as thei may goon,
285 Onto a strete whech was pathed with ston.

Well is him that may a fagott bere
To brene the clerkys! The emperour was there,

Sett in a stage, for he wold see the ende.
The fyre is made, blokkes are leyd on hepe,   *logs; in a heap*
290   Fagottes gan thei amonge the clogges bende.   *logs spread*
There is not ellys but fech, renne, and lepe;
Blow now fast — the foweres shuld not slepe.   *flames*
Thei bynde her fete, thei throw hem in the fere,
But thei are glad and full mery of chere,   *i.e., the philosophers*

295   Thankyng God that all thing made of nowte
That thei may dey for swech a Lordes sake.
Thei pray to Him ryght as He hem bowte
Her soules tyll Him now that He wold take.
What schuld I now lengere this tale make?
300   Thus are thei dede, her sowles onto blysse,
Eke tyll her bodyes oure blyssed Lorde grauntyd thyss:

Skyn ne flesch was non of hem brente,
Ne hede, ne clothe, ne heere of berde ne of heede.
Thei lay there dede with browes fayre bente,
305   With fayre face colourde bothe whyght and reede,
For lyk as the fyre makyth the rusty leede   *lead*
Bryth and schene, so makyth the fyre this mené —   *company*
Whoso knew hem before myth ken hem and see.   *recognize*

In her peynes, men seyd, thei cryed thus:
310   "Blyssyd be God that we nevyr knew ere,
Blyssyd be Cryst! Honourde be oure Lorde Jhesu!
For of this tormente have we now no fere."
This was a scole mervelows for to lere:
That thei in torment myrth and joy schuld make.
315   Onto God only her sowles gan thei take;

Thus deyed this mené in Novembyre the thirtene day.
Aftyr her deth thei semed not to a be dede: *have been dead*
As slepyng men in fayre coloure thei lay,
In handys, body, legges, eke, and heede,

320	With coloure fresch, lovely, and also reede.	
	This see the puple and mervelyd wondyr sore;	
	God thei preysyd for than and evyr more,	
	For be this miracle converted was that day	
	Meche folke to Cryst, and for devocion	
325	Bothe of the clerkys and eke of the may,	*maiden*
	Thei token the bodyes with solempne orison	
	And biried hem there in dyvers mansion,	*estates*
	Trostyng to spede bettir for her cause.	*to prosper by having them*
	Thus endyth her martirdam rith in this clause.	

Chapter 7

330	Thoo sey the emperour: "There is non othir botte	*remedy (i.e., way to deal with)*
	Onto this mayden whech is so stedfast	
	But fayre wordes, whech draw womanhoode	
	And makith hem often othir thingis to tast	
	Than thei shulde do if thei wold be chast."	
335	Therfor this mayden rith thus thoo he glosyth:	*flatters*
	"Kateryne," he seyth, "there is no man supposith —	
	"Nothe ye youreselve — that I wold but goode	*As you know*
	Onto youre persone. But this grete distresse	
	To which I putte you, spellyng yet as no bloode,	
340	Was forto chast you fro that sekenes	*drive you from*
	Whech that ye have caute of fonned holynes,	*foolish*
	And left the rytes that oure elderes before	
	Receyvyd and honouryd as for sovereyn lore.	
	"This was the cause why that I distressyd you soo.	
345	But love have I onto you sekyrly	
	As to the best of alle, save on and no moo.	
	And why I do soo, if ye will wete why,	
	Youre beuté it causith, youre cunnyng eke; and I	
	Love you so wele that, if ye lyke to consent,	
350	And thurifye to Jupiter that is omnipotent	*offer incense*

"Ye shall have honour — no woman shall be you lich.
O swete virgyne, enclyne youre love to me!
O fayre visage of bewté now most rych,
O woman most worthy of imperiall degré,
355 O very merveyle, parfyth felicité,
Wold god ye knowen what care I have for yow
And what beheest I have made in myn avowe.

"Why wold ye despyce oure goddis immortall?
Why wold ye calle hem so venemous a name?
360 Why seyd ye that thei are develes infernall?
Why slaunder ye so her endewed fame?
For this blasfeme, iwis, ye are to blame:
'Deceyvoures of the puple,' as ye seyde.
Chaunge youre langage, ye noble goodly mayde!

365 "Chaunge betyme, for though thei suffir longe,   *strike*
At the last thei smyten and taken hey venjaunce.
Tendir youre thought, speke no more wronge:
Thus shall ye best her yre swage.   *their wrath assuage*
Take youre offeryng yet, in schort langage,   *to be brief*
370 And plesith hem so thei may be youre frendes,
And sey nevyr more that thei be fendes.

"If ye wil don as I you now counsayle,
This shall ye have: next aftir the qween
Shall ye be to us, withouten fayle;
375 To youre comaundment all men shall bene
Obeyng, but whom that ye will susteyne
He shal be favoured with all myth and mayne,   *in every way possible*
And whom that ye hate, compendiously to sayne,   *briefly*

"That man shall levyn in full gret distresse.
380 Comforth youreselve, dispice not good counsayle,
Makith not youre frendis to levyn in hevynesse,
Lete myn wordis sinken in youre entrayle:
Fle swech that may not avayle.
Withinne my kyngdam may ye have this ryght:
385 What that ye will shal be fulfyllyd as tyth.   *tithe (see note)*

237

"If that ye will exilen ony man,
That man shall goo — there shall no good him save.
More plesaunce to you graunt I ne can
But suffir youre will all that ye will have.
390   For this decré shall I nevyr more wave:
Whom that ye list of grace for to avaunce,
In joyfull dayes that same man may daunce.

"Betwix the qween and you shal be non distaunce
But only this: because of oure spousayle   *marriage*
395   Sche must of me have more dewe plesaunce —
The love betwix us, I trow, shall nevyr fayle;
But to you shall long both lawe and counsayle
Thorow all oure reme to governe at youre wille: *realm*
Rith as ye bydde all men shall fulfylle.

400   "Yete shall I make in the market place   *Furthermore*
A solempne ymage lich an empresse.
As man of craft will counterfete youre face
It shal be made. Ilke man, more and lesse,   *Each*
Shall honour that with ful grete besynesse,
405   Whan thei comen forby shul fallen on knes anon.
This ymage shall not only be made of stone,

"But of clene metall, gylt full bryght and shene.   *shiny*
Whoso comyth forby with sufficient evidens
Shall knowen full wele that sche was a qwene
410   Whos ymage stante there, and that in grete offens
Shall he falle that doth noo reverens
To that ymage. And whoo flee thertoo,
What maner offens that evyr he hath doo,

"Shal be forgeve at the reverens of yow, mayde.
415   Thus may ye be deyfyed, if ye will it take."   *deified*
Swech maner wordis untill hir he sayde:
He wold a tempill all of marbell make,
Of ful grete cost rith for hir sake,
Wenyng evyr with swech feynyd plesauns   *Believing*
420   To bryng this mayde oute of hir good perseverauns.

238

Chapter 8

Sche lowe a lytill whan sche had herd all this,　　　　*laughed*
And than she spake with mery countenaunce:　　　　*cheerful*
"Full happy am I," she seyd, "unto blys,
Whan that the emperour will me thus avaunce　　　　*promote*
425　　To reren a ymage of so grete plesaunce　　　　*raise*
In worchip of me and of so grete pryse.
Summe men wolde seyn that I were nyse　　　　*foolish*

"If I refused it, for of gold it schal be
If I comaunde, but yet at the lest
430　　Of sylvere he wyl it make and of swech quantyté
The chaungours schul stryve and be in no rest　　　　*money changers*
To bregyn so mech tresoure oute of the nest
To make a memoryall of Kateryne the mayde!"
Swech manere wordes at that tyme sche sayde:

435　　"And thow this ymage be made of marbyll grey,　　　　*even if*
Suffysyth it that to my laude eterne　　　　*praise*
Every man schall come be the wey
Where that schal be sett in a herne,　　　　*corner*
On bothe knes him must fall yerne　　　　*eagerly*
440　　And do his omage, elles must him deye.
What manere wordes hope ye thei shall seye?　　　　*expect*

"'Heyl ymage, made ryght in memoryall
Of a lady full wyse and ful of prudent;
Heyle statue that art now as eternall;
445　　Heyl sygne, made ryght to this entent —
The grete beawté of Kateryne to present!'
Wyll not this be full grete plesaunce
Tyl hem that loven this worldly lusty daunce?

"But this wold I knowyn or we this thinge make:
450　　Of what matere schall my legges be?
What manere werkman that dare undyrtake
To make hem to meve and walke in her degré?　　　　*go*
My handys, eke, I wolde wete how that he

239

Shuld make to fele and of what matere —
455 Or we goo ferther this wold I lere.

"The eyne eke whech this ymage schall have,
If thei schul loke ryght as I do in dede,   *in person*
Where is that werkman that swech thinges can grave?
He were wel worthy to have ful grete mede!
460 I leve nevyr that this werk shuld well spede.   *believe*
Thys matere thus sotely to congelle,   *solidify*
There is no werkman in erthe that can it fulfylle.

"A tunge, eke, if he shuld it make
Onto this ymage to speke and to crye:
465 Where is he that dare this undirtake?
If he do thus, he werkith a grete maystry,   *marvel*
But for this cause that there is no man so slye.   *clever*
Therfor I conclude thus, in a shorte sentens:
Whan ye have wared youre witte and youre expens   *worn out*

470 "To make this ymage, it shal be unsensible,
Stond lyke a stone, and byrdes that flyes ther abowth —
As I suppose it shal be right possible
Ther shall comyn sumtyme a full grete rowth —   *flock*
Here unclene dunge shall thei there put oute
475 And lete it falle rith on the ymage face.
Loo, swech a guerdon I may now purchace   *reward*

"That men shuld dredyn and foules shuld defyle!
But whan deth hath shake on us his blast,
And that oure mynd be passed a lytyl whyle,   *memory*
480 I am aferd this werke shall not last —
Wherfor to make it me thinkyth but a wast.
To trosten in fame and in veynglory
It is but feynyng a fekyl flatery.

"And thou thei make it as fayre as thei can,
485 Yette shall dogges defylen it every day.
For thow it honoured be of every man,
The small childeryn that come by the way

240

Shul sumtyme make there ful fowle aray.
Shall I for this leve my God forevyr
490 And fro His frenchip my sowle now desevyr

"To worchep develes that standen in tempil here,
Kepte as beres? Do way! It shall not be —   *bears*
There shall no joy ne peyne me nevyr stere
To leeve my Lorde, to leve my felicité,
495 To renne in apostasie. Fye! It will not be!
Lette be youre labour, sere, let be youre promysse;
Thei shall not maken me nevyr to do amysse.

"What, shuld my lyffe bettir ben in ese   *be more comfortable*
For swech a statue? What shuld it profyth
500 Onto my soule — me thinkith it coude not plese
No good man, for thow it were to the syth
Ful delectable, with coloures schynyng bryth,
Onto oure dayes it shuld non encres,   *increase*
Onto oure sekenes it shuld non reles,

505 "Onto oure lyffe it shuld be no myrth,
Onto oure deth it shuld non comforth be.
None avayle to end ne to byrthe:
To what part longith it of felicité?
If it mowte kepe my flesh in swech degré
510 It shuld not rote, I shuld it nevyr weyven,   *reject*
But as profitable I wold it than receyven.

"I have a promysse made of a gretter Lorde,
Of gretter fame than I will now expresse,
And made aforne persones of recorde   *witnesses*
515 In whech is graunted, truly withoute gesse,
A memorial of parfyth stabilnesse,
As ye shall knowe, many that here be.
Leveth youre besynes as now onto me —   *preoccupation with*

Labour no more to wynne me to youre parte.
520 It shall not be, I wil be as I am,
It will not avayle youre sotilté ne youre arte —

He is my spouse whech is both God and man;
I am His mayde. I wil do that I can
To haven His love; He is my swetnesse,
525 He is my joy, He is my gentilnesse."

Chapter 9

Thoo chaunged the emperour both word and chere,
And to the mayden he seyd as I rehers:
"The benynglyer that we treten you here,   *more benignly*
As me semeth, the more ye revers.   *oppose [me]*
530 This shall ye have, shortly in a vers,
Deth or joy whech you levest: *prefer*
If ye will leve in solas and in rest,

"Than shal ye now with hey devocion
Thurifye to that magesté   *Offer incense*
535 Of grete Appollo. His exaltacion —   *worship*
As ye knowe wele, for it is no secré —
Redressith this word with hete whech that he   *Repays; world; heat*
Spredyth upon iche mayde. Obey thertoo!
There is no choys; this thing must nedis be doo.

540 "Fayre spech avaylith noth to you in no wyse.
I wold wele with solas a led youre gentilnesse,   *have directed*
But at my promysse ye sett lytill prysse —
Ye schal repent it sothly, as I gesse.
There is the fyre: dispose you to holynesse,
545 Do it with good will; ye schal the soner purchace
Pardon of synne and encres of grace.

"If ye do noth, in schort tyme ye shal be dede,
Rith in example of the puple that is here: *as an example for*
Her hertis arne hangyng hevy as leed;   *their*
550 A man may perseyven rith be her chere
It may not passen lyghtly, swech matere —
It must be punchid, rith for fere of othir.   *punished; other (i.e., imitation)*
He shuld be dede thou he were my brothir."

242

Chapter 10

     "Peyne is welcome to me," seyd she than,
555   And deth, eke, I wil it noth forsake,
     For thou ye smyth, fle, sle, or banne,   *though; smite, flay; banish*
     It skyllith me rith noth for my Lordis sake   *It makes no difference*
     Swech myschevys for His love to take.   *afflictions*
     He toke for me mych more wrechydnes
560   Whill He lyved her in this worldly wyldernes.

     "Poverté He suffered than full buxumly   *humbly*
     Whan that He myth an had riches at His will;   *have had*
     The same myschef yete suffered nevyr I,
     But if it com, I will obey thertyll.   *accept it*
565   Ageyn blasfemewrs stod that Lord ful styll,
     Gevyng exaumpil til us of paciens:
     Why shull His servauntis maken ony resistens

     "Whan the wykyd purposyd to don hem wrong?
     For His cause, His feyth, or His love
570   I am now redy, be it short or long,
     To suffer despite, peyne, and reprove.   *contempt*
     I wote wele it will falle to myn behove   *credit*
     Whan I am gone: the more I suffyr here,
     The more joy shal I haven elleswhere.

575   "He offered himselve to the Fader of blys
     An host ful clene, undefyled with synne,
     And I wil offyr my body, for it is His,
     Onto His plesauns whech I wold wynne.
     Loke ye youreselve whan ye will begynne,
580   For I am redy in body and in goost:
     Sle or flee, fry or ellis roste.   *flay*

     "There shall come tyme thu shalt repent full sore
     Of cruel domes whech thu usest here.   *judgments; imposed*
     Of thi power settest thu ful gret store,
585   Whech shal rew thee ful sore aftir thi bere.   *aggrieve; bier (i.e., after your death)*
     Crystes servauntis hast thu brent in fere —

In tyme comyng therfor thu shal be schent   *ruined*
Whan that thu with fendes in helle shal be brent.

"The more thu thretyst, the more glad am I;
590   The moo peynes thu applyest to me,
The more my joyes encres sekyrly.   *certainly*
I go not alone whan that I part fro ye,
For whan I dey many of thi mené
Of thin howsold shal folow me ful sone.
595   Of Cryst my Lord have I askyd that boone:

"That of thi meny rith a full grete parte
Shul trow in Him and levyn her ydolatrye.   *renounce*
Wayte aboute with all thin sotyll arte —
Thu shal fynd that I make no lye.
600   Her soules fro peyn frely thus shul flye
Streyte to hevyn, and thu shalt brenne in helle.
This thing is trew that I ye now telle."

Chapter 11

Than was the emperour ny wode for ire.   *nearly crazy*
He comaund his men that stodyn hem abowte
605   To fetche yerdis of ful sotyll wyre;   *thin*
He chase men that were of body ful stouth.   *chose; strong*
Till hem he seyd right thus without douth:
"Take this mayden and strippe hir moder-nakyd.   *naked as when she was born*
I trow she shal sone of hir slepe be wakyd!

610   "Bete hir wele, rith for hir blasfeme
To feryn hem that trostyn in hir doctryne.   *scare*
Lete hir no more spekyn of that Bethleme,
Ne of Galile shal she no more dyvyne.
I trow that peyne shal hir rather enclyne
615   Onto oure wille than may oure plesauns.
Do ye youre dever, thou that she falle in trauns!"   *duty; even if*

The tormentoures have taken hir on syde,
Made hir naked backe and armes thertoo.

244

With eyrend wandes, as fast as thei may glyde,   *iron*
620   Thei beten hir body; the blode cam fast hir froo.
Whan thei were wery, than don fresh men moo:
Thus is she betyn for hir spouses love.
Sche trostith on comforth that comyth fro above.

These weren hir wordes: "Lord send me paciens,
625   Make me strong to suffir this penauns.
If that I have ronne in Thi offens   *offended You*
Lete it be purged be this same grevauns.
Thankyng be evyr unto Thi purvyauns,
Lord, maker of man and best.
630   Of Thi servauntis, I that am the leest,

"Thanke Thee more for this same betyng
Than for the welthes that Thu sent me befor,   *riches*
For wele wote I that this tormentyng,
It is to me as a grete tresowre.
635   Farewel the werd now forevyr more:
Stele and robbe the goodes that I have;
I care noth now neythir for toure ne cave."

The tyraunt aske among this byttir peyne,   *amid*
Whan all was blode and the beters wery were all:
640   "What sey ye mayden? Will ye yete susteyne
Youre elde heresye in whech ye be falle?
If ye will mercy of oure goddes calle,
Ye shall it have, and ellys new game —   *or else another round of punishment*
Or that ye goo, I trow ye shal be tame."

645   Sche answerd thus: "Sere, know this wele:
That I am strenger in body and in goost
Than evyr I was to sufferne every dele
Al maner turment, wheyther thu wolt fry or roost.
But thu, my schamful dog ful of boost,
650   Do what thu wilt, for I shall stronger be
In my sufferauns than thu in thi cruelté.

"Bethink thee wele, on ilke maner syde,
Whom thu may fle or bryng on dawe   *put to death*
The Crysten puple that knowen is so wyde,
655   Whech do no wrong but kepyn a ful trew lawe.
I shall dey and passen this worldes wawe,   *woe*
Folow my Lorde and dwelle with Him in blys,
Wher that no thing is thout ne do amys.   *thought or done*

"Ther schall I dwelle in joye and in solas
660   Whan thu thiself schalt be in horrybyll peyne.
Thou schalt than desyre, but thu schalt have no grace;
Thou schalt be bounden with that wofull cheyn   *chain*
Of obstynacy; thu schalte repente and seyn,
'Allas that evyr I wrowth swech torment
665   Onto youre hevenly blyssyd covent!'   *assembly*

"Thus schalt thu wayle qwan thu sest us in blysse,   *when*
And thu in sorowe withouten remedye,
Lyeng in peynes whech shul nevyr mysse,
This shalt thu knowe uphap hastyly.   *perhaps*
670   Therfore fulfylle now of ire thi malencolly,   *madness*
And I shall suffyr for the love of God of heven."
Thus seyd the lady with a ful bold steven.   *voice*

Chapter 12

The emperour comaunded onto his servauntis anon,
"Ye take this mayd and into prison hir lede.
675   I will ye put hir in the depe cave of ston,
No man so hardy in no maner hir to fede.
I will," he seyth, "that this be done in dede:
All these fourty dayes whech that I shall ryde,
Lete hir no mete have to slake therwith hir pryde.   *diminish*

680   "Geve hir no drynke, ne lete hir no drynke have.
Whoso otherwyse do ageyn my comaundment —
So holy Jubiter mote my soule save —
Whan I come home, sone shall he be brent!
I will that ye fulfylle all myn entent

685   Even streytly, withoute delacion: *delay*
            No man so hardy of no maner nacion

            "Bere hir mete or drynke or eny lyght."
            This cruell maundment and this same decré
            Made the emperour thus ageyn the law o ryght
690   And is redyn forth with his mené
            Up into the lond for cause whech that he
            Had for to don as potestates have.   *To do what potentates (rulers) have to do*
            And thus is this mayde left alone in cave,

            Withouten ony comforth or ony solas.
695   But Cryst hath noth forgetyn His wyffe
            All these fourty dayes, of His good grace,
            He wolde noth levyn hir like a caytiffe.   *wretch*
            He sent down His servauntis fro the hows of lyffe —
            His aungelis I mene — to comforth this mayde.
700   Swech maner wordes thoo til hir seyd thei:

            "Oure Lord comaund that ye shuld be glade —
            Suffir this desese with sobir paciens.   *discomfort*
            Mete shal ye have — ye nevyr swech had;   *Food*
            Lith hath He sent yow with oure presens.   *Light*
705   The emperour for youre cause renneth in offens
            Whech he shall sumetyme ful sore repent."
            Thus was she comforted in hir torment

            With lyght of heven and with hevenly mete,
            With presens of aungelis. For thei that hir kepte,
710   Thei myth here the noyse, how thei hir trete.   *how [the angels] treated her*
            Thei myth sene lyght as it gan strepe   *crept*
            Thorow the slarrys — thei myth not slepe.   *cracks*
            So have thei merveyle of all this thing,
            But rith noth told thei onto the kyng.

715   But to othir folke in the courte there
            Sprong this word there, how that this mayde
            Was kept fro lyth, in ful grete fere,
            And fro mete eke, as I ere sayde,

And how the jayloures were so afrayde
720   Of certeyn lyght at the dongon dore:
This word in the courte goth aboute sore.

Chapter 13

The tydens are come onto the qwenes ere
Of the cruel sentens and of the lith eke,
How that the mayden without ony fere
725   Had answerd the clerkys in the tothir weke,
And how that the mayden with wordes meke
Had turned hem to Cryst, and how thei were brent,
And she for that cause in prison is ny shent.

The emperour was absent, as I seyd before,
730   Forth unto the lond redyn in hast.
Thei tolde the qween that he comaunded sore
That she neythir mete ne drynke shuld tast,   *i.e., Katherine*
But for pure hungyr she must dey and wast —
These last wordes seyd he on the heth:
735   "No man gefe hir mete ne drynke ne lyght in peyn of deth."

This meved the qwen of very womanly peté   *pity*
To have compassion of these peynes alle
Whech that this lady, be very cruelté
Of the kyng, had suffered. Thus is she falle,
740   The qwen, all in stody walkyng in the halle,   *rapt in thought*
Thinkyng besyly upon this mayde,
And til hirself pryvyly thus she sayde:

"These Cristen folke, thei do no man wrong:
Alle that thei bye trewly therfor thei pay;
745   Onto her God thei syngyn ful goodly song
New and new, as men seyn, every day;
Wastfull are thei noth in no maner of ray;   *not; clothing*
In gloteny ne drunkchip wil thei nevyr be —
This same lyffe full wele it plesith me.

750	"And on of hem had I ben or nowe,
	Had not oure lawe forfend us that scole.
	If it were sene that I to hem drowe,
	Men schuld seyn that I were a fole.
	It myth turne me eke to mekyl dole
755	If that my lorde myth this changyng knowe.
	But yete in my herte there begynnyth to growe

I would have been
forbidden
was attracted to them

conversion

      "A grete desyre for to sene this mayde.
      Allas, how shall I fulfylle myn entent?"
      Thus be hirselve the lady thought and sayde.
760   But in this stody even as she went
      Happyd to come, as thow God had him sent,
      A noble knyth, a wysman in all thing,
      Pryvy of counsayle ryght speciall with the kyng,

      Governowre of knytes, leder of hem alle,
765   A very fadyr to yong folke that shuld lere —
      Porphery the storyes rith thus thei him calle.
      Onto the qween he kneled with ful sad chere.
      "I am glad," she seyd, "Porphery, that ye be here.
      Ye ben a man that may mych avayle.   *accomplish*
770   To you now I will tellen my pryvy counsayle.

      "I am so trobilled newly with Crysten lawe
      I can noth slepe, I may neythir ete ne drynke.
      Every day, or it begynnyth to daw,   *dawn*
      And eke all nyght, on this matere I thynke —
775   I trow I am ful ny my lyves brynke,
      But I have comforte ryght thus." Thoo sche sayde,   *Then*
      "Goode Porphyry, me muste nedes se yon mayde.

      "Orden ye the meene ryght as ye can —   *Arrange a means*
      Gefe the gaylere gold and sylvyr enowe;   *jailer*
780   Ordeyn so that ye and I may than
      Speke this ladye. To Godd I make a vowe,
      Loke my lorde nevyr so wrothe and rowe,
      I must nedes speke hir or I schal be dede,
      For in this matere myn hert is hevy as lede."

785   Porphyry seyde, "Madame, it schal be do:
    I schal parforme this thing, trost in me.
    In swech degré the dorys schal be ondoo
    There schall no man be pryvy but we thre —
    That is to seyn, the gaylere, I, and ye.   *jailer*
790   Drede yow noth, ye schal have your entent.
    With this matere have I sore be torment:

    "Me thinkyth grete wrong that this lady suffereth here
    So horribily beten, kept fro mete and drynke,
    And she no harme doth in no manere.
795   Ful often tyme she made me on hir to thynke
    Sithin I hir herde the noble argumentis clynke   *resound*
    With the clerkys, whan she convycte hem alle.
    Therfor, madame, falle what so befalle,

    "We wil se hir, and with good leysyre,
800   And speke with hir this same nyte folowyng.
    Grete giftis shall I geve to the gaylere   *jailer*
    To kepe counsayle and speke of this nothing.
    Goo ye to chaumbir and whan I geve warnyng
    Comyth forth alone and lete youre women slepe —
805   Loke ye be redy whan I shall you clepe."   *call*

Chapter 14

    Thus be consent the qwen and Porphiry,
    Whan all men slepyn to prison are thei goo
    Alle alone, rith seyth oure story.
    Whan thei comen there, thei too and no moo,
810   So grete lith in prison sey thei thoo   *light*
    That thei fallen down withouten spech or breth —
    Thei hopyd nevyr to a ben so ny her deth,   *expected; near their*

    For that brytnes was lych a lythnyng
    Whech thei sey than, so wondyrfull and bryght
815   Her wytt is goo, and down in stameryng
    Are thei falle for fere of that syght.
    There was a savour, also, with the lyght;

Thei felt nevyre swech, the story seyth, certeyne,
For with that savour her comfort cam ageyn.   *courage*

820   Tho spake the mayden swech wordes to hem:
"Ryse up syster, ryse up brothir in fere.
Cryst that was bore in the cité of Bethleem,
He hath callyd yow onto His servyse here.
Be glad and mery, be of ryght goode chere;
825   Oure Lord hath chose yow newly to His grace —
For that cause He sent yow to this place."

Thei behelden the mayde at that tyde,
How that sche sate on knes full mekely.
Many aungell sey thei on every syde,   *saw*
830   With swete gummes anoyntyng hir softly;   *[medicinal] gums*
Evyr as thei touchede with handys by and by   *again and again*
The flesch was helyd, the skyn closed ageyn,
With mech more beauté, sothely for to seyn,

Than evyr it was whyle that it was hole.   *whole*
835   Thus can oure Lorde redresse all dolour
Whech men suffre, be it in hede or soole.   *i.e., foot*
He can in lesse tyme than in halfe a houre
Hele oure sores, comfort oure laboure.
These folk there hadden a blysfull syght,
840   Ful of comforte, ful of hevynly delyte.

There satte besyde eke sundry ful elde men
Gevyng comforte ontyll hir hevynesse.
There were in cumpanye no mo than nyn or ten —
Of her noumbre have I no sekyrnesse —
845   Thei were sent thedyr, sothely as I gesse,
Because this woman was withoute solace,
Hir to comfort with summe hevynly grace.

On of hem helde in his hande a crown   *One of them*
Fayre and reall — we can it not dyscryve —
850   Ryght fro his hande Kateryne toke it down.
Onto the qwen thus she seyd belyve: *directly*

"This crown, systir, with these braunches fyve
Shall ye haven and weryn upon youre heed
As for asay; but aftir, whan ye be dede,   *To try on*

855   "Than shall ye have it for reward evyrlestyng."
Onto the old men tho turned that mayde
Whil she helde the crowne, in the settyng,
Thus tyl hem with meke voys she sayd:
"For these personys to my Lord I prayd
860   Thei shul be writyn in the boke of lyffe.
Therfor, seres, as I, Crystes wyffe,

"Graunted be patent, so wil I that ye wryth
These too names in that boke forevyr.
Clense her synnes, make so that hevy with   *evil being (i.e., the devil)*
865   Fro my Lord nomore hem desevyre.   *separate*
I pray to God that now mote thei falle nevyre
Aftir the tyme that thei reseyvyn the feyth."
On of the eldest ageyn onto hir seyth: *said to her again*

"O preciouse spouse of God that syttyth above,
870   O gemme reall schynyst in chastyté,
Whatevyr thu aske of Cryst that is thi love,
It cannot fayle, so precious to you is He.
Onto thi persone, therfore, trost thu to me:
This lady shall preve onto grete perfeccion,   *attain*
875   This knyte shall have eke swech progression   *knight*

"In vertuous lyffe that thorow his gode counsayle
Too hundred and moo fro her fals beleve   *their*
Shall turne to Cryst and ful sore for her synne wayle
Her fals feyth whech thei cannot preve."
880   Thus have these folke of Kateryne take her leve,
Walkyng to chaumbyr with hertis suspens,   *anxious hearts*
Kepyng this matere alle cloos in sylens.

252

Chapter 15

This mayden is kepte in prison evyr stylle
With swech comforth as ye have herdyn here.
885   Of mannys comforth hath she neythir lettir ne bylle —   *missive*
No man dare doo it, swech is now her fere.   *fear*
Fourty dayes full thus was she kepyd there
Withouten mete, but in all these dayes   *food*
Of hevenly mete had she swete assayes.   *samples*

890   For He that fedde Danyel the prophete in the lake   *lion's den*
And caryede Abacuc so ferre oute of Jude   *Habakkuk; Judea*
To bryng him vytayle, that same Lord myth make
That in prison this mayden thus fedde shuld be.
In storyes that I rede, in dyvers too or thre,
895   A fayre dowe fro heven brouth hir mete —   *dove*
Wheythir bodyly or goostly it is hard for to trete,   *determine*

For, as Austen seyth, that same seede
Whech oure faderes receyvyd in wyldernes,
Whech served hem than in stede of brede —
900   This very doctir seyth in sothfastnes —
That possybyll it is swech seedes more or lesse
Shuld be noryshyd in the eyyere be supposicion,   *air; placement*
In the lowere part whech hath desposicion,

Sumwhat to the erde acordyng in nature:
905   This is his sentens, whoso wil it rede,
In his boke whech tretyth in Scripture.
I trow this same was don here in dede:
The Holy Gost this goodly mayden gan fede
With hevenly thyng whech had erdly kynd:
910   Thus wene I, but I wil no man bynd,   *commit himself*

But if he will for to levyn my tale.   *believe*
She was fedde — that have we of treuth.
If God had left hir in so byttyr bale
Withouten comfort it had ben grete reuth.   *pity*
915   In that pryson she lyved withouten sleuth   *weariness*

Alle fourty dayes, but in the last of alle
As she in prayyer ful besyly gan calle

Onto Cryst, she saw an hevenly syth:
Oure Lord Himselve to pryson is com down,
920   With many aungellys shynyng wondir bryth,
With many maydenes of ful grete renown —
For very joy Kateryne fell in swown.
Oure Lord comforth hir with ful goodly chere:
"Dowtir, lokyth up whom ye se here.

925   "Know youre makere for whom alle this dysese
Ye have suffered. Take it evyr in pacyens —
The more ye suffyr, the more ye Me plese.
Kepe youre constans, drede no worldly offens,   *constancy*
Thinke 'not long,' leve noth with herte suspens.
930   I am with yow, I shall you nevyr forsake.
Many an hert ful redy shul ye make

"Onto My servyse or ye part fro this lyffe;
Grete nombre of puple shall ye returne —
Many a husbond, mayd, widow, and wyffe
935   Fro her maumentrye shall ye hem returne,
Onto My feyth ledyn hem to sojorne."   *rest*
Whan this was do oure Lord went up to hevyne
With grete brythnes as it were a levyne.   *beam of light*

She lokyd aftir tyll she sey no more,   *saw*
940   Returnyth to prayyer, as evyr was hir usage,
It was to hir a ful grete tresore
That Jhesu lyst to make that pylgrymage.
Hir hertly sorow so for to swage   *heartfelt*
With His presens, blyssyd evyr He be,
945   And be this mayden comend to Him be we.

Chapter 16

Whan his causes arne brouth fully to the ende
With that he rode forth — Maxens now I mene —

254

He is comyn home. Anon he gan to send
For hir be sex knytys, rith as I wene.   *six knights*
950   If thei be fals, sone it shall be sene,
Thei that kepte hir; it shall hem ovirthynke   *regret*
If it be provyd thei goven hir mete or drynke!

Alle the cyté is gaderyd to sene this syth,
A grete puple; summe for cruelnes,
955   Summe are there that han ful grete despyth
At the emperour for his wykkydnes —
Thei thinke this lady is put to grete distresse
For no cause only but for gode.
The emperour seyd with ful sturdy mood,   *furious words*

960   "Bryng forth this woman, bryng forth this concionatrix!   *conjurer*
Bryng forth this scolde or a wycche; no man may turne hir herte!
In hir errour is sche made so fyx
That fro it no man may make hir sterte.   *go*
But if it she do, ful sore shall she smerte."
965   Thus is she brouth before his presens.
He supposed veryly that for hir abstinens

She had be pynyd even to deth.   *afflicted*
Now lokyth she fresch with colour.
For very angyr his hert ny it sleth,   *slays*
970   For she is fayrere than she was that hour
Whan he comaunde to ledyn hir to that tour.
"Traytoures," he seyd, "ye shal dey ilke one
But ye telle me in this place anon

"Who hath fedde ageyn oure comaundment
975   This froward caytyff that no man may evyr lede!   *perverse wretch*
I swere be Jubiter, which is omnipotent,
It shal be wist who that dede this dede.
There shall no man for no maner mede
Do this thing whech we forfend soo."   *forbade*
980   He dede hem bynd with eyryn be too and too.   *iron*

Than the mayden to excusen hem alle
Seyd to the kyng swech maner wordes certeyn:
"Thu art a lord, an emperour men thee calle;
Thu art ordeynyd all treuth to susteyn.
985   Thei that don ageyn thi lawe or seyn,
Hem shuld thu ponyshe, but innocentes non:
If thu dost, thu dost ageyn thi trone,

"For these men whech had kepyng of me
Brout me neythir mete ne drynke, thu undirstand.
990   I was susteyned all in anothir degré
Be my Lord whech is alle weldand,   *almighty*
For be His messangeres sent He me to hand
Alle my sustenauns — no dore myth hem lette,   *hinder them*
To spere hem out thu canst not gette.   *lock; achieve*

995   "Therfore these innocentis, do hem no torment;
Thei be not worthi, sere kyng, I sey thee whi: *tell you why*
Be holy aungellis my Lord me mete sent —
Non erdly creature was therto pryvy —
For hungyr He wold not suffyr me to dey.
1000   He is my love, I am His forever;
Joy ne sorow shall us not desever."

Chapter 17

Tho these wordes the tyraunt with dobylnesse   *Then*
Answerd ful fayre, that thei that stodyn abouth
Shuld not suppose in him swech cruelnes —
1005   The sturdy hert in him whech was so stouth   *fierce; furious*
Was hid with langage as venyn in a clouth;   *poison in disguise (cloth)*
Ful fayre wordes at that tyme he sayde:
"I am for yow ful sory, most goodly mayde.

"Ye born a kynges dowtir, of kyng and of qwene,   *[were] born*
1010   Cosyn to lordes many that servyn me:
The best born woman of this cuntré ye bene,
Thus are ye namyd, and all this with sotylté
Of certeyn wytchis — cursyd evyr thei be —   *sorcerers*

256

Is turnyd and lost, for othir joy is there non
1015 But Jhesu Cryst, Mary, Petyr, and Jon,

"Whech are tratoures proved be the senate
And dampned to the deth for treson and heresy.
Whi will ye lesse thus youre honourabil astate
And gevyn attendans to witchcraft and lye?
1020 It had ben bettir to a kepte the same sophye   *have; learning*
Whech that ye lerned fyrst in scole.
This maner lernyng will prove yow a fole.

"Eke ageyn oure holy goddes servyse
Ye speke and cry, and that so malicyously,
1025 With word and chere ungoodly hem despyse:
This causeth me, I sey yow sewirly,
That, notwithstand, so mote I have mercy,   *even if I were to have mercy*
That I wold save yow, I must nede punysh this pryde
Ryth for my puple that stand here besyde.

1030 "Therfore chese now wheydir that ye will deye
With swech deth as law will dampne you too,
Or ellys youre feyth, if ye will reneye,   *renounce*
Than shall ye have mercy and worchip eke alsoo.   *honor*
Com of anon, let se what ye will doo: *Come on*
1035 Offir to Jubiter, youre god omnipotent;
Youre tendyr body with yrn shall ellys be rent."   *iron*

Chapter 18

The mayde answerd to the emperour ageyn:
"Thou that my lyffe be ful swete to me   *Although*
Yet had I lever with a swerd be slayn
1040 Than that my lyfffe in ony maner degré
Shuld offend the blyssyd majesté
Of my Lord God. I sey thee, Cryst is my lyffe
And grete encres, thow I dey on a knyffe,   *though*

"So that I dey in charyté and for His sake.
1045 Therfore, thow deth come to me this houre,

257

For His lufe ful mekely I wyll it take;
I schall nevyr with myght ne with laboure
Gruch ageyn my Lorde, my savyoure.   *Complain against*
Deth schall avaunce me with gret emolument.
1050   Deth is a chaungoure: fro this lyffe present   *one who causes change*

"To bettyr he ledyth us. This is oure beleve:
Oure dedely bodyes whech are coruptible,
Whan that he comyth, he bryngeth hem to this preve,
That thei schall rest and rote as seyth oure byble.
1055   Aftyr that restyng, yet it is possible
Onto oure Lorde the bodyes to rere ageyn   *raise*
In fayrrer forme than evyr thei were seyn.

"Therfore, thu teraunt with thi feyned langage,
Do what thu wylt: put me to torment,
1060   Brenne me with brondys, thin yre for to swage.
I wold offyr to Cryst whech is omnipotent
Summe plesaunt offeryng, summe delectable present;
Kyin and calveryn or schepe I all forsake —   *Cows; calves*
Myn owe body to offeryng wyll I take.

1065   "But for I may not lefully do it myselfe   *i.e., commit suicide*
As make this offeryng, therfore thi cruelté
Schall bydde thi servauntys eythere ten or twelfe
With veniable hert to make a hende of me.   *vengeful; end*
Too Him that was offered in Calvery on a tre,
1070   To Him I offyr my flesch, my blode, and my felle.   *skin*
But for thi cruelnes, yet eft I thee telle,

"Thou schalt ful sore hereaftyr this thing repent
Not oonly in helle, whech thu schal be inne,
But here in erde schal thu fayle thin entent:
1075   For thi dedys, whech are full of synne,
God schall rere a lorde the whech schall wynne   *raise*
Alle thi londes fro thee and make the pore,
Take awey thi worchepe and thi tresoore.

"Yet schal he slee thee as thu art worthy:
1080 That wykkyd heede he schall make of smyte,   *have chopped off*
Thi blode shall be offered than full solemply
Onto thi goddys ryght for despyte.
Loke my wordys that thu note and wryte:
This man that shall brynge thee thus a dawe   *put you to death*
1085 Schal be a lorde of the Crysten lawe.

"Yet may thu skape all this grete myschauns
If thu wyll turn ye and aske God mercy
Of thi wykedenes, if thu have repentauns
And forsake the maumentys whech stand on hye!"
1090 These are the wordes whech that this ladye
Seyd at that tyme this man to convert,
But all hir wordes sett he not at hert.

Tho semeth it wele this lady for holynesse
Was so avaunsed whyll sche was lyvande
1095 That God made hir as a prophetesse
To tell thinges that were aftyr comaunde,   *coming*
For this same deth, as I undyrstande,
Had this same Maxence as sche seyd, trewly.
For in storyes I am well avysed that I

1100 Have red of him that he went to Rome
To fyght with oon whech had governauns
Of all that cyté, and oonly onto his dome   *under his sole rule*
Stode all that cuntré with all her pusauns,   *puissance*
Bothe Ytayle and Almayne, Ynglond, Spayn, and Frauns —   *Germany*
1105 Constantyn he hyght, whech thoo baptyzed was
Of Seynt Sylvestere be a ful specyall grace.

This same Constantyne discoumfetyd in batayle   *defeated*
This forseyd Maxence, for all his pompe and pryde,
As this lady in prophecye whech myght not fayle
1110 Had seyd before — the fame was bore full wyde
And merkyd full wele, the day and eke the tyde,

Of sundry men whech aftyrwarde full wele knewe
All that sche seyd was full stable and trewe.[1]

Chapter 19

But whan these wordes were seyd of this mayde,
1115 He cryed lowde to the puple abowte,
So was he with hir wordes afrayde.
What he shall do now is he fall in dowte.
Swech was his crye: "Fy on swech a rowte   *crowd*
That schall thus suffyr a woman here defame
1120 Oure hye goddys, her servyse, and her name!

"How long schall we this whych thus susteyne? *witch; tolerate*
How long schall we suffyr this cursidenes?
To all good leveres it schuld be very peyne   *true believers*
To here a woman with swech sturdynesse   *audacity*
1125 Ageyn all men, the more and eke the lesse,
Thus evermore crye — ley on hondys, for schame — *seize her*
Ye stand as men me thinkyth were lame!"

Thus cryed this tyraunt with full lowde noys,
Thus berkyd this dogg ageyn that hevynly name,
1130 Ageyn Jhesu that was hangyd on croys.
His men abowte him thus gan he to blame:
"Com forthe anon; loke ye tak this dame,
Bete hir and rende hir with yrn and plumbys of lede —
Leve not youre labour tyll that sche be dede!"

1135 Sche was bete now than befor his face
So dispytously that schame it was to see,   *pitilessly*
For many a man that stode thoo in that place
Myght not loke on hir for reuthe and pytee.
The tyraunt wold nevyr sey, "Now leve ye,"

---

[1] Lines 1110–13: *the report [of her prediction] was widely circulated, / And various men who carefully noted the day and time (i.e., the details of her prediction) / Afterwards knew that / Everything she said was reliable and true*

1140   But evyr he cryed, "of hir make an hende,   *end*
        For if sche lyve oure puple wyll sche schende!"

Chapter 20

        Thus is sche bounde and led forth in the town.
        The puple that folowyde on hir thus gun crye:
        "O noble mayde, why wyl ye not fall down
1145   Onto the emperour and of him aske mercy?
        We are full sory that youre fayre body
        Is so rent, youre skyn is all to tore;
        But ye aske mercy, ye are lost for evyrmore.

        "What woman are ye that so despyse your age,
1150   Youre body, your beuté, that ye set at nought?
        Ye may have worchepe, ye may be set in stage   *platform*
        Ryght as a goddesse — where on is youre thowte?
        And all the world for beuté schulde be bowte:
        Here myght thei fynde it; thei nede no ferther seke.
1155   Syth ye be wyse, syth ye be holde so meke,   *are held to be*

        "Why wyll ye not obey onto the kynge?
        Bettyr it is to bowe than vylensly to be dede.   *cruelly*
        In youre bokes I trow ye lerned this thinge:
        The grete dygnyté may ye not down trede;
1160   It longyth to yow to obey onto your heede.
        Syth it is ryght, why will ye not it doo?
        We wolde do thus if ye councelled us soo.

        "Ye lese the flour of youre virgynyté,
        Ye lese that Godd plenteuously in yow sette,   *what*
1165   Ye lese your herytage, ye lese youre degré,
        All for a worde whech that is youre dette!   *obligation*
        Ovyrsolenly think we that youre hert is sett   *Too singularly*
        Whan that no counseyle may yow lede ne rayle,   *constrain*
        Most specyaly whan it is your avayle."

1170   Swech wordes spake the puple there abowte:
        "Remembre yow, mayde, what ye schall now lese

All for youre hert, for it is so stowte.
Feynyth summe plesauns, syth ye may not chese —
Both body and bonys with betyng wyll ye lese;   *lose*
1175   Onys mercy may avoyde all this.   *At any time*
Thys is oure consell — it may yow bryng to blys.

"Youre whyght skyn that schyneth as the sune,
Ye wyll schende it and make it pale and wan,   *destroy*
For very betyng it wyl be all dunne;
1180   Youre blode reall whech now that no man   *royal*
In these dayes remembyr no hyer can,
This wyll ye spylle ryght upon the grounde.
Youre counsell in this is neythir sane ne sounde!"

Chapter 21

"O wykkyd counsell," seyd the mayde ageyn,
1185   "Goo to your werkys and think no more on me.   *about your business*
Fy on beuté that wyll with wynde and reyn
Be steyned ful sone; my fayrnesse whech that ye
Compleyn so sore, thow that I lyve, pardé,   *Lament*
And fall in age, yet wyll it than apeyre.   *deteriorate*
1190   Than for my flesch fall ye not in dyspeyre,

"But trost ye this as for a sekyrnesse:
All youre bodyes, be thei nevyr so bryght,
Shall dey and roote in her wretchydnes,   *rot*
For this same deth longyth onto us of ryght,
1195   Condempned for synne be the provydens and the syght
Of God, oure Lord. What, shall we than so wayle
For febyll beuté that so sone will qwayle?   *decline*

"Every man must thus as of necessité
Deye and rote but of the speciall grace
1200   Be graunted to summe of that deyté —   *deity*
For summe with clennes be that there purchace
Swech dispensacion that in what maner place
They be leyd, thei shall nevyr roote,   *rot*
Flesshe ne senowis, veynes, shete ne coote: *sinews; shroud; garments*

1205 "This specialté is to hem graunted here
That kepe her bodyes fro all unclennes
Of lust and fylth and fro that love unclere   *impure*
Whech thei calle lechery — no love, I gesse,
I calle it rather a wyld rage of wodnesse.
1210 But now to purpos: thei that kepe hem clene,   *to the point*
Thei have this pardon graunted, as I wene.

"And if my Lord, my love, wil graunt me
That aftir my deth my flessh shall not roote,
Than am I more bound onto His deité
1215 Than evyr I was and this I Him behoote: *promise*
There shall nevyr man make me so to doote   *be so foolish*
That I shall leve His love or His plesauns.
Therfore, ye puple, leve this observauns,   *ritual*

"Folowith no lenger, goth home to youre werke;
1220 Wepe noth for me but for youreselve ye wayle.
I shall dey bodyly, but because I have the merke
Of Crystis baptem, I shall scape that grete asayle
Of all the fendys whech with grete travayle
Are ful besy oure soules for to gete
1225 Onto her prison, where thei shall hem bete.

"This shall I escape and eft ryse ageyn
In fayrer forme than evyr ye sey in me —
I beleve and trost this thing as for certeyn.
Therfor, seres, for youreselve wepe ye,
1230 For youre errour, that ye in derkenes be;
For if ye deye in this same errour,
Youre reryng ageyn shall cause you grete dolour."   *resurrection*

Many of hem that here hir thus speke   *hear*
Were converted to Cryst oure savyoure.
1235 Ful pryvyly her maumentis dede thei breke
Whech that thei had in ful grete honour,
Withdrow hem fro synne and wayled her errour,
And pryvyly, sole hevy as ony leed,
For naturall fere that thei shuld noth be dede.

Chapter 22

1240 Ther was a man in Alysaunder at that tyme,
    Meyer and leder of alle the puple there   *Mayor*
    Undyr the emperour, puncher of all cryme,   *punisher*
    Of whom the cyté had full mechill fere.
    Venemhous in angyr was he as ony bere;   *bear*
1245 Dispitous, veniabill, without discrecyon:
    Cursates thei called him thorowoute the town.

    He sey the emperour in angyr and woodnes
    And, of pure malice, sette him more on fere: *aflame*
    "O emperour," he seyd, "thi wisdam, as I gesse,
1250 Shuld make thee ashamyd of this matere here,
    That o wench shuld bryng thee thus in dwere —
    Thu standyst stoyned as thow thu were bounde.
    Lystyn my counsayle therfor now a stounde: *while*

    "This mayde Kateryne sey yett no torment
1255 Whech shuld fese hir to make afrayed.   *attack*
    Therfor, sir, I telle you myn entent:
    We shall make a thing so horrybyly arayed
    It shal be dred or it be fully asayde.
    Lete hir se onys this thing that I shall devyse —
1260 She shall leve sone than, I trow, all this gyse.   *behavior*

    "Comaund werkmen for to obey to me:
    I shall be maystir, thei shall do her werke,
    For I have conceyved now a new cruelté —
    Ful sekyrly therof have I take my merke.   *made measurements*
1265 In this matere both controllere and clerke   *accountant*
    Will I be and no man but myselve.
    Werkmen will I have with me ten or twelve.

    "This have I dyvysed in my besy thoght:
    Foure grete qweles thus schul we make,   *wheels*
1270 Swech maner wise shall thei be wrought
    What maner thing that evyr thei take
    Anon in pecys thei shul it rende and shake

With her sharpnes whech thei shul have,
For all the spokes that com fro the nave   *hub*

1275   "Shul have nayles sharp as a knyffe
I-fasted to the sercles round all abowth.   *perimeters*
There is no man now that beryth lyffe,
Be his herte nevyr so styffe and stowth,
And he be onys ine he com not oute
1280   Or he be deed and alle to pecys drawe,
Rith be experiens this thing shall we knawe.

"Sharp sawes shull thei have sumwhat crokyd,
Nayled onto the qwelys on the utter syde.   *wheels; outside*
In swech maner forme thus shul thei be hokyd:
1285   Ech of hem be othir ful sotilly shall glyde;   *past the other*
Summe shall com upward with her cours wide,
Summe shall go downward, and thus shall thei rend
All thing betwix hem and therof make an ende.

"Therfor lete these qweles be mad in hast.
1290   Sett the mayd right be hem whan that thei goo —
Sche shal be afrayed or sche hem tast.   *frightened before; experiences*
There is no man lyvyng hath sey swech whelys moo!   *seen*
This same devyse shall plese youre lordchip soo,"
Seyd this Cursates. "Ye shull cun me thanke.
1295   Yondyr will we make hem right on the banke."

The emperour comaunded, and that in hasty wyse,
These qweles shuld be made and that anon
Rith as Cursates thus gan devyse.
Thei are called forth, both Robyn and Jon,
1300   Carpenteres and smythes, as fast as thei may gon.
Thei hewe and thei blewe ful sore, levyth me:
The qweles must be redy withinne dayes thre.

Chapter 23

Now is it com that same third day.
The qweles are redy, sette as thei shall be;

1305	She is brought forth, Kateryne, this same may,	
	Right betwix hem sett now is she.	
	Too qweles goo downward, as we seyd, pardé,	
	And too rend upward; there is non that it seyth	
	But for fere he gruggeth with his teth.	*gnashes his teeth*

1310	O nobil mayd, how shall thu scape this thing?	
	This irous emperour, he is noth thi frend;	*wrathful*
	The meyhir is cruel in his ymagenyng,	
	For he hath stodyed with all hert and mend	
	Thi virginal body to distroy and shend.	
1315	There is no comfort but fro the court above:	
	He wil not fayle thee, Jhesu that is thi love.	

	Thus is she sett and lykly to be rent.	
	With all her labour the servauntis dresse her gere:	*gear*
	Thei tary sumwhat because that hir entent	
1320	Thei wene to chaunge rith for very fere.	*expect*
	Hir yne and handis ful mekely gan she rere	*eyes; raise*
	Up onto heven — swech was hir oryson:	
	"Lord God," she seyd, "that made sunne and mon,	

	"Lord that art allmyty in majesté,	
1325	Thu can all thing and may fulfylle in dede;	*know and can do [everything]*
	Lord that nevyr hydyst Thi grete pyté	
	Fro thoo folke that cryne onto Thee at nede,	
	O Lord of lordes, my prayer Thu may spede.	
	I pray Thee, Lord, with ful besy entent,	
1330	That Thu distroy this horribyll new torment —	

	"Make Thi thundir descend now with Thi levene:	*lightning*
	Brenne it, breke it, thys tyme I me thus pray.	
	Schewe Thy power, open now Thy hevyn	
	That men may know Thi lordchip at this day.	
1335	It is full esy to Thee make here swech afray	*for You to; attack*
	And to the puple it is full mervelows.	
	Good blyssyd Lord that art so graciowus,	

"Thys aske I not for oure fere of deth
But for Thi puple that stand here abowte.
1340   Me thinkyth, Lorde, her langage myn herte sleth,
That thei with tungys and wordys prowde and stowte   *furious*
Schuld blaspheme Thi name and put in dowte
Thi trewe feyth. This is, Lorde, my cause,   *goal*
To schryve me schortly to Thee in a clause: *confess; sentence*

1345   "That thei shuld trost Thi myght and Thi powere
And honour Thi name and be converted eke,
Be turned fro maumentis whech thei worchep here,
The Lord Godd only for to seke.
This pray I Thee with hert lowe and meke:
1350   Graunt me this as Thu art omnipotent —
Suffyr not Thi servauntes with maumentys be circumvent."   *deceived*

Chapter 24

Whan that this lady had endyd hir orysoun,
Anon a angell was sent down fro hevene —
With wynde and thundyr thoo cam he down.
1355   There cam with him eke an horryble levene.   *lightning*
The hour of the day thei sey it was but sevene,
But or eyte he with wynde and fere   *eight; fire*
Breke all this qwelys — thei fley here and there,   *wheels; flew*

Thei spryng abowte be pecys in the place.
1360   Summe man hathe harme on legges and on knees,
Summe are hurt on handys and on face
There fley fere ful wondyrly with the trees.   *flay many; spokes*
Mech of the puple have take there her fees: *got what was coming to them*
Thei that blasphemyd oure Godd with cruell hert,
1365   Fro this venjauns thei may not lyghtly stert.   *go*

The lady sate stille, for she felt no grevauns,
Makyng hir prayer with grete devocion.
Thus can oure Lord for His make purvyauns,   *i.e., followers; provision*
Thus can He shape hem her savacion.   *ordain*
1370   Thus dede He sumtyme in the Calde nacyon   *Chaldean*

Whan that His servauntis in the ovene were sette
Wher that the fere of his myth was lette,   *fire was deprived of its power*

For thei in the ovene were no thing brent,
But thei about it, thei toke the harme.   *the bystanders*
1375   This lady is lych hem in this myracle present:
The fyre fley abouth hir and in hir barme   *bosom*
It restyd oftyme, but she was not warme,
Ne hurt, ne harmed in no maner degré,
Yet was this fere so horrible that he

1380   Brent the qweles and throw hem aboute,
Brent men, eke, and thoo were not fewe —
Foure thousand seyth oure story, withouten doute,
Were dede with the blast, leyd all on rowe,
Of hethen caytyves, schrew rith be schrewe.   *wretches; villain*
1385   Heraudes noumbred hem for thei coud best.
The lady sate stylle in hir holy nest,

Kneland devoutly in sobyr prayere.
The aungell and fere both thei toke her wey   *companion; departed*
To place thei cam fro; men myth hem here
1390   Both in her comyng and goyng, thei sey.
Mech folke for fere were in poynt to dey,
Save that the comforth of this swete may
Lyft hem ageyn fro that affray.

This is the ende of this costfull werke: *expensive*
1395   Who are now woo but hethen men there?   *sad*
Who are now mery? Who gune her fruntes merke   *foreheads*
But Crysten folke whech hath scapyd this fere?   *fire*
Summe men for venjauns may not go ne stere: *i.e., are crippled or dead*
Thus o syde is in joye, the othir in sorow and care;
1400   Of swech maner venjauns lete every man beware.

Chapter 25

Now is the emperour oute of mesure wood,
For all fayleth and fallith that shuld now stand.

For very angyr he rent habyte and hoode.
"Saturne," he seyd, "whi take ye not on hand
1405   Youre owne cause? For, as I undirstand,
This venjauns is repugnyng to youre deité.
Wher is now youre myth? Wher is now he,

"Jubiter youre sone, that hath the governauns
Ovyr these Ciclopes, smythis I mene,   *Cyclopes*
1410   Whech with her thundir make the erde to dauns
So it is aferd of tho strokes kene?
But ye defend you, youre offeryng wil be lene!   *lean*
Ryse up, ye goddes, and suffir not this wrong!
Me thinkith ye abyde wondirly long."

1415   In all this care the qween that stod above,
Hey in a toure for to behold this syght,
Whech on that tyme had bore the love
Full pryvyly in hert of God almyth,
Now will she pleynly ryth before his syth
1420   Uttir hir hert, falle therof what falle.   *come what may*
She is now com down, and hir servauntis alle,

To presens of hir lord. Thus than she sayd,
"Thu wretchid husbond, what hast thu i-doo?
Why tormentist thu so wrongly this goodly mayde?
1425   Ageyn the grete God whi wrestyllist thu soo?
What wodnes makith thee with care and woo   *madness*
To pursew Goddis servauntis with peyne and deth?
O cruell best, whan thu shalt yeld thi breth,

"Whedir wilt thu send thi wretchid goost?
1430   Thou fytyst ageyn the prycke that shall thu fynd,   *attack*
For whan thu art hyest and in pryd moost,   *most proud*
Oure Lord God ful sore shall thee bynd.
Turne thi bestialté to mannes mynd!   *i.e., be rational*
Know the powere of thi God above
1435   Whech werkith so wondirly for hem that Him love!

"The grete myty Godde of Crysten men —
Se what He dede this ilke same day:
With a thundir clap, of thi lordes ten
Smet He to the deth — thu thiselve it say —   *saw*
1440   Foure thousand of thi comonys in her aray,   *your subjects*
Thei ly yondyr dede. Who shall hem reyse?   *resurrect*
If Appollo do it I will him than preyse.

"He that with a stroke may swech thing make,
He is a lord; know Him for thi kyng.
1445   Thi fals maumentrye I rede thee forsake.   *advise*
Turne thee to that Lord that mad all thing:
The synnes that we dede whil we were ying   *young*
He will forgeve us if we mercy crave —
Aske mercy of Him and thu shall it have!"

1450   Whan the tyraunt herd what the qwen sayde,
"Woman," sayd he, "wote ye what ye say?
I am full sekyr ye spoke with the mayde
Whan I was oute this othir day.
Avyse you sumwhat or that ye asay   *lest; experience*
1455   The orible peynes whech that ye shul have.
Youre frendes ne youre kynrod shall you not save,

"For, be that hy majesté of the goddes alle,
And be that provydens of Jubiter the kyng,
But ye fro this fonnednes and that in hast falle,   *foolishness*
1460   Dame, ye shall have as foule endyng
As evyr had woman, eythire eld or ying,
In youre dayes. Therfor, avyse you weel,
For thow youre God hath brokyn oure wheell

"Be witchcraft or be nygromancy,
1465   Trost me in this: we shall ordeyn a mene
For to distroy youre fals tretchery.
What, art thu now, dame, led on that rene?   *by that rein*
Thi witte counte not to a bene worth   *amounts; bean*
Whan thu forsakist the goddes protection
1470   And, as a fole, takyst the Crysten illusyon."

270

Chapter 26

Thus in his angyr and in his grete ire,
He byddyth his mynystris to take the qwen.
With sotil launces made of yrne wyre
Thei schul rend hir tetys ryth anon bedene.   *teats; immediately*
1475   In his presens thei shall do it, for he will it sene —
Long sorow he will that his wiffe shall have.
"Lete se," he seyth, "if Cryst shall hir now save!"   *Let [it be] seen*

Aftir this is done he will thei hir take,
Lede hir to the felde there traytouris alle   *where*
1480   Have as thei deserve, teye hir to a stake,
Smyte of hir heede and let it down falle,
Let it lye there — hungry doggys it schalle
Ete and devoure in despyte of Jhesu.
As the tyraunt badd, his men dede pursew:

1485   Thei pullyd hir tetys in ful horrible wyse
Ryght from hir breste — pyté it was to se
The blode in the veynes with the mylke ryse.
All rent and ragged, all blody was sche,
Yet onto Kateryne sche fel down on kne,
1490   Prayng ful dolfully, and evyn thus sche sayde:
"O Crysten pelere, o most holy mayde,   *pillar*

"Pray now for me onto thi Lorde above,
That this peyn whych I suffyr here
Only for His worchep, His feyth, and His love,
1495   May be to my sowle a suffycyaunt chere   *accomplishment*
Whan I schal come to that blys full clere
Whech thu behyght me not long agoo.   *promised*
Pray eke for me that I may kepe alsoo

"The same good purpos whech I am inne,
1500   That this peyn horrible make me not reneye   *renounce*
This holy lyffe to turn ageyn to synne.
I am sore aferde my flesch, or that I deye,
For very drede the contrarye of this shulde seye.

271

Wherfore, lady, all this lyghte in thee: *alights upon you*
1505 Pray thu to Godd that He may kepe me."

The mayde seyd onto the qween ageyn,
"O blessed lady that hast forsake all thing,
Crowne and joye, schortly for to seyn,
And wonne the lufe therfore of oure kynge,
1510 Cryst I mene, make now no stakeryng   *have no doubt (staggering)*
As in this matere, for He shall make thee stronge
For Whos lufe thu sufferest now this wrong.

"Suffyr hertly all this grete dyssesse: *discomfort*
It schal not lest but a lytyll space.   *last*
1515 Cryst youre Lorde herwith shall ye plese,
Whech hath graunted of His specyall grace
That this same day shall ye se His face.
A mervelous chaunge, lady, shall it be
Whan ye com before the Trynyté:

1520 "For temporal londe ye shul have hevenly blys,
For erdly husbond youre spouse shal be He
That may amend all thing that is amysse —
A Lord that dwellith evyr in felicité,
A Lord that hath nevyr non adversité.
1525 Thus shul ye chaunge, lady, onto the best.
I shal not long be absent fro that nest."

Thus is she comforted, this noble Crysten qwene,
Thus is she stabylyd mytyly in oure feyth.   *supported mightily*
Thus is she led, with knytys as I wene;
1530 And evyr the emperour onto his men seyth
Ful bostous wordes, strokes eke he leyth   *arrogant*
Upon her backes that thei shuld make a ende
Of this woman, for hir tetys now thei rend,

As I seyd ere, and aftir that grete peyne
1535 With sharpe swerd hir hede of thei smyth.   *off*
Oure Lord Godde strenghid hir to susteyne
With grete pacyens all this same unryth.   *injustice*

Thus is she passed; hir soule is to that lyth   *light*
Whech was endles, rith as we beleve!
1540   The thre and twenty day of Novembyr, rith at eve,

And on a Wednysday, was this martyrdam
Thus consummat. Hir body whan it was dede
Was left stylle, in despyte of Crystyndam,   *out of scorn for*
Lying there full white and eke full rede,
1545   No man so hardy to wynd it in cloth or lede,   *wrap; lead*
Thus had the emperour of his cruelté.
That she lay thus mech folke thouth pyté.   *thought*

Chapter 27

Now is the nyth com and onto her rest
Is every man go that was abydyng there.
1550   Porphery thouth it was honest
And eke medfull this body for to rere,   *meritorious; lift up*
Eke to the byrying devoutly it to bere.
Therfor called he certeyn knythis onto him,
And whan the weder was ful derke and dym,   *weather*

1555   Rith in the wyntir aboute seynt Kateryne day,   *i.e., November 25*
He cam to the body with full holy entent.
Evene in hir lyvand, rith as she lay,
With full swete and costful onyment
He baumed hir body and forth with it went,   *anointed*
1560   With prayer wepyng and full besy cure;
Thus thei led it to the sepulture.

The next day is there grete questyon:
Who beryed the qwen? Who was so hardy
To falle in grevous transgression
1565   To remeve or bery this same body?
Only of suspecion certeyn folke openly
Were arestyd be the offyceres ther,
And Porphiry ful boldly withouten fere

Aperyd to the emperour and thus he sayd:
1570   "Sith thu art a lord and justyce shuld kepe,
Whi hast thu tormentyd this holy mayde?
Thin owne wyves hede of dede thu swepe —   *did you smite off*
Grete cause hast thu sore for to wepe!
These innocentis, eke, this is thin entent,
1575   Withouten cause now to torment.

"Chese of thin ire, cese of thi wrong;   *Chase*
Leve thi besynes in inquisicion.
I telle thee pleynly, thow thu me hong,
I am that man whech with devocion
1580   Byried thi wiffe; me thout it no treson
But full acordand onto nature
To bryng that body onto sepulture.

"Wher hast thu seyn swech cruelnes?
Yete to thevys and robouris whan thei are dede
1585   Her frendis have leve of the law, I gesse,   *permission*
To wynd hem in clothis, in bord of lede,   *coffin*
To solace her neyboris with drynke or brede.
All this is turnyd ageyn discrecion,   *sound judgment*
Ageyn kynd eke ageyn religion!

1590   "Wher lered thu evyr that bestis shuld ete
Bodyes of men, of all creatures best?
Thus oure auctoures wryth and thus thei trete:
It is neythir worchipfull ne eke honest
Onto mankynd to foule his own nest.
1595   Sere emperour, I confesse here this dede have I do —
Punch not these innocentis, but lete hem goo!"   *Punish*

Chapter 28

These wordes of Porphirie thei aren a wounde
Onto Maxens hert, for he made a cry,
Whan he had sorowed a lytyll stounde,   *while*
1600   So grete and so loude the halle whech was hye
Sounded with the noyse; the very malencoly

Made him so wood he wist not what he sayd, *mad*

But sone aftir swech wordes he up brayd: *roared*

"O me, most wretchid of all men that lyve,

1605 Wherto brought Nature me to lyffe?

Whi wold she to me swech astate gyve *prosperity*

Whan she thus wretchidly hath take my wyffe?

Had she suffered me with sharp knyffe

Be stykyd in my cradyll she had do the best. *stabbed*

1610 Now am I reved of all my dewe rest, *deprived*

"For Porphery here, of whom I most trost,

Porphirie here, the best frend I have,

My Porphirie, my knyth, thus is he lost,

So deceyved of witchcraft that he begynnyth rave.

1615 Evene as the spokys rest in her nave, *spokes [of a wheel] rest in their hub*

So in his brest stood all my comforth;

To swech anothir frend can I nevyr resorte.

"He deceyvyd my wyffe, but she is dede,

He hath deceyved himself, that grevyth me most.

1620 My hert it waxith hevy as the lede,

So am I acomered with thoutis in my goost. *assailed*

Allas, my Porphirye, I durst a made a boost, *would have sworn*

Thow all my kyngdam had me forsake,

Fals to my crown no man shuld thee make.

1625 "Yete thow thu have do this grete despite —

Deceyvyd my wyffe but deceyvyd thiselve —

Yete of thi treson thu shall have respite:

Ten dayes I graunt thee or ellis twelve.

Leve this Crysten cumpany, forsake that elve *elf*

1630 Jhesu of Nazareth — He dede nevyr man good.

He is cause of spyllyng of mech gentil bloode.

"If thu wilt leve this new cursyd scole,

Thu shall have grace, thu shalt not dey.

So wyse a man now made a fole,

1635 Who caused him thus sone to reneye *renounce*

The holy religion, the eld trew wey
Whech that oure faderes kept withoute mynd?
Allas, man, allas — thi reson is ful blynd!"

Chapter 29

    Right with this langage the emperour dede calle
1640 All knytes of the court be on and be on.   *one by one*
    He examyned himselve that tyme hem all,
    How that thei thoutht this matere shuld goon.
    Ful dolfully to hem he made his mone:
    "Beholdith," he seyth, "how my Porphyrye
1645 All sodenly is i-falle onto this myserye.

    "I hope it is to you but ignorauns
    If that ye favoure him in his dede,
    But be ye ware of that grete venjauns
    Whech that may falle withouten drede   *without doubt*
1650 On swech renegatis that othir men lede
    Fro her trew lawes. How will ye answere?"
    Alle seyd thei thus that stoden there:

    "Be it knowe to thee now, ser emperour,
    That God and Lord whech this same man
1655 Honourith at this tyme, Jhesu oure savyoure,
    This same God, with all that we may or can,
    Will we serve, curse thu or banne,
    Endith thou and smyth with tormentis straunge —
    Leve this wele: thu shall us nevyr chaunge.   *Believe*

1660 "Fere of deth or love of lyffe swete
    May nevyr depart oure hertly love
    Fro Jhesu Cryst, the trewest prophete
    That evyr was sent fro heven above.
    What peynes are applyed than shall thu prove
1665 That alle oure hertis are sette in one,   *i.e., we are of one mind*
    In this same feyth, as stabill as the ston."

The emperour comaund in hasty wyse
Thei shuld be led onto her passion,
For of swech renegates he wil be justese
1670   To venge the wrong which that was don
Upon the goddes, the sunne and the mone.
Thus are thei ledde forth to her ende,
Save Porphirye alone now thei have no frend,

For he to comforth hem with full myty feyth
1675   Onto the emperour presyd where he stoode.
Swech maner wordis at that tyme he seyth:
"Men will wene that thu be ny wood
To sle this puple sodenly in her bloode
And lete me scape whech stered hem all.
1680   For perell, I counsell, whech that may falle

"Onto thee and eke onto thi londe,
Evene with the membris take now the hede!"
Thus sayd this man, as I undirstond,
To comfort hem thus or thei be dede.
1685   Because thei were of vysage hevy as leed
He was adrede ful sore that thei schuld fayle
If thei withoute him had go to this batayle.

Therfore, evyn aftyr his holy hertys desyre
Is he now servyd: bounde and forthe eke leed.
1690   Thei were not brent as heretykys in fyre,
But in her martyrdam thus were thei spede: *hastened*
Too hundred were there, of whech not on flede,
Her hedys the emperour bad thei shuld of smyte.
This was her ende, schortly to endyte.

1695   The bodyes were left that doggys shuld hem ete,
For very despyte ryght of Crysten feyth —
On of the auctoures whech this legend trete
In very sothenesse thus wrytyth and seyth.
The day of her deth eke ful fayre he leyth
1700   Of Novembre moneth, the foure and twenty day, eke
The fyfte day of that same weke.

Chapter 30

The next day folowyng, he clepyth this mayde
Before his tribunal; now is she present.
With ful sotyll langage onto hir he sayde
1705 Alle this male corage and his evyll entent: *wicked heart*
"Thow thu be gylty," he seyd, "of this torment
Of Porphyrye, of my wyffe, and my knytes alle —
(Fer fro her feyth thu made hem to falle,

"With sorcery and myschauns thu hast turned hem;   *wrongdoing*
1710 Thei coude nevyr resort onto her modyr wytte.   *common sense*
Thei dede more for thee than for fadyr or eem.   *uncle*
I cowde nevyr perceyve the knottys that ye knyte,
But deede are thei alle and we repent not yyt.) —
Mayden, thu may lyve, if thu hafe grace,
1715 Notwythstondyng thi treson and thi trespace.

"Wherfore I counsell now onto thi foudenesse: *foolishness*
Forsake thi magyke, wepe sore, and wayle
That evyr thu were so bolde in folehardynesse
To geve the qwene or Porphyrye swech evyl counsayle.
1720 Fro thin eyne lete the watyr now thi chekys rayle,   *flow down*
Fle thi deth now, for thow thu dede this gylt —
That is to sey, thu art cause of blode that is spylt —

"Yet may thu amend it with devocyoun,
To make an offeryng to the holy Saturne.
1725 We all wyll folow thee ryght in processyoun,   *right behind you*
So that thu wylt to this counsayle turn.
Allas, woman, how long wylt thu sojorne
In this grete cursydhed, oute of all resoun?   *accursed state*
Yet wyl I forgeve the all thin elde tresoun.

1730 "Thu schal have, mayden, al thoo behestis alle
Whech I promysed thee to bryng to astate.
Tary no lengere for perell that may falle:
Chese the bettyr or ellys sey chek-maate.
But if thu offyr, we too are at debate,   *we two are at odds*

278

1735   For thu schalt deye and that in ful hasty wyse.
      Thi deth anon on this maner I wyll devyse:

      "I wyll make smyght of thi heed with a blade
      Scherpe on bothe sydes whech may not fayle —
      He waraunt it, the smythe that it made,   *guarantees*
1740   That it was sewyre at ilke maner asayle,
      Were it flesch, were it bone or mayle,   *mail*
      It schuld it kerve. Therfore, mayd, consent,
      And of thin errour, I counsell thee, repent."

Chapter 31

      The mayde answerde than with full meke voys:
1745   "Evyr hafe I seyd that I am redy to deye
      For His love whech was hang on croys.
      This day schal be, schortly for to seye,
      A gret spectacle to the worldylys eye,
      To se a qween forsake londe and halle,
1750   So sodeynly to deth for to falle.

      "Sume men ween we Crysten, whan we dey,
      Sume men wene the fall is reprovable,   *reprehensible*
      Sume men ween the fall is myserye.
      We lese thing to us that is ful supportable —   *tolerable*
1755   I sey we lese thyng that is deceyvable,
      I sey we lese a lyvyng ful of stryffe
      And wyne a regyon whech is the lond of lyffe.

      "For grete sekenes, there schall we have helth;   *In exchange for*
      For wepyng teres, we shall have lawhyng joye;   *laughing*
1760   That place haboundeth evyr more in welth,   *abounds*
      That place in sikir hath nevyr no noye,   *harm*
      It is more sikir than evyr was the toure of Troye   *tower*
      Fro schot and treson; therfor thedir I glyde.
      Whan I shall dey, Cryst shal be my gyde.

1765   "Wherfore I wil no lenger now thee drawe   *lead*
      With veyne termes: do as thu hast thought.   *intended*

I despice thi goddis, thi offeryng, and thi lawe;
Alle thi maumentis eke I sett at nought.
To Him I goo that hath me ful dere bought;
1770   To Him I will, I covett to se His face.
The angellis song whech is in that place,

"If thu myth here it, astoyned shuld thu be.
Thou hast no grace swech mysteries to approche.
Farewele my frendys, farwele all my mené,   *companions*
1775   Farewele my castels that stand hye on roche!   *cliff*
A new drynke my love will me abroche   *tap (as a keg)*
Aftir my blood be spylt here on the ground.
Farewele the world that is shape so round!

"I shall folow the Lombe that washid with His blode   *Lamb*
1780   Oure blody synnes, wretchid and unkynd,
I folow the Lombe whech is full meke and good,
Whos steppes folow virgines withouten mynd.   *innumerable*
Come of, tyraunt, sle and do thi kynd: *off; i.e., do your worst*
I abyde not elles but deth and goo to lyffe;
1785   I drede no fere, water, swerde, ne knyffe!"

With these wordes sentens was gove anon:
She shal be dede, as was devysyd before.
Forth is she drawe. Men and women ilkon
Folow on fast and folow on wondir sore,
1790   Wepyng and cryeng evyr more and more:
"O holy mayde, whi wilt thu thus wretchidly
Take thi deth and with sweche velony?"   *dishonor*

Sche seyd ageyn, "Moderes and maydenys alle,   *replied*
Wepe not for me, lette noth my passion,   *hinder*
1795   Leve youre wordes with whech ye on me calle;
For if nature enclyne you to consolacion,
To have mercy on myschefe and desolacion,
Wepe ye than rith for youre owne synne
Whech ye have haunted, in which ye be inne.   *committed*

1800	"Wepe for youre errour whech shall you bryng	
	Onto brennyng fyre where youre goddes dwelle.	
	Thow that youre prestis rede to you and syng	
	Of the goddes holynesse and mech thing you telle,	
	I sewir you this that thei ben in helle	*assure*
1805	And evyr withoute ende in that place shal be;	
	But if ye amend you, eke so shall ye."	

Chapter 32

	Aftir this is sayd, she is come to the place	
	Where she shall dey, and of the man thoo	
	Whech shuld hir smyth she prayed space	
1810	For to have, or she fro this world goo,	
	That she may sey wordes on or too	
	In pryvy meditacion onto God above,	
	Which is hir makere, hir Lord, and hir love.	
	The man graunted and sche kneled down	
1815	With eyene and handes lift up to hevene.	
	On swech sentens sche made hir oryson:	*In this vein; prayer*
	"O myty God whos name for to nevene	*to name*
	Is ful mervelous, makere of planetes sevene,	
	Helth of hem all that trostyn in Thi mercy,	
1820	Hope of all virgines that to Thi helpe cry,	
	"O Jhesu, most swettest, whech hast nonbred me	*numbered*
	Rith into Thi college among Thi maydenes all,	*assembly*
	Do with Thi servauntis aftir Thi benygnyté.	
	Spred me with Thi mercy; lete me nevyr falle	
1825	Into my enmy handis. Lord, to Thee I calle.	
	Do me this mercy for Thi hey name:	
	That what maner man, the rith or the lame,	*i.e., not lame*
	"Whech hath my passion in rememberauns,	
	Eythir in his deth or ellis in sekenes,	
1830	Or in his persecusion or eyther grevauns,	*or else*
	If he with devocion and hertyly besynes	*diligence*
	Aske ony relees, Lord, of Thi worthynes	

Graunt him his bone, Lord, for my sake,   *request*
As I now my deth for Thi love take.

1835   "And all thoo that my passion have in memorye,
Pestilens ne deth mote hem nevyr greve,
Hungyr and sores and othir myserye,
And all evyll eyres, on morow or on eve,
Suffyr hem not to have, but rathere hem geve
1840   Abundauns in hervest and ethir temporate;   *air*
Let not her londys abyde desolate

"But graunt hem plenté of her greynes alle.   *grains*
Because thei love me, Thu schalt hem love.
Behold, Lorde, for Thi cause I mote now falle
1845   Down into deth. Take to Thi behove   *Use; benefit*
Thing that this bochere may not hale ne schove: *butcher; extract*
Tak Thu my sowle, no man may but Thou.
O Jhesu Cryst, my sowle I comende now

Onto Thi handys; I pray Thee Thu it take.
1850   Lett Thin aungellis whech that se Thi face
Come down fro hevyn for Thi maydenes sake,
Suffyr hem to come now onto this place,
To lede my soule, Lorde, onto Thi grace,
Onto that feleschepe whech Thu me behyght   *promised*
1855   Among Thi seyntys that schyne with Thee full bryght."

Chapter 33

Sche had scarise made hir conclusyoun   *scarcely*
Of this prayere but anon sodenlye
Fro the hevene thei herd thoo a sownde soun,   *loud sound*
A swete voys, and thus it gan to crye:
1860   "Myn owne spowse, My wyffe and mayde holy,
Come now to Me, come now onto thi rest,
For in My feyth thu hast labored as best.

"The blyssed gate of hevyn is now ope:
It is made redy to thee that mansyoun,   *for you; dwelling place*

282

1865   For thi feyth, thi charyté, and thi hope,
          Schall thu have my specyall benysoun.   *blessing*
          There abyde the persones of thi nacyoun
          For to reteyne thee to that eternyté,   *serve*
          Where thu schalt joye before the Trinyté.

1870   "Maydenes are redy to bryng thee thi crowne,
          Aungellis are redy ordeynde thi sowle eke to lede.
          As for a tyme cast of thi fleschly gowne —   *off*
          Thu schall receyve it in anothyr stede.
          Come forthe in hast; lok thu have no drede
1875   Of thi petycyons, for I graunt hem alle:
          What manere man that on thee wyll calle

          "Or worchip with hert thi holy passion,
          What maner myscheffe whech he be inne,
          I will relese it, and all transgression
1880   Of her defautes or of her eld synne,
          If thei will leve it and new lyffe begynne,
          For thi sake I will forgeve hem all,
          Conferme hem eke nomore aftir to falle."

Chapter 34

          The mayde leyd forth hir necke fayre and qwyte,   *white*
1885   And thus she sayd onto the smyter thoo: *i.e., executioner then*
          "I am called to fest now of God almyth:
          Doo thu thin office, the tyraunt bad thee soo,
          Fulfille his comaundment, and than may thu goo
          Without daunger, stand eke in his grace;
1890   I pray to God forgeve thee thi trespace."

          The man was glad to do the comaundment
          Of his lord; wherfor, with besy corage
          He applyed holly all his entent
          Sumwhat to spare this yong tendir age,
1895   For with a stroke that was ful wode and rage   *violent and passionate*
          Hir hede he parted from hir body there.
          Too grete myracles anon men myth lere.

On was in tokyne of virginall clennesse: *One*
In stede of blood, mylke ran at hir necke,
1900   Whech of hir purité that tyme bare wytnesse.
Ther myth non othir thing ren at that becke
Than swech as was befor in the secke —
I mene thus to put you oute of doute:
Swech thing as was in hir, swech thing ran oute.

1905   It ran so plenteuously, it wattered all the grounde
That lay aboute hir. O most mervelous welle:
Here is the hede, the mylke aboute all rounde.
What shulde I more of this myracle telle?
Save Mari alone, of maydenhode she hath the belle —   *i.e., ranks first*
1910   That witnessith wele this present vision
Whech may no wey be called illusion.

Anothir myracle eke was seyn at yye:
Aungellis aperyng in full mervelous aray.
Bodys lich men, wynges had thei to flye,
1915   Thei cam down ful sodenly, auctouris say,
Thei toke the body and sone bore it awey
Onto the mount where Moyses the lawe toke —   *i.e., Mount Sinai*
Of this myracle rith thus seyth oure boke.

The hill in whech God gave the wretyn lawe
1920   Onto the Jewes, ledyth to that perfection
Of Crystis Gospell and of His vertuous sawe,   *teachings*
In whech we fynd full swete instruction,
Poule in his bokes maketh swech induction —
He seyth it longith to Jerusalem as in servage,   *servitude*
1925   With all his childirn here in pylgrymage.

Than sith that this hill is as it were gyde
Onto that mownt whech that stant in blysse,
It is full good to us that we full hastily ryde
Aftir this mayde that she may us wisse   *show*
1930   A stedfaste lore for to amend oure mysse.   *sins*
So shall she be in manere of a figure
To bryng us to hevyn aftir oure sepulture.

This mount, thei sey, stand in Arabie;
It is fro Alisaunder of lond ful gret distauns.

1935 In twenty dayes, if that I shuld not lye,
Myn auctour seyth, thow man had purvyauns
And gydys good and eke gret pusauns
Full scarsly shuld he laboured in theis dayes —
There leve but fewe that hath mad asayes.

transportation
guides; stamina

have attempted it

1940 This passion was, as oure story seyth,
On a Fryday, rith for this entent:
That syth she fauth so strongly for oure feyth,
Men wene therfor it was convenient
That this same day whech oure Jhesu went

fought

1945 Oute of this world, that same day his mayde
Shuld dey for Him; thus oure auctour sayde.

The grete myracles whech be at hir grave
Are ny onknow, rith for grete distauns
Betwix that and us, but this knowlech we have:

1950 That oyle it rennyth evyr in habundauns,
With wheche oyle of sores alle grevauns
Whech men suffyr, it wil be helyd anon.
Summe men say that if thei bere a ston

oil
injury

Of that same grave, whedir that thei it bere

1955 It will swete evyr that same holy licour;
Thus sey the pylgrymes that have be ther.
This sey oure bokes whech be made in honour
Of this swete mayde, of this vertuous flour:
It longith to floures swech licoures to swete.

From; wherever
sweat

sweat

1960 I herd men eke of othir myracles trete,

Of lampis hangyng before hir sepulture,
Fylt with that oyle whech brenne a mannys lyve
And of her lyth nevyr make forfeture
Thou thei brenne yeres ten and fyve.

for a lifetime

1965 In this matere pleynly I will me schryve:
I may wele leve that swech merveyles ther be,
But for because I have non auctorité,

explain myself

I dare not write here her declaracion
Lest that I poyson all my forseyd werke;
1970   Lest that eke men of myn own nacion
Shuld ymagen that I, which am a clerke,
Mith of swech thingis take a wrong merke.   *be misguided*
Wherfor I comytte all this thing in fere   *together*
Onto discression of hem that shull it here,

1975   For I will determyne no conclusion
As in this matere. But fully I beleve
That whoso myth se that solempne stacion,   *holy place*
He shuld know thing to which we cannot preve.
Of this matere thus I take my leve.
1980   God, oure Lord, for His hye mercy
Graunt us hevene aftyr this mysery.

Per Capgrave.   *By*

Notes

Prologue

8   *Thou ledyst the daunce.* According to the OED, "to lead the dance" is a figurative expression meaning "to take the lead in any course of action" (dance, 6a). However, the rejoicing of the saints in heaven is often represented as a dance. See, for example, *The Book of Margery Kempe*, ed. Lynn Staley (Kalamazoo, MI: Medieval Institute Publications, 1996), p. 60, line 1150, and p. 62, lines 1199–1200.

16–43   *alle the privileges . . . / . . . thi loveris alle.* Following Jacobus de Voragine's *Legenda aurea*, Capgrave presents Katherine as a sort of omnibus saint, who has obtained all the favors God has granted his other saints, including John the Evangelist (Jesus visited his deathbed), Nicholas of Myra (oil flowed from his grave), the Apostle Paul (blood mixed with milk ran from his severed throat), Margaret of Antioch (God promised to honor requests made in her name), and Clement of Alexandria (angels adorned his grave). That Margaret, Clement, Paul, and Nicholas are mentioned is not accidental, for these are the saints with whom Katherine is most frequently paired in medieval iconography. For a translation of Jacobus de Voragine's Katherine legend, which was the most widely known life of that virgin martyr in the late Middle Ages, see *The Golden Legend*, trans. William Granger Ryan, 2 vols. (Princeton: Princeton University Press, 1993), 2.334–41.

59   *all that scharp whele.* An allusion to the emperor Maxentius' attempt to mangle Katherine with a torture instrument consisting of revolving spiked wheels. See 5.1240–1400.

62   *Ryth for straungenesse of his derk langage.* This story of how Katherine's *Life* must be transcribed from an illegible source bears a striking resemblance to the story of the genesis of Margery Kempe's *Book*.

78–112   *a revelacyoun / . . . God ofte sythe.* The priest's vision is a humorous reenactment of Ezekiel 2:8–3:3, in which a heavenly messenger commands the prophet to eat a scroll. Unlike Capgrave's priest, Ezekiel does as he is told without protest. A nearly identical incident occurs in Revelation 10:8–10; John, like Ezekiel, immediately swallows the scroll.

101   *clospe ne hook*. The covers of medieval manuscripts were often equipped with clasps and hooks.

119–26   *Amylion fytz Amarak . . . / . . . ye schall more clere*. Capgrave places Amilion's discovery of the MS in the 1360s, during the reign of Peter I of Cyprus and the papacy of Urban V.

143   *all the sevene artes*. Defined by Martianus Capella in the fifth century, the Seven Liberal Arts was an educational curriculum consisting of the *trivium* (grammar, rhetoric, dialectic) and the *quadrivium* (music, arithmetic, geometry, astronomy). Capgrave details Katherine's pursuit of this curriculum in 1.302–99. For more on the subject, see David L. Wagner, ed., *The Seven Liberal Arts in the Middle Ages* (Bloomington: Indiana University Press, 1983).

150   *be* is repeated in MS.

163–68   *Byschop in Alysaunder . . . / . . . syng and rede*. Capgrave is identifying Athanasius with the fourth-century theologian and bishop of Alexandria who, according to longstanding tradition, originally composed Katherine's passion. *Mech adversyté* (line 165) refers to Athanasius' struggle to discredit the views of the Alexandrian priest Arius, who denied the divinity of Christ. Because Arianism was favored by emperors at the time, Athanasius was repeatedly forced into exile. Apparently eager to anticipate all questions, Capgrave admits he does not know whether Katherine's biographer also wrote the so-called "Athanasian Creed," which was recited during *prime*, one of the eight liturgical hours that structured communal worship in medieval religious houses.

198   *A hundred yere aftyr*. Capgrave is attributing Arrek's Latin translation to the late fifth century (somewhat more than a century after Athanasius' death in 373).

236–38   *that hevynly reyne / That Apollo bare abowte . . . / . . . mannes soule*. Apollos was a learned Alexandrian convert (Acts 18:24–28) whom Paul commends for "watering," or nourishing, the newly sown Christian community at Corinth (1 Corinthians 3:5–9).

Book 1

53–54   *Oute of the harde thorn brymbyl-tree / Growyth the fresch rose.* "The rose springs
          from the brier" was a common expression at the time. It was often used to
          describe saints born of pagan parents. See B. J. Whiting, *Proverbs, Sentences, and
          Proverbial Phrases from English Writings Mainly Before 1500* (Cambridge, MA:
          Harvard University Press, 1968), R206.

71   *keye.* Citing Capgrave's usage, the OED ("key," 5) reads, "a place which from the
          strategic advantages of its position gives its possessor control over the passage
          into or from a certain district, territory, inland sea, etc."

79–81   *hir fredomys . . . grete repayre.* Freedoms were the rights and privileges granted
          to a city. Capgrave is saying that Amalek prospered because it was a good place
          to conduct business.

100–05   *Seynt Mark . . . for to beleve.* Eusebius reports Mark's missionary work in Egypt
          in Book 2 of his *Ecclesiastical History*.

107–18   *Rede Philo . . . I trow not he may.* Philo (20 BC–AD 50) was a Jewish exegete
          who influenced the Alexandrine school of theology. In his *De vita contemplativa*
          (*On the Contemplative Life*), to which Capgrave is probably alluding, Philo
          describes a large community of contemplative men and women who settled
          outside Alexandria and who had some of the earmarks of Christian hermits.
          Eusebius claims these contemplatives were Mark's Christian converts (*Ecclesias-
          tical History* 2.16–17) — a view that was widely accepted during the Middle
          Ages. Regardless of whether Philo's ascetics were Christian, Christian monasti-
          cism is generally held to have originated in Egypt, when, during the fourth
          century, men like Katherine's teacher Adrian retreated to the desert to devote
          themselves to God and wage war against demons through their asceticism. See the
          prototypical life of St. Anthony, composed by Katherine's putative biographer
          Athanasius.

127–33   *on Pathenus . . . called* Stromatum. Pantaenus is the first known head of what
          would become, under his successors Clement of Alexandria (author of the
          Stromateis, or *Miscellaneous Studies*) and Origen, an influential school of
          theology.

134–47   *Thys same Alysaundre . . . mote thei spede.* This passage explains why Katherine is known simply as Queen of Alexandria, though her realm encompasses many other cities and lands.

180   *fothyr.* According to the OED, "used for an enormous quantity, a 'cart-load' of money" (fother, 1c).

182–89   *Zacharye and Elysabethe stode . . . in this degré.* Capgrave is following the conventional practice of certifying Katherine's holiness by pointing out that her life conforms to familiar Biblical patterns. His allusion is to Luke 1:5–25, 57–59.

201   *rose oute of thorne.* See note to lines 1.53–54.

213–15   *For of that penaunce . . . ful holy men.* Christ's mother, Mary, was held to have escaped the normal agonies of childbirth because she was untainted by original sin.

221   *Sarcynrye.* By Capgrave's day, this and other terms referring to the Muslim faith had come to signify heathendom generally.

227–36   *This chyld for to hylle . . . Thus is it kept.* Capgrave's attention to the baby Katherine's nurture reflects a widespread interest in childhood during the fifteenth century, when guides on child rearing and stories about children proliferated. For a discussion of the fifteenth century's "fascination with childhood," see Barbara A. Hanawalt, "Narratives of a Nurturing Culture: Parents and Neighbors in Medieval England," in *"Of Good and Ill Repute": Gender and Social Control in Medieval England* (New York: Oxford University Press, 1998), pp. 158–77 (quote on p. 161); and Seth Lerer, "Reading Like a Child: Advisory Aesthetics and Scribal Revision in the *Canterbury Tales*," in *Chaucer and His Readers: Imagining the Author in Late-Medieval England* (Princeton: Princeton University Press, 1993), pp. 85–116. The contents of one of the MSS containing Capgrave's *Life of Saint Katherine*, British Library MS Arundel 168, evince a particular concern with the education of children. This manuscript includes an alphabet poem, a translation of Benedict Burgh's *Distichs of Cato*, and two other virgin martyr legends that emphasize the saint's relationship to her parents: William Paris' "Christine" and an anonymous verse life of St. Dorothy. Capgrave evinces his particular interest in nurture in his prose life of St. Augustine, which devotes considerable attention to Monica's troubles raising her unruly son.

246 ff.   *Thus provyd this princesse.* Though more attention was being devoted to women's education in Capgrave's England, the rigorous liberal arts training described below would not have been available to actual women, who were barred from attending such institutions of higher learning as universities. For useful discussions of the education of women in late medieval England, see Nicholas Orme, *Education and Society in Medieval and Renaissance England* (London: Hambledon, 1989), pp. 153–75; and Caroline M. Barron, "The Education and Training of Girls in Fifteenth-Century London," in *Courts, Counties, and the Capital in the Later Middle Ages* (New York: St. Martin's Press, 1996), pp. 139–53. For a discussion of St. Katherine as a possible model for medieval English girls, see Lewis, "Model Girls?: Virgin-Martyrs and the Training of Young Women in Late Medieval England."

264   *as I seyd ere.* See Prol., line 144.

270–73   *hir play . . . was hir wylle.* The saint's aversion to entertainment is a ubiquitous hagiographical convention.

337–64   *The kyng dyd make there for hir alone . . . in hir stody thoo.* These lines explain why Katherine is so astounded when the hermit Adrian appears in her study in 3.401–06.

379   *tawt.* MS: *tawter*

393   *astronomye.* "Astronomy" was in the Middle Ages more like what we would call astrology. The two disciplines were not distinguished in Capgrave's day.

402–27   *All the grete clerkys . . . / . . . that there wore.* This encounter foreshadows Katherine's debate with the fifty philosophers in Book 4. The pitting of a young woman's intelligence against the craft of clerks occurs also within romance tradition. Compare John Gower's "Tale of the Three Questions," *Confessio Amantis* 1.3067–3402 and the Tale of Apollonius of Tyre, 8.271–2008. See note to lines 633–35 below. For more on the broader tradition of "disputing women," see Helen Solterer, *The Master and Minerva: Disputing Women in French Medieval Culture* (Berkeley: University of California Press, 1995).

441–42   *He is logged there with lordys of his kyne / Whech deyd withouten feyth.* Medieval theologians generally took a dim view of the fate of a pagan like Costus, who, though a good man, lived after the birth of Christ and, hence, could at least in theory have become a Christian. Gordon Whatley provides a useful survey of medieval views of righteous pagans in "Heathens and Saints: *St. Erkenwald* in its Legendary Context," *Speculum* 61 (1986), 330–63.

494   *Famagost.* Capgrave is translating the city's name as "The fame of Costus," where "Costus" is written with a *G* instead of a *C*.

518   *no man wyst why.* Meliades may be trying to pre-empt an organized opposition to her daughter's ascension. To judge from the laments following Costus' death, many citizens of the realm cannot imagine Katherine as their new monarch (1.454–57).

526 ff.   *for the kynrode of hir.* Technically speaking, the antecedent of "hir" is "the qween" (line 512), Katherine's mother. Hence, it is tempting to see in Capgrave's attention to Meliades's genealogy the same deliberate "focus on women as progenitors of the sacred" that is evident in fifteenth-century representations of the Holy Kinship. See Pamela Sheingorn, "Appropriating the Holy Kinship: Gender and Family History," in *Interpreting Cultural Symbols: Saint Anne in Late Medieval Society*, ed. Kathleen Ashley and Pamela Sheingorn (Athens: University of Georgia Press, 1990), pp. 169–98 (quote on p. 173). Yet Capgrave's subsequent account of "the kynrode of hir" ends with Costus (line 681)! This inconsistency raises a number of questions: Did Capgrave intend "hir" to mean Katherine all along? Did he merely forget that he had originally intended to rehearse Meliades's genealogy? Does his inconsistency register the same anxieties about issues of family and gender that Sheingorn finds in representations of the Holy Kinship?

619–21   *Antiochus . . . Jewes yet him banne.* Antiochus' atrocities and ultimate punishment are recorded in 2 Maccabees 4.7–10.9.

633–35   *In* Appollony of Tyre *ye may rede the storye . . . problemes evyn.* To avoid losing his daughter/lover, Seleucus devised a riddle for prospective suitors. The man who solved it would win the daughter; those who failed to solve it were executed. For a popular Middle English version of the romance, see Book 8 of Gower's *Confessio Amantis*.

663   *Fortune.* See note to lines 1.868–75.

686–93   *In this reknyng . . . ordre and degré.* A different version of Katherine's genealogy is given in the popular prose *Lyf of Seynt Katerine*, which shows Katherine's relation through her father to the emperors of Rome. See *The Life and Martyrdom of St. Katherine of Alexandria,* ed. Henry Hucks Gibbs (London: Nichols, 1884), or "The Life of St. Katherine," trans. Winstead, in *Chaste Passions.*

701–04   *I answere hereto as do Seynt Jerome . . . that was His wylle.* See Jerome's Commentary on Matthew (under Matthew 1:1–17).

734   *and in halle.* Not in MS.

755   *Save summe spoke of love.* Earthly love is not to anyone's "behove" (line 756) in a saint's legend.

763   *puttyng at the ston.* A competition to see who could throw a given stone the farthest. Compare "putting the shot" in modern track and field competitions.

788   *wit.* MS: *wyght.*

804–12   *So was Cornelius . . . thus seye these clerkys.* The story of Cornelius is told in Acts 10.

839–40   *He may . . . / Make goddes of men.* Katherine explains this point in her debate with the philosophers. See 4.2025–32 and my note to line 2032.

868–75   *thu blynd Fortune . . . art thou unstable.* Fortune was conventionally represented as a lady turning a great wheel set with people (kings, bishops, nobles, etc.), some happily ascending, others losing their crowns as they tumble down. Following Book 2 of Boethius' influential *Consolation of Philosophy* (AD 524), Christian moralists used Lady Fortune and her wheel to reflect upon the inevitable transience of all earthly pleasures. For a discussion of this theme in fifteenth-century England, see Rosemary Horrox, Introduction, *Fifteenth-Century Attitudes,* pp. 6–10.

901   *To sette the standard the wengys on the syde.* A standard is a pole used to display a military emblem. In this case, the sculpted figure of a bird is presumably mounted on the standard and turned so that the enemy can easily see its wings spread. A loose translation would be "And flaunt your battle emblem in the enemy's face."

931–50   *that ye wyll have mercye . . . hertys hayle!* It might seem that the lords are addressing Meliades in language more appropriate to a courtly lady than to a queen mother. However, rhetoric used in letters addressed to social superiors is suffused with the language of love, as Diane Watt notes in "'No Writing for Writing's Sake': The Language of Service and Household Rhetoric in the Letters of the Paston Women," in *Dear Sister: Medieval Women and the Epistolary Genre*, ed. Karen Cherewatuk and Ulrike Wiethaus (Philadelphia: University of Pennsylvania Press, 1993), pp. 126–29.

976–77   *To lyve alone in stody, it was nevyr seyn / That ony lady ony tyme dyd so.* Though I know of no English examples, a number of Italian women chose to forgo marriage in favor of a life devoted to scholarship. See Margaret L. King, "Book-Lined Cells: Women and Humanism in the Early Italian Renaissance," *Beyond Their Sex: Learned Women of the European Past*, ed. Patricia H. Labalme (New York: New York University Press, 1980), pp. 66–90. Many medieval Englishwomen would, however, have appreciated Katherine's reluctance to give up the freedom that a single woman enjoyed. Records from the 1377 poll tax indicate that at least 30% of adult women in England had never been married. See Maryanne Kowaleski, "Singlewomen in Medieval and Early Modern Europe: The Demographic Perspective," in *Singlewomen in the European Past, 1250–1800*, ed. Judith M. Bennett and Amy M. Froide (Philadelphia: University of Pennsylvania Press, 1999), p. 46. Moreover, evidence suggests that when working conditions were good for women, they delayed marriage. See P. J. P. Goldberg, *Women, Work, and Life Cycle in a Medieval Economy: Women in York and Yorkshire, c. 1300–1520* (Oxford: Clarendon Press, 1992), pp. 360–61.

Book 2

11   *found*. MS: *foud*.

14   *Sche knowyth not yet the rode*. A crucifixion pun: *rode* means both way and cross.

24   *us*. Not in MS.

36   *othyr*. MS: *odyr*.

55–66   *For thus it menyth . . . and thi love*. Capgrave is adapting the etymology of Katherine's name provided in Jacobus de Voragine's *Legenda aurea*.

250   *It is more sykyr a bryd in youre fyste.* The first known record of the popular proverb, "A bird in hand is worth two in the bush." See Whiting, *Proverbs*, B301. The speaker continues with two more proverbs, "The gray hors whyl his gras growyth / May sterve for hunger" (lines 253–54; compare *Proverbs*, G437) and "The sore may swelle long or the herbe / Is growe or rype" (lines 256–57; compare *Proverbs*, S504).

260   *now.* Deleted in MS.

267–71   *To se the boweles cut oute of his wombe . . . be foure and be fyve.* Reference to the method of executing traitors by hanging, drawing, and quartering.

276   *se men flete and also se hem synk.* Probable allusion to a judicial ordeal (the "cold-water ordeal"), dating from c. 800, wherein the accused was cast into water; sinking indicated innocence, floating guilt. See Henry Charles Lea, *The Ordeal* (1866; rpt. Philadelphia: University of Pennsylvania Press, 1973), pp. 72–88.

307   *And yet of this punchyng oft he knew ryght nowt.* In other words, Costus did not personally supervise each and every execution.

         of. Repeated in MS.

470   *you.* Not in MS.

476   *I wepe so sore I may no lengere ryme!* Here and elsewhere (for example, 3.1251, 4.1666), Capgrave's characters betray an almost Brechtian consciousness that their stories are unfolding in rhyme royal stanzas.

510–23   *Nabugodonoser . . . Goddys grace.* Daniel's dealings with Nebuchadnezzar are recounted in Daniel 1–4. According to Daniel 6, Darius (not Nebuchadnezzar) threw Daniel to the lions.

510–67   Capgrave is establishing Katherine's propensity towards conversion: her knowledge of and respect for Scripture (Genesis, Daniel), her desire to know more about Daniel's god, and her purely perfunctory reverence for her own pagan gods (lines 564–67). Katherine's study of Scripture, however, might have made her a problematic example for fifteenth-century lay readers.

580   *Ovyde seyde.* Capgrave is paraphrasing views in the introduction to the *Remedium Amoris*.

582   *medecyn comyth ovyr late.* Proverbial: Whiting, *Proverbs*, M484.

735–42   *Valerye . . . in this forsayd werke.* The *Dissuasio Valerii ad Ruffinum philosophum ne uxorem ducat* was a popular misogamous tract written by Walter Map in the late twelfth century.

786   *that astate I trede all undyr fote.* Capgrave may be alluding to popular representations of Katherine of Alexandria trampling the emperor Maxentius. See Introduction, p. 2.

825   *Aristoteles* Elenkes. Aristotle's *De sophisticis elenchis* (*On Sophistical Refutations*) was a standard textbook for late-medieval students of dialectic. Aristotle dissects the various rhetorical tricks employed by sophists, whom he defines as people who wish to *appear* wise without actually being so. In so doing he provides a veritable treasure trove of rhetorical fallacies, which Katherine accuses her opponent of using.

883   *ye.* MS: *eye.*

909   *othir that have abyden long.* Capgrave evokes the stories of various lovers (Troilus, for example, or Dido) whose initial resistance to love resulted in a tragic romance.

958–59   *mo wyse hedes . . . the bettir is it.* Proverbial. See Whiting, *Proverbs*, H227.

961–93   *qwy / That o man above many shall have governing . . . cuntré abowte.* The view that kingship results from the voluntary submission of free people to another's authority (*pactum subjectionis*) is found in the work of various late-medieval political theorists, including Marsilius of Padua (*Defensor pacis*, especially 1.8–9), Duns Scotus (*Ordinatio* 4.15.2), and Nicholas of Cusa (*Concordantia*, especially 2.21–41, 3.4). The idea goes back to Greek and Roman times, for example, Cicero's *De officiis* (especially 2.21–41) and Aristotle's *Politics* (especially 3.14). For general discussions of consent theories and related matters, see Jeannine Quillet, "Community, Counsel and Representation," in *The Cambridge History of Medieval Political Thought, c. 350–c. 1450*, ed. J. H. Burns (Cambridge: Cambridge University Press, 1988), pp. 520–72; and Anthony

Black, *Political Thought in Europe, 1250–1450* (Cambridge: Cambridge University Press, 1992), pp. 136–85.

994   *thei.* Not in MS.

1106   *whil.* Rawlinson reads *wyll*, a careless scribal error. I have emended for sense according to Arundel.

1116   *grype ne take.* The lord is literally saying that no one can overcome Katherine's arguments, but, since the overall debate concerns Katherine's marriage, we may infer a sexual innuendo.

1124   *To Gorgalus tyme.* See 1.568 ff. for Capgrave's account of Gorgalus, king of Syria, and his descendants.

1154   *as wyse.* Repeated in MS.

1159   *he.* Not in MS.

1167–68 *ten or twelve / Schuld geve exaumple rathere than schall oone.* John Gower expresses the same opinion in his discussion of government in the *Confessio Amantis* (Prologue, lines 157–58).

1191–92 *syth ye sey that I am now so wys, / Than have I o thing.* See line 1148.

1204   *in₂.* Not in MS.

1231   *Athenes, of wysdam it beryth the key.* Athens was the home of such renowned philosophers as Plato, Socrates, and Aristotle. In Chaucer's Knight's Tale, when Theseus is said to be "lord and governour" of Athens (I [A] 861), the implication is that he is wise, a man renowned for "his wysdom and his chivalrie"(line 865).

1247 ff. *lych a griff am I.* The Apostle Paul develops and explores this simile in Romans 11:13–24.

1286   *Mynerve.* Minerva, Roman goddess of wisdom.

1304   *Babel*. See 1.533–95. Alexandria was founded by the sultan Babel, who named the city Babylon after himself. When Alexander the Great conquered Babylon, he renamed it Alexandria.

1354   *The Fyrst Mevere*. See Aristotle, *Natural Science*, Book 8, and *Metaphysics*, Book 12.

1371   *do*. Not in MS.

1467   *we₂*. Not in MS.

Book 3

6   *is*. Not in MS.

36   *onto*. *to* not in MS.

45   *was* MS: *wall*.

52–53   *Athanas, of whom . . . / We spoke befor*. Prol,, lines 127–69, 1.260–73.

88   *Were thei growen, were thei bare or balled*. In other words, no distinction was made between the various orders of religious — those that required a tonsure, those that allowed members to be hairy or go bare-headed, etc.

114 ff.   *He saw a syght*. To have a saint approached by a divine commission that directs him to go to an intimidating pagan to convert that person is not uncommon in medieval literature. Compare Ananias' fear of approaching Saul in *The Conversion of Paul*.

142 ff.   *Gramercy madame!* The humor of this scene, in which one of God's chosen people is completely oblivious of whom he is speaking with, is strongly reminiscent of the humor of mystery plays. For example, in the Towneley Noah play, after God has descended from heaven, conveyed his displeasure with humanity, announced his intention of flooding the earth, and instructed Noah to build an ark, the patriarch burbles: "A benedicite! What art thou that thus / Tellys afore that shall be? Thou art full mervelus! / Tell me, for charite thi name so

gracius." *The Towneley Plays*, ed. George England, EETS e.s. 71 (London: Oxford University Press, 1897), p. 28, lines 63–65.

175   *Yet hath sche of me knowyng nevyr a deele.* See below lines 470–78 for Capgrave's careful distinction between having God in one's heart and being aware of God.

178   *Grete Babell.* Compare 1.534–41, where Capgrave notes that Alexandria had been called "Babilon *the lasse*"! (line 540).

208–09   *sche schall love bettyr the hayre / Than any reynes.* Though *reynes* refers to a fine cloth made in Rennes, Brittany, the Virgin may be making an off-color pun, for *reynes* can also mean "the male generative organ" (MED, *reine* 2b). Such a pun would not be too surprising in this narrative, whose saints are hardly naives. Later in this book (lines 1104–05), the Virgin will make sure that Adrian is temporarily blinded before Katherine is stripped for her baptism. And Katherine herself insists that, though she may be a virgin, she knows a thing or two about sex (lines 637–44).

212   *Sevyn Scyens.* The Seven Liberal Arts (see note to Prol., line 143).

327   *Lollard.* An English heretic whose views derived from the teachings of the Oxford theologian John Wyclif.

369   *Poule seyth this best.* 1 Corinthians 1:26–29. This is one of two instances in which Capgrave invites his readers to consult Scripture (the other is 4.2279–81) — a radical invitation for the 1440s in a work addressed to a popular audience. Fearing the spread of Lollardy, the Church had taken strict measures to curtail lay access to the Bible.

401–06   *Sche lokyd on him and was astoyned sore . . . wondyr fast.* Capgrave takes pains to detail Katherine's security measures in 1.337–64.

413   *All heyll, madame!* Adrian echoes the angel Gabriel's greeting to the Virgin Mary at the Annunciation. Capgrave elaborates the analogy between Gabriel's visit to Mary and Adrian's visit to Katherine in lines 465–76.

470–76   *Ryght as Gabriell . . . we wyll take hede.* For a useful discussion of patristic and medieval views of the Annunciation, see Jaroslav Pelikan, *Mary Through the*

Centuries: Her Place in the History of Culture (New Haven: Yale University Press, 1996), pp. 81–94.

524 ff.   *sche is modyr and also clene virgyne.* Adrian is referring to a central tenet of Marian theology, namely, the perpetual virginity of Mary. Like many late medieval writers, Capgrave insists on Mary's singularity as a virgin mother, but he also does everything possible to humanize her by portraying her as a sensitive and affectionate mother-in-law. His emphasis on Mary in the legend is consistent with the intense devotion to the Virgin that marked late medieval piety. Also typical is his depiction of Christ as a fully humanized suitor.

553   *Eleyn the fayre lady of Grees.* Helen, famous beauty and wife of the Greek king Menelaus, whose abduction by Paris precipitated the Trojan War.

611   *in pytte.* A depression in the body, perhaps a dimple or the hollow of the neck.

635   *And yet sche is a mayden at asay and sale.* According to a popular tradition derived from the apocryphal *Infancy Gospel of James* (c. 150), a midwife tested Mary's virginity after she had given birth to Christ. An East Anglian dramatization of the incident that is roughly contemporaneous with Capgrave's legend can be found in the Nativity play of the N-Town Cycle. See *The N-Town Play*, ed. Stephen Spector, EETS s.s. 11 (Oxford: Oxford University Press, 1991), pp. 152–63.

644   *he.* Not in MS.

694–707   *How may ye couple . . . offendyth phylosophye!* Katherine's objection to a Christ "coupled of contraries too" (line 702) anticipates a point one of the philosophers will raise with her in 4.1703–05.

724   *That ye were bounden sumetyme with a bonde.* Capgrave refers to the practice of swaddling infants, that is, binding their limbs with narrow strips of cloth so that they cannot move freely.

730   *onto. on* not in MS.

766   *The Fyrst Mevere.* See note to 2.1354.

799–804   *Of the men of Sodom aboute Lothis hous . . . thei schull not see.* The blinding of the Sodomites is recounted in Genesis 19:11.

826   *That be the aungell led Abacuc to the lake.* In verses 33–39 of *Bel and the Dragon*, an addition to the Book of Daniel composed in the second century BC (appearing among the Apocrypha in the Revised Standard Version and as Daniel 14 in the Vulgate Bible), an angel intercepts the prophet Habakkuk as he is bringing food to workers in the field, telling him to take the meal to Daniel, who has been cast into a lions' den in Babylon. When Habakkuk protests that he does not know any such place, the angel carries him there and back by the hair.

856   *Ye hafe set your trost hyere than myselve.* Katherine's surpassing of her spiritual teacher echoes her surpassing of her secular teachers in 1.414–19.

874–75   *as David fro the schepe / . . . if we take kepe.* See 1 Samuel 16:11–13. Samuel summoned Jesse's youngest son, David, from his job herding sheep and anointed him King of Israel.

887   *dun.* MS: *downe.*

919   *We can not speke it.* Capgrave is repeating a commonplace of mystical literature, namely, that people who have a direct experience of the godhead cannot describe their experiences (and hence Capgrave cannot relay them).

927–29   *Seynt Poule hymselve . . . in that secree.* For Paul's comments on his heavenly vision, see 2 Corinthians 12:1–7.

933   *holy crisme.* Sacramental liquid consisting of a mixture of oil and balsam.

949   *Wolcome of clennesse very swete rose.* On the odor of Christ that signifies purity, "an odor that leads to life," see 2 Corinthians 2:14–16. Compare Tiburce in Chaucer's Second Nun's Tale who, in the presence of St. Cecile, smells the scent of lilies and roses: "The sweete smel that in myn herte I finde / Hath chaunged me al in another kynde" (VIII [G] 251–52). The red rose is affiliated with martyrdom and here may anticipate the conclusion to Capgrave's saint's life. It is also traditionally associated withe Virgin Mary, the heavenly rose in eternal bloom, because her body is not destroyed by death.

967–68   *certen tokenes thei bere . . . another bare.* Martyrs were typically associated with emblems recalling their passions. For example, Agatha, who had her breasts torn off, usually bears a platter with a breast, while Lawrence, who was roasted, carries a grill. When Katherine joins the assembly of martyrs, she will be carrying a wheel. In some late medieval paintings, these emblems are embroidered on the saints' garments.

993–1001   *Hir body . . . se His face.* Katherine cannot approach Christ or see his face because she has not yet been cleansed from sin through baptism, as Christ reminds his mother in lines 1032–49. Mary forthwith translates Christ's theological explanation of the sacrament into language that Katherine would surely understand: "It is a goodely usage . . . / Who schal be weddyd onto duke or kynge / Befor hir weddyng to hafe a bathynge" (lines 1069–71).

1025   *a.* Not in MS.

1053   *A prest hafe ye redy.* Christ's insistence that Adrian perform both the baptism and marriage ceremonies affirms the clergy's prerogative to dispense sacraments and mediate between God and human beings — a role that was hotly contested by the Lollards.

1226–31   *My modyr wyll here. . . . Consent ye Kateryne?* Christ's emphasis on Katherine's free choice ratifies a position the Church had taken since the twelfth century, namely, that a valid marriage required the consent of the parties being married and not just their parents. Ideally, as in this case, the parents and children would agree. See James A. Brundage, *Law, Sex, and Christian Society in Medieval Europe* (Chicago: University of Chicago Press, 1987) and John T. Noonan, "Power to Choose," *Viator* 4 (1973), 419–34.

1232   *wilt.* Not in MS.

1251   *schortly to ryme.* See note to 2.476.

1258   *Befor hem all schal ye go in the daunce.* See note to Prol., line 8.

1272   *Whan Thu commendyd Jon me untoo.* John 19:26–27.

1286   *calcedony*. For a discussion of the properties of this stone, see *English Medieval Lapidaries*, ed. Joan Evans and Mary S. Serjeantson, EETS o.s. 190 (London: Oxford University Press, 1960), pp. 29–30, 49, 75.

1301   *Sponsus amat sponsam*. A chant sung at the liturgical office of Matins on the feast of Saint Katherine.

1307–08   *This chyrch must folow . . . / The chyrch above in all that it may.* Seen from a somewhat different angle, Capgrave's *chyrch above* is following — or at least endorsing — *this [earthly] cherch . . . in all that it may*. Witness the emphasis on individual consent in marriage and on the sacraments of baptism and marriage.

1316   *fere.* MS: *dere.*

1332   *Eyt dayes.* The eighth day is associated with the Resurrection, and hence with a new life and a new beginning, as Jacobus de Voragine explains in the *Golden Legend* 1: 216–17.

1343   *think 'not longe.'* The allusion is to John 16:16–22, the "little while" of pain before bliss in Christ. See also 5.1514 where Katherine reassures the queen that the torture will last but "a lytyll space."

1390–1421 *Oure Lord Godd is of swech a kynde . . . ye wel, madame.* Adrian is explaining the doctrine of the Trinity, that three distinct persons make up one God. For a discussion of this complex dogma, see Jaroslav Pelikan, *The Emergence of the Catholic Tradition (100–600)* (Chicago: University of Chicago Press, 1971), pp. 172–225.

1428   *Swech langage in synfull tunge is but brok.* Capgrave seems to be endorsing the orthodox view that the vernacular is a poor medium for expounding doctrine. For a discussion of the clergy's disparagement of the vernacular, particularly for religious exhortation, see Nicholas Watson, "Censorship and Cultural Change in Late-Medieval England: Vernacular Theology, the Oxford Translation Debate, and Arundel's Constitutions of 1409," *Speculum* 70 (1995), 822–64. See also Rita Copeland, "Why Women Can't Read: Medieval Hermeneutics, Statutory Law, and the Lollard Heresy Trials," in *Representing Women: Law, Literature, and Feminism*, ed. Susan Sage Heinzelman and Zipporah Batshaw Wiseman (Durham: Duke University Press, 1994), pp. 253–86. By Book 4, Capgrave's scruples about expounding theology in English seem to have vanished.

Book 4

1 ff.   *These erdely dwellers . . . Are lykened to the bees.* Virgil's comparison of human
            society to a bee-hive in *Georgics* 4.3 was frequently quoted by medieval political
            theorists and well known in Capgrave's day.

23   MS: *For that thei here thowte they have delectacyoun.* I am accepting the reading
            of MS Arundel 396, which makes more sense.

78–148   *In the tyme of Costus . . . in Rome al alone.* Capgrave's rather garbled account of
            events during the late third century — which will not be found in standard history
            books — can be summarized as follows: Maximinus Galerius, Maximian, and
            Diocletian were co-rulers of the Roman empire. After Maximian and Diocletian
            resigned, Maximinus appointed three sub-emperors: Maximinus to rule the East;
            Severus to rule Lombardy, Tuscany, and Germany; and Constantine to rule
            Britain. Maximinus Galerius was killed in battle and the Romans chose his sub-
            emperor Maximinus' son Maxentius (Katherine's nemesis) to be the new Roman
            emperor. Unhappy with this arrangement, Maximinus set out for Rome but died
            en route. Equally unhappy, Severus waged war against Maxentius but was
            eventually killed by his own soldiers. Maxentius remained emperor of Rome until
            his excesses and iniquities drove the Roman people to rebellion.

119   *Salysbury playn.* Location of Stonehenge, legendary burial place of King Arthur's
            father, Uther Pendragon; Arthur's successor, Constantine; and 450 Breton nobles
            killed by the Saxons in the fifth century.

290   *with gunnes and wyth myne.* "Gunne" refers to a machine used to cast missiles
            during a siege. A "myne" was a tunnel dug to undermine a fortification.

310   *used.* Not in MS.

381   *There was no matens seyd, servyse, ne pryme.* Capgrave is referring to the
            liturgical offices that were recited daily in religious houses.

389   *some.* Not in MS.

395–96   *Saturne . . . With his sekyll in hand.* Saturn was conventionally represented with
            a sickle because, after settling in Italy (see below, lines 638–40), he taught the
            Italians how to reap grain with that tool.

406 *I owe him non, for maumentrye I despyse.* A playful jab at contemporary lovers, who, in the parlance of romances and love lyrics, were still Cupid's servants.

468 *All tho myshappys whech were seyd before.* An allusion to the dire predictions made by Katherine's lords during the Marriage Parliament of Book 2.

478–79 *now is the hour / Whech sche behestyd.* See 3.1478–87.

551 *With mace.* In this context, "mace" refers to a rod of office.

586 *With bath of picth and beverych of lede.* Methods of torture.

633 *Rede in your boke.* A possible allusion to the *Hierâ Anagraphe* (c. 300 B.C.) of Euhemerus of Sicily, which proposed that the gods were men who were only after their deaths reputed to be divine. Augustine of Hippo refers to Euhemerism at several points in his *City of God.* Most of Katherine's assaults on Maxentius's religion — the scandalous behavior of the gods, their outrageous rituals, and so forth — appear to have derived from the first seven books of the *City of God.* For a fifteenth-century discussion of Euhemerism, see *The Assembly of Gods*, lines 1707–08.

636 *telle.* MS: *telles.*

676 *woundis fyve.* A reference to the five wounds the crucified Christ received on his hands, feet, and side.

752 *ye.* Not in MS.

876–89 *He hite hir . . . / . . . now take.* Maxentius iterates and elaborates on these promises in 5.372–420. His promises and Katherine's response constitute one of the most memorable scenes in most versions of Katherine's passion.

1063 *Why.* Crossed out in MS.

1125 *chese.* Not in MS.

1143 *in prison.* Not in MS.

1163   *And as Thu graunted Thin apostles here.* Matt. 10:17–20, Mark 13:9–11, Luke 12:11, 21:12–15.

1185   *As Thu graunted Ester to plese hir Assuere.* Esther 4–5 relates that, in an attempt to save the Jews from destruction, Esther risked death by approaching her husband, King Ahasuerus, unsummoned in the inner court of his palace.

1195   *voutes sevene.* Capgrave may be thinking of images in popular prayer books, or Books of Hours, which often represent martyrs standing in multi-vaulted prison cells.

1233–34 *a trew messagere / And as no feyned spyryte.* Demons were notorious for impersonating angels on their visits to imprisoned saints, as in the legend of the virgin martyr Juliana.

1268   *he.* Not in MS.

1271   *new Ulix.* Representations of Ulysses as a crafty, scurrilous deceiver with a golden tongue (in the tradition of Ovid's *Metamorphoses)* were common in the Middle Ages.

1344   *Phylystyoun.* Philistion was a physician identified with the Sicilian school of medicine founded by Empedocles in the fifth century BC.

1371   *philosophye.* MS: *philophye.*

1499–1512 *thei be but figures / Representyng othir manere thing . . . schuld go therby.* This scholar is using the same arguments that the Church used to defend images and statues of Christ and the saints from Lollard claims that venerating such representations amounted to idol-worship. For a popular statement of this orthodox Catholic argument, see Thomas Hoccleve's 1415 "Address to Sir John Oldcastle," in *Hoccleve's Works: The Minor Poems,* ed. Frederick J. Furnivall and I. Gollancz, EETS e.s. 61, 72–73 (London: Oxford University Press, 1892, 1925), vol. I, p. 21, lines 409–24. It is perhaps not surprising that Katherine does not refute this argument but rather changes the subject.

1534   *Vulcane was cruell and yet was he cokholde.* For a pithy account of how "cruell" Vulcan took vengeance on his wife, Venus, and her lover, Mars, see Book 4 of

Ovid's *Metamorphoses*. This topic is a favorite among medieval vernacular writers.

1587–88   These lines are reversed in the MS with a mark that they should be read in the order in which I have placed them.

1592   *The Kyng of Thebes a book had hir sent.* Augustine criticizes the allegorization of the Roman Pantheon in his *City of God*, primarily in Books 6–7. He attributes that allegorization to Marcus Terentius Varro, whose work on theology (*The Antiquities)* is unfortunately lost. I thank Chris Manion for suggesting Varro as the author of Katherine's book.

1667 ff.   In her instruction of the unenlightened through the figure of the Trinity, Katherine alludes to a common doctrinal practice. Compare St. Cecile's instruction of Tiburce in Chaucer's Second Nun's Tale (VIII [G] 333–41). The length and complexity of her exposition, however, is unprecedented in any Middle English saint's life.

1674   *creature.* MS: *creatour.*

1723–25   *He that reysyde Lazare fro the grave . . . He that Petyr in the see dyd save.* See, respectively, John 11 and Matthew 14.

1724   *four dayes.* Both MSS Rawl. poet. 118 and Arundel 168 read that Lazarus lay in the grave for "fourti [Ar. Fourty] dayes." I have emended "fourti" to "four," an emendation supported by MSS Arundel 396 and Arundel 20 as well as by John 11:39.

1729–31   *He that so mervelously onto heven gan glyde . . . mervayles.* Mark 16:19.

1748   *leke.* MS: *loke.*

1752–57   *Sybylle . . . nevyr sey nay.* Capgrave is quoting the so-called Tiburtine Sibyl, whose pronouncement is quoted, among other places, in Jacobus de Voragine's *Golden Legend,* trans. William Granger Ryan, 2.170. For a discussion of the medieval Sibylline tradition, see Bernard McGinn, "*Teste David cum Sibylla:* The Significance of the Sibylline Tradition in the Middle Ages," in *Women of the Medieval World,* ed. Julius Kirshner and Suzanne F. Wemple (Oxford: Basil Blackwell, 1985), pp. 7–35.

1844   *Be armes, bones, and be blode.* The emperor, ironically, is swearing by Christ.

1871   *marred.* MS: *marreth.*

1882   *thousandis fyve.* The allusion is to the feeding of 5,000 in John 6:1–14.

1951–52 *Youre prophete seyde . . . / bete and bynde.* Psalms 2:9.

1972   *In the tre was joy bore and in the tre woo.* An allusion to Christ's cross (redemption) and to the Tree of Knowledge (the fall).

1975   MS has a chapter heading indicated at this line.

1986–88 *I red in a Crysten prophete . . . that ye be goddes alle.* Psalms 82:6. The Old Testament was considered an integral part of the Christian tradition, its prophets and scholars deemed fundamentally Christian thinkers.

2000   *Baal.* References to Baal, a Phoenician god worshipped by wayward Israelites, occur frequently in the Old Testament. The "thre hundred prophetis" spoken of in lines 2001–02 may allude to 1 Kings 18:19 and 18:22, which mention 450 (not 300) prophets devoted to Baal.

2024–50 *And be nature is He God . . . that auctorité.* Jaroslav Pelikan explains the distinction made by various medieval theologians between Jesus, who was God's natural son, and the saints or faithful (called "gods" in Psalms 82:6), who were God's adopted sons, in *The Growth of Medieval Theology (600–1300)* (Chicago: University of Chicago Press, 1978), pp. 55–56.

2032   *And sones of Him that syttith hyest.* Katherine is supplying the portion of Psalms 82:6 that the pagan scholar omitted in his allusion (line 1988).

2055–57 *Thoo same prophetis . . . thei dampned were.* 1 Kings 18:40 relates that, after winning a contest with the prophets of Baal, the prophet Elijah rounded up his 450 rivals and killed every one of them.

2080   *comoursly.* This word is not attested in the MED, though three of the four *Katherine* MSS give that reading. Horstmann emended it to "concoursly," but the MED cites only the noun "concours," meaning an agreement or a flocking/ crowding together. MS Arundel 20 reads "anon."

2082   *Noys*. Bernardus Silvestris develops this concept at length in his *Cosmographia*.

2158–77   *Of oure ladies clennes in hir concepcion / . . . sittith thus hye.* In answering
Ariot's objection, Katherine affirms the doctrine of the Immaculate Conception,
namely, that Mary was miraculously conceived without the "original sin" that
Adam and Eve passed on to their descendants. That teaching was highly
controversial during the later Middle Ages (in part for the reason Ariot puts
forward — how could a woman whose parents had inherited original sin be
sinless herself?). Mary's Immaculate Conception was endorsed by the 1439
Council of Basle, though the legitimacy of the Council was later contested.

2179–84   *His comyng was lich the sune schynyng bryth . . . cam down here.* This simile was
commonly employed by both poets and theologians to describe Mary's concep-
tion of Jesus. See Marina Warner, *Alone of All Her Sex* (New York: Knopf,
1976), p. 44; and Gail McMurray Gibson, *The Theater of Devotion: East Anglian
Drama and Society in the Late Middle Ages* (Chicago: University of Chicago
Press, 1989), p. 146. For an example of the simile in Middle English devotional
lyrics, see "Marye, mayde mylde and fre," in *Middle English Marian Lyrics*, ed.
Karen Saupe (Kalamazoo, MI: Medieval Institute Publications, 1998), p. 165,
lines 73–76.

2194–96   *It is ful hard swech thingis forto ryme . . . to the Incarnacion.* Capgrave may be
needling conservative clerics who declared that doctrine should not be discussed
in the vernacular. He concedes that it is hard to discuss matters like the Incarna-
tion "in langage of oure nacion" (line 2195) — all the more so when one is trying
to rhyme — but instead of curtailing his treatment of those topics, he embellishes
his putative source with "othir auctouris" (line 2199). See the note to 3.1428.

2235   *coude*. Not in MS.

2262–68   *Davyd . . . whan he thristid sore . . . bare this thing.* 1 Chronicles 11:15–19.

2278   *dilatacion*. MS Rawl. poet. 118 reads "delectacion"; the other MSS read
"dilatacion."

2281   *That myth it here if that hem list.* This reading is significantly different from the
readings of Arundel 398 ("That men myght plod in hir, if that hem lyst") and
Arundel 20 ("that men myght plode in hyre yff that hyme lyste,") which suggest

(rather daringly) that readers consult Scripture for themselves. Arundel 168 reads "That men myght plede in here, if that hyme list."

2341   *It is ful convenient that we shuld do soo.* The scribe of MS Arundel 20 apparently disagreed that this would be an appropriate place to end Book 4, for he finishes narrating the philosophers' martyrdom before beginning Book 5.

Book 5

6   *fyve braunchis.* Five is a number traditionally associated with Mary, with her five joys and five sorrows. Lydgate composes *The Lyfe of our Lady* in five books. Chaucer's poem on Mary in the Prologue to the Prioress' Tale is in five stanzas. Capgrave seems to be linking Katherine's life structurally to that of her Lady; n.b. his linking her to a red rose of five branches and five leaves in lines 10ff., the rose being a primary feature of Marian iconography. See Saupe, ed., *Middle English Marian Lyrics*, for numerous examples of the analogies. Five is also associated with the Passion — with the five wounds of Christ and with the five pains of the Passion. (For the latter, see Jacobus de Voragine, *Golden Legend* 1.203–06.) The significance of five is perhaps most fully elaborated in Middle English literature in *Sir Gawain and the Green Knight*'s description of the five-sided star Gawain sports on his shield and the system of five fives it represents: five fingers, five senses, five joys of the Virgin, five wounds of Christ, and five virtues.

23   *Betokynyng.* MS: *Betokynyth.* This emendation is supported by Arundel 168 and 396.

62   *Thus shall it be translate now new fro Lateyn.* As Capgrave explained in his prologue (lines 57–60), the English priest whose work he had been transcribing died before he had completed his translation.

65   *credulyté.* MS: *crudelyte.* MSS Arundel 20 and 396 support this emendation.

69   *Wherfor.* I have changed MS Rawl. poet. 118's "for" to "wherfor," a reading supported by the other three MSS.

146   *nevyr plant.* MS: *into oure hert plant.*

165   *these.* MS: *that.* Emendation supported by the other MSS.

209–80   *that we schuld ben baptized or we deye . . . trost me now trewly.* The philosophers
           are expressing an eminently orthodox view — that baptism is necessary for
           salvation. Given current controversies surrounding the sacraments, however, it
           is surprising that Katherine should draw attention to *baptem of the Goste* (line
           274) as an acceptable alternative to baptism by water or blood. For a discussion
           of baptism's place in sacramental controversies, see Sarah Beckwith, "*Sacrum
           Signum:* Sacramentality and Dissent in York's Theatre of Corpus Christi," in
           Criticism and Dissent in the Middle Ages, ed. Rita Copeland (Cambridge:
           Cambridge University Press, 1996), pp. 270–71. For a discussion of spiritual
           baptism, see *Summa Theologiae* III.68.2, wherein Thomas Aquinas says that
           people do not need to be actually physically baptized to be saved if they intended
           to be baptized and died before such a rite could be performed (he makes particular
           reference to martyrs).

275–76   These lines are reversed in the MS with a mark that they should be read in the
           order in which I have placed them.

339   *putte you.* Not in MS.

342   *rytes.* MS: *riches.* The emendation is supported by the other three MSS.

346   *save on and no moo.* Maxentius is referring to his wife. See below, lines 373–74,
           393–96.

385   *fulfyllyd as tyth.* Tithes were the one-tenth portion of one's goods that a person
           owed to the Church during the Middle Ages. Maxentius is thus saying that he will
           take Katherine's wishes as seriously as he takes his religious obligations.

394   *oure.* MS: *youre.* This emendation accords with the reading of all the other MSS.

422   *she.* MS: *che.*

535–37   *Appollo . . . Redressith this word with hete.* Maxentius refers to Apollo's capacity
           as sun god.

543   *schal.* MS: *schon.*

547   *schort tyme.* MS: *ryght.*

576   *An.* MS: *And.* Emendation supported by the other MSS.

647   *I.* Not in MS.

707   *torment.* MS: *tornament.* The emendation follows the other three MSS.

710–11   These lines are reversed in the MS with a mark that they should be read in the order in which I have placed them.

785   *seyde.* Not in MS.

817   *a savour.* See note to 3.949.

852   *braunches fyve.* Capgrave echoes a theme he developed at length in the prologue to Book 5. For the significance of the number five, see the note to 5.6.

857   *Whil she helde.* MS: *Wille she elde.* The emendation accords with the reading of the other three manuscripts.

887   *Fourty dayes.* Katherine's days in prison correspond to Christ's days of temptation in the wilderness (Matthew 4 and Luke 4). Compare Chaucer's allusion to Christ's feeding of the Egyptian Mary in the desert (*CT* II [B[1]] 498–501). See Paul M. Clogan, "The Narrative Style of the Man of Law's Tale," *Medievalia et Humanistica* 8 (1977), 217–33.

890–92   *For He that fedde Danyel . . . Lord myth make.* See note to 3.826 above.

891   *Abacuc.* MS: *abouth.*

893   *fedde.* Not in MS.

897–906   *as Austen seyth . . . In his boke whech tretyth in Scripture.* See Augustine's *Exposition on the Psalms*, Ps 95:11–12, on verse 9, where he discusses the feeding of manna to the Israelites in the desert (Ex. 16:13–35).

929   *Thinke 'not long.'* See note to 3.1343.

935   In the MS this line follows line 942 with a marker that it should be positioned as I have here.

1006   *hid*. Not in MS.

1052–57   *Oure dedely bodyes . . . In fayrrer forme.* For medieval views of bodily resurrection, see Caroline Walker Bynum, *The Resurrection of the Body in Western Christianity, 200–1336* (New York: Columbia University Press, 1995).

1105–06   *Constantyn . . . baptyzed was / Of Seynt Sylvestere.* See Jacobus de Voragine's account in *The Golden Legend*, 1.279. The tale is also told in Gower's *Confessio Amantis* 2.3187–3496.

1133   *plumbys of lede*. Weights at the end of a whip.

1153   *world*. MS: *worde*.

1160   *It longyth to yow to obey onto your heede.* On the analogy between society and the body, with the king as head, see Anthony Black, *Political Thought in Europe, 1250–1450* (Cambridge: Cambridge University Press, 1992), pp. 14–18.

1198–99   *Every man must . . . Deye and rote but of the speciall grace.* A corpse's preservation was taken as an indication of sanctity.

1299   *both Robyn and Jon.* Generic names, roughly equivalent to "Tom, Dick, and Harry."

1370–74   *Thus dede He sumtyme in the Calde nacyon . . . thei toke the harm.* See Daniel 3, where Shadrach, Meshach, and Abednego survive the fiery furnace.

1395   *woo*. MS: *who*.

1433   *mannes*. MS: *moonys*.

1474   *rend hir tetys.* The tearing off a woman's breasts is typical of the sexualized torture in virgin martyr legends; it occurs in the legends of Agatha, Barbara, Christine, and many others.

1480–81   *teye hir to a stake, / Smyte of hir heede.* This is the method of execution Margery Kempe desires in *Book* 43.677–81: "Hyr thowt sche wold a be slayn for Goddys lofe, but dred for the poynt of deth, and therfor sche ymagyned hyrself the most soft deth, as hir thowt, for dred of inpacyens, that was to be bowndyn hyr hed and hir fet to a stokke and hir hed to be smet of wyth a scharp ex for Goddys lofe."

1572 *dede.* MS: *yede.*

1593–94 *It is neythir worchipfull ne eke honest / Onto mankynd to foule his own nest.* Proverbial: Whiting, *Proverbs*, B306.

1594 *foule.* MS: *folow.*

1697 *On of the auctoures.* The Vulgate *Vita* reads: "*consummata itaque est horum passio mense Nouembrio die uicesima quarta, feria quinta.*" Ed. S. R. T. O. d'Ardenne and E. J. Dobson, *Seinte Katerine*, EETS s.s. 7 (Oxford: Oxford University Press, 1981), p. 199.

1699 *of.* MS: *aftyr.*

1704–05 These lines are reversed in the MS with a mark that they should be read in the order in which I have placed them.

1714 *Mayden.* MS: *May.*

1762 *the toure of Troye.* Treason ultimately allowed the Greeks to capture Troy and win the Trojan war.

1779–82 *I shall folow the lombe . . . wihouten mynd.* Revelation 21–22.

1873 *Thu schall receyve it in anothyr stede.* Christ is alluding to the resurrection of the body after death. See note to lines 1052–67 above.

1923 *Poule in his bokes maketh swech induction.* See Galatians 4:22–31.

1939 *There leve but fewe that hath mad asayes.* One devotee of St. Katherine who made this journey (1480–83) was Felix Fabri, a Dominican friar from Ulm, Germany. His account of the trip has been translated by Aubrey Stewart, *The Wanderings of Felix Fabri*, 2 vols. (1887–97; rpt., New York: AMS Press, 1971). Felix's devotion to Katherine's relics is the point of departure for Sheri Holman's provocative novel, *A Stolen Tongue* (New York: Atlantic Monthly Press, 1997). For another fifteenth-century pilgrim's account of his visit to Katherine's shrine, see Pero Trafur, *Travels and Adventures, 1435–1439*, trans. and ed. Malcolm Letts (London: George Routledge and Sons, 1926).

1950   *That oyle*. As Capgrave explained in his prologue (lines 26–27), curative oil flows from Katherine's tomb — a sign of God's special favor.

1965 ff.   *In this matere pleynly I will me schryve*. Capgrave's concerns about his perceived credibility and the authenticity of miracles are unusual for a saint's life. Perhaps not surprisingly, the scribe of British Library MS Arundel 20 replaced the final four stanzas of the poem with a more conventional invocation of Katherine's blessing on himself and his readers. The same scribe did other things to "tidy up" Capgrave's text: he omitted the unusually long and complex prologue and ended Book 4 with the execution of the philosophers rather than in the middle of the philosophers episode.

Glossary

a *have*
acorde *agree*
aftir *according to*
Alisaundre *Alexandria; Alexander*
and *if*
anon *immediately*
aray *company, clothing, circumstances*
asay *test*
astoyned *astonished*
Athanas *Athanasius*
avise *consider*
avisement *deliberation*

bale *suffering*
ban(ne) *curse*
baptem(e) *baptism*
bare *bore*
be *by*
bedene *together*
behestis *promises*
blinne *cease*
bone *request*
bost *boast*
brenne *burn*
brent *burned*
brith *bright*
but *unless, except*

chere *appearance, disposition*
Cipré *Cyprus*
cité *city*
clennes(se) *purity*
clepe *call*
conceyte *idea, thought*

convenient *appropriate*
convicte *overcome*
cuntré *country*

dauns *dance*
ded(e) *did; dead*
degré *rank, manner*
delve *dig, study*
desese *discomfort*
dole *grief*
dome *judgment*
drede *doubt; fear*
dresse *apply (oneself), prepare*
dwere *doubt; dissension, trouble*

e(e)m *uncle*
eke *also*
elles/is *else, otherwise*
enow(e) *enough*
ermyte *hermit*
even(e) *exactly, just*
eyne *eyes*

fayn *eager(ly), glad(ly)*
fele *many; feel*
fell(e) *skin*
felle *fierce, cruel*
fer *far*
fere *fire; fear; company,* **in fere,** *together*
fith *fight*
for *since, because*
fothere *a great amount*
fre *free; noble; generous*

Glossary

ful *very; full*

gan *did, went, began*
gesse *guess*
gide *guide*
go(o)st *spirit*
gove(n) *given*
gramercy *mercy!*

hast *haste*
hem *them*
her *their*
herde *earth*
hevy *unhappy*
hir *her*
hith *be called*
hope *expect; expectation*
hye *high*
hyere *salary*
hyght *was called*

ilk(e) *each; same; very*
iwis *indeed, certainly*

knyth *knight*
kyn(rod) *family*

lede *lead*
lees *lies*
lere *learn; teach*
lese *lose*
let(e) *let, allow, cause; prevent, hinder*
leve *leave, abandon; permit; believe; live*
levene *lightning*
ley *lain*
lich *as, like*
list *wish, desire*
lith *light*
loke *look*

long *belong, be appropriate, pertain*
lore *teaching, lesson*
loy *lain*
lyvande *living (people)*

make *mate*
maumentis *idols*
maumentrie *idolatry*
may *maiden*
mech *much*
mede *reward*
meke *meek*
mende *mind*
mené *mean; means; retinue*
mete *food*
mith *might*
mo(o) *more*
mone *moon; cry, complaint*
mote *must*
motif *proposition*
munke *monk*
myty *mighty*

nowt(e) *nothing*
ny(e) *nearly*
nyth *night*

o(o), on *one*
of *of; off*
onys *once*
or *before*
owte *anything*

pardé *By God!*
party *partly*
pe(e)s *peace*
Pers *Persia*
peyn(e) *pain*
plat *flat*

Glossary

prees *crowd*
presens *presence*
preve *prove; proof*
pryvy *private, secret, special*
punch *punish*
puple *people*

qweles *wheels*

real(le) *royal*
rede *read*
renne *run*
rere *raise*
reuth *pity*
rith *just, exactly; right*
rote *rot; root*
row(e) *order, row; rough*

sad *somber, serious*
sciens *learning; discipline*
se(e) *see; sea*
secré *mystery; inner recess*
seke *seek; sick*
sentens *substance, content; reason*
ser(e) *sir*
sex *six*
sey *say; saw*
sith *since*
sle *slay*
sobtill *subtle*
soft(e) *quiet, gentle, slow*
sole *alone*
sone *soon*
sore *intensely, eagerly, greatly, very*
soth *truth; true*
space *time, while*
spille *abandon, ruin*
stede *place*
sterve *die, perish*

stoyned *astonished*
straunge *uncommon; foreign*
Surré, Surry *Syria*
swage *assuage*
swech *such*
swow *swoon*
synne *sin*

tast *taste; test; experience*
terme *argument, reason*
tetis *teats*
tho(o) *then; those*
thorow *through*
thouth *thought*
thow *though*
thowt(e) *thought*
tide *time*
to(o) *two*
towe *tough*
trow(e) *believe*

usage *custom*

venjauns *vengeance*

wage *reward; wages*
wan *won, conquered; pale*
want *lack; need*
wene *suppose, think*
were *war; worse, worst*
wers *worse*
wete *know*
wise *way, manner*
wist *knew; known*
with *person*
wode, wood *mad, crazy*
worchep, -chip *honor*
wordly *worldly*
wot(e) *know*

Glossary

wroth(e) *angry*
wrout(e) *did; done*

ying *young*
yye *eyes*

Volumes in the Middle English Texts Series

The Floure and the Leafe, The Assembly of Ladies, and *The Isle of Ladies*, ed. Derek Pearsall (1990)

Three Middle English Charlemagne Romances, ed. Alan Lupack (1990)

Six Ecclesiastical Satires, ed. James M. Dean (1991)

Heroic Women from the Old Testament in Middle English Verse, ed. Russell A. Peck (1991)

The Canterbury Tales: Fifteenth-Century Continuations and Additions, ed. John M. Bowers (1992)

Gavin Douglas, *The Palis of Honoure*, ed. David Parkinson (1992)

Wynnere and Wastoure and The Parlement of the Thre Ages, ed. Warren Ginsberg (1992)

The Shewings of Julian of Norwich, ed. Georgia Ronan Crampton (1993)

King Arthur's Death: The Middle English Stanzaic Morte Arthur and Alliterative Morte Arthure, ed. Larry D. Benson and Edward E. Foster (1994)

Lancelot of the Laik and Sir Tristrem, ed. Alan Lupack (1994)

Sir Gawain: Eleven Romances and Tales, ed. Thomas Hahn (1995)

The Middle English Breton Lays, ed. Anne Laskaya and Eve Salisbury (1995)

Sir Perceval of Galles and Ywain and Gawain, ed. Mary Flowers Braswell (1995)

Four Middle English Romances: Sir Isumbras, Octavian, Sir Eglamour of Artois, Sir Tryamour, ed. Harriet Hudson (1996)

The Poems of Laurence Minot (1333–1352), ed. Richard H. Osberg (1996)

Medieval English Political Writings, ed. James M. Dean (1996)

The Book of Margery Kempe, ed. Lynn Staley (1996)

Amis and Amiloun, Robert of Ciseyle, and Sir Amadace, ed. Edward E. Foster (1997)

The Cloud of Unknowing, ed. Patrick Gallacher (1997)

Robin Hood and Other Outlaw Tales, ed. Stephen Knight and Thomas H. Ohlgren (1997)

The Poems of Robert Henryson, ed. Robert L. Kindrick (1997)

Moral Love Songs and Laments, ed. Susanna Greer Fein (1998)

John Lydgate, *Troy Book: Selections*, ed. Robert R. Edwards (1998)

Thomas Usk, *The Testament of Love*, ed. R. Allen Shoaf (1998)

Prose Merlin, ed. John Conlee (1998)

Middle English Marian Lyrics, ed. Karen Saupe (1998)

Four Romances of England: King Horn, Havelok the Dane, Bevis of Hampton, Athelston, ed. Ronald B. Herzman, Graham Drake, and Eve Salisbury (1999)

John Metham, *Amoryus and Cleopes*, ed. Stephen F. Page (1999)

The Assembly of Gods: Le Assemble de Dyeus, or Banquet of Gods and Goddesses, with the Discourse of Reason and Sensuality, ed. Jane Chance (1999)

Thomas Hoccleve, *The Regiment of Princes*, ed. Charles R. Blyth (1999)

Other TEAMS Publications

Documents of Practice Series:

> *Love and Marriage in Late Medieval London*, by Shannon McSheffrey (1995)

> *A Slice of Life: Selected Documents of Medieval English Peasant Experience*, edited, translated, and with an introduction by Edwin Brezette DeWindt (1996)

> *Sources for the History of Medicine in Late Medieval London*, by Carole Rawcliffe (1996)

> *Regular Life: Monastic, Canonical, and Mendicant Rules*, selected with an introduction by Douglas J. McMillan and Kathryn Smith Fladenmuller (1997)

Commentary Series:

> *Commentary on the Book of Jonah, by Haimo of Auxere*, translated with an introduction by Deborah Everhart (1993)

> *Medieval Exegesis in Translation: Commentaries on the Book of Ruth*, translated with an introduction by Lesley Smith (1996)

> *Nicholas of Lyra's Apocalypse Commentary*, translated with an introduction and notes by Philip D. W. Krey (1997)

> *Rabbi Ezra Ben Solomon of Gerona: Commentary on the Song of Songs and Other Kabbalistic Commentaries*, selected, translated, and annotated by Seth Brody (1998)

> To order please contact:

MEDIEVAL INSTITUTE PUBLICATIONS
Western Michigan University
Kalamazoo, MI 49008–3801
Phone (616) 387–8755
FAX (616) 387–8750

http://www.wmich.edu/medieval/mip/mipubshome/html